T0318716

Contracting Out
in Government

JOHN A. REHFUSS

CONTRACTING OUT IN GOVERNMENT

A Guide to Working with Outside Contractors
to Supply Public Services

J o s s e y - B a s s   P u b l i s h e r s

San Francisco • London • 1989

CONTRACTING OUT IN GOVERNMENT
A Guide to Working with Outside Contractors
to Supply Public Services
by John A. Rehfuss

Copyright © 1989 by: Jossey-Bass Inc., Publishers
350 Sansome Street
San Francisco, California 94104
&
Jossey-Bass Limited
28 Banner Street
London EC1Y 8QE

Library of Congress Cataloging-in-Publication Data

Rehfuss, John A.
    Contracting out in government: a guide to working with outside
contractors to supply public services / John A. Rehfuss. — 1st ed.
        p.   cm.—(The Jossey-Bass public administration series)
    Bibliography: p.
    Includes index.
    ISBN: 978-0-470-63115-7
    1. Contracting out—United States. 2. Contracting out.
I. Title. II. Series.
HD3861.U6R44 1989
350.7'0973—dc19   88-30702
                                                          CIP

The paper in this book meets the guidelines for
permanence and durability of the Committee on
Production Guidelines for Book Longevity of the
Council on Library Resources.

JACKET DESIGN BY WILLI BAUM

FIRST EDITION

Code 8910

The Jossey-Bass
Public Administration Series

Contents

PREFACE

Enormously strong political pressure for cutting back government has been increasing at all levels of government, particularly during the Reagan administration. One form this pressure has taken is privatization, a movement that includes a number of activities ranging from self-help to disposal of government assets. One form of privatization is *contracting out,* or having a governmental service provided by outside work forces under contract. Contracting out has long been used to procure goods and services. In the United States, it is the most common form of privatization, even though some purists insist that this is not true privatization, since the government still controls provision of the service. To such purists, contracting out is merely a weak gesture toward less government. To others, contracting out is an unnecessary evil, weakening public services and displacing experienced public employees. Clearly, contracting out is a controversial practice that will continue to be disputed as more services are contracted out and the type of contracted services changes.

The growth in the practice of contracting out is discussed in a number of works dealing directly or indirectly with this topic. These books fall generally into two categories. The first includes advocacy pieces, whose authors ardently applaud privatization and usually relate success stories and happy endings (failures are rarely mentioned) involving contracting out. The other category can be considered users' manuals; these books are written for the manager who has already chosen to or is deeply interested in contracting out. *Contracting Out in Government* falls into neither of these camps. It is a sympathetic but balanced look at contracting out, with specific suggestions for the manager. The book is neither a manual nor a polemic. While pro contracting, this book is cautiously optimistic, rather than Pollyannaish.

Contracting Out in Government places contracting out in perspective with other forms of privatization. The book traces the recent growth in contracting out, indicates those services in government where contracting out is increasing, provides advice on specific provisions in the contract designed to protect the contractee, and gives general guidelines on when and when not to contract out. Finally, the book provides a list of do's and don'ts for managers considering contracting out.

The book richly portrays the varied situations that make up contracting out. Six actual contracts or portions of contract specifications are presented, as are three extensive case studies, five shorter cases, and over a dozen vignettes of contracting out. Many of these case studies present contracts that were successful in order to give the reader a realistic view of the process. While some contracts are unsuccessful (primarily owing to employee and union resistance, followed by problems of corruption), the vast majority of contracting out experiences work well. Using the techniques and guidelines presented in this book will help managers increase even further the prospects for success.

The book blends actual experience with an understanding of the environment in which contracting out exists. The cases, sample contracts, and suggested contractual provisions represent the current state of knowledge in the area. The discussions on politics, international contracting out, privatization, and trends in contracting out provide the reader with enough background to clearly evaluate the prospects for contracting out. The book explains the contracting out environment for those looking for a broad perspective and provides specific contracts, guidelines, and contract provisions.

Intended Audience

This book is designed to reach several audiences. It is primarily directed toward upper-level managers. Managers who are familiar with contracting out will find useful the background perspective on privatization and the scope of contracting out; those managers who have less experience with contracting out will appreciate the specific suggestions and sample provisions. The case studies and perspectives presented in the book are useful in explaining contracting out to community leaders as well as to their governing boards.

These community influentials constitute a second audience. Legislators who make decisions on contracting out and other community leaders, such as League of Women Voters or Chamber of Commerce members, will find in this book a balanced view of the contracting out process that can be of considerable help when the process is being considered for use.

The book also serves an educational purpose in several ways. It provides an overview of contracting out to departmental officials who have responsibilities for this area. Such an overview can aid in the training of line officials whose job it is to monitor contracts. Another educational use is helping procurement or contracting officers understand the process. Administrative officials or management aides who need an overview of contracting out before beginning internal feasibility studies or comparative analyses can also benefit from the book's treatment of the topic. Finally, this book can be an important tool for use in the academic classroom as a supplemental work for classes that include studies of contemporary administrative issues.

Overview of the Contents

Part One introduces the reader to the dynamics of contracting out. Chapter One puts contracting out into context as part of the broader issue of privatization. This chapter covers the range of contracting out at all three levels of government, closing with a discussion of the major advantages of contracting out. Chapter Two covers some major trends and focuses

on three new developments in contracting out: its use in social
services and in prisons and correctional facilities and the use
of private financing for such public projects as wastewater systems. Chapter Three discusses when not to contract out, drawing on the criteria set forth in Chapter One as well as on widely
held "conventional wisdom."

Part Two covers the technical aspects of contracting out.
Chapter Four considers the many activities that take place, from
the initial feasibility study to the final signing of the contract.
These are technical activities, but their effective execution can
positively affect the acceptability of the contracting out process.
Chapter Five discusses a most crucial process: effective monitoring of the contract. This process can make the difference between a satisfactory and an unsatisfactory contract. Chapter Six
deals with common contract provisions to safeguard the agency
and discusses their effect.

Part Three compares the three kinds of contractors and
then examines some actual contracts. Chapter Seven contrasts
for-profit, nonprofit, and government contractors and the reasons that each contractor type predominates in certain areas.
Chapter Eight presents four typical contracts for services directly
affecting the public. Chapter Nine presents two contract documents for acquisition of services or for in-house services not
directly affecting the public.

Part Four emphasizes the political aspects of contracting
out. Designed to help avoid the mistakes of previous contracts,
this part provides many case studies of successful and unsuccessful contracting out experiences. Chapter Ten examines
several political aspects of contracting out, such as corruption
or excessive ideological zeal. The most common political issue—
dealing with employees and unions—is covered thoroughly in
Chapter Eleven. This chapter considers the political issues raised
by employees and their unions and provides ten vignettes of contracting out when it is opposed strongly by these groups. Chapter Twelve concludes the book by offering eight very general
do's and don'ts for managers considering contracting out. The
Resources contain a number of case studies and some important additional material on contracting out. The case studies

in the Resources section include material on intergovernmental contracting under the famous Lakewood plan; data processing in Prince George's County; an attempt at private management of public works in South San Francisco; a successful switch to private rubbish collection in Berwyn, Illinois; cases of contracting failures, two from the federal government; and an account of international contracting out—in Great Britain (under the privatization program of the Thatcher government), in Canada, and in Denmark (under the Falck private fire protection plan).

Acknowledgments

It is a pleasure to thank all the people who have helped me complete this book. The School of Business and Public Administration at California State University, Sacramento, particularly my Department of Organizational Behavior, provided me some badly needed released time from teaching. I was also helped by two anonymous referees who reviewed the first draft of the book and were of great assistance.

Three graduate assistants—Vicki Cromwell, Kerri Drake, and Cathy Leland—provided copyediting, research, and proofreading assistance that helped smooth many rough edges of the book. Finally, thanks are due to my wife, Carol, who cheerfully accepted my long-term affair with the computer word-processing program that produced this book.

Sacramento, California   John A. Rehfuss
November 1988

THE AUTHOR

John A. Rehfuss is professor of public management at California State University, Sacramento. He received his B.A. degree (1956) in political science from Willamette University and his M.S. (1958) and D.P.A. (1965) degrees in public administration from the University of Southern California.

Rehfuss's recent research interests have been in contracting out public services, particularly the governmental manager's responsibility for monitoring the contractor. Rehfuss has written *Public Administration as Political Process* (1973), *Urban Politics in the Suburban Era* (1976, with Tom Murphy), *The Job of the Public Manager* (1989), and *Contracting Out in the Public Sector* (1989). He has also written over thirty-five professional articles on topics such as urban management, senior management systems, and public budgeting.

Rehfuss was city manager of Palm Springs, California, before entering academic life. He has taught at two California State Universities, San Jose and Sacramento, and at Northern Illinois University.

Contracting Out
in Government

PART I

The Dynamics of Contracting Out for Services

This book is divided into four parts, each with three chapters. Part One is an introduction to the dynamics of contracting out. Part Two deals with the mechanics of the contracting out process, while Part Three introduces the different kinds of contractors and some actual contracts. Part Four looks at political aspects of contracting, concluding with some suggestions for success in contracting out.

Chapter One considers the scope and practice of the contracting out process and begins by considering contracting out as part of the broader issue of privatization. Contracting out has been a management option for much longer than privatization, but the current upsurge of interest in contracting out is partly due to interest in privatization. Contracting out, particularly at the local level, is common for engineering, architectural services, or other such personal services. Most contract services are technical, noncontroversial services, such as building maintenance or landscaping, but contracting is now expanding into direct services to citizens. At the federal level, contracting out is heavily used, mostly by the Department of Defense in weapons procurement. Three cases portray the much-criticized procurement system. State contracting varies widely, with much con-

1

tracting used for such diverse activities as social services, economic development, and welfare.

The chapter closes with a discussion of the major reasons for contracting out: cost savings, operational flexibility, and increased responsiveness and control.

Chapter Two covers some major trends and innovations in contracting out. In general, one major trend at the local level is that contracts are tending to go to private, rather than other, governments. Social services are increasingly being contracted out to nonprofit organizations, although the distinction between profit and nonprofit can become blurred.

A new trend is the use of contracting out in prisons and correctional services. Contracting out in the prison industry, both for the use of inmates and to manage industries, is now commonplace. A current use of contracting out is in the financing of jails and correctional units, since private money can speed construction of facilities and alleviate overcrowding. Some private contractors are actually operating, as well as constructing, juvenile or jail facilities, although not facilities for housing felons.

Private parties are financing many public works projects as well as prisons and correctional institutions. Wastewater plants, waste-regenerating facilities, and even tollroads are being financed, designed, constructed, and operated by private financiers. Spurred by tax advantages early in the 1980s, privatization may make the issue of contracting out (operating a facility) a subsidiary question to the financial package for the facility.

Chapter Three deals with some specific topics: When is contracting out a good idea and when is it not? Building partly on the advantages of contracting out explored in Chapter One and partly on conventional common sense, this chapter suggests some reasons for and against contracting out. Times when it is a good idea to contract out include when the intent is to reduce costs, when the contract can be well monitored, when technical or complex services are required, when benchmark job costs must be set, and when it is important to avoid management or policy constraints. Contracting out should not be done when the intent is to disguise service level cuts as cost savings, when contracting will result in heavy employee/union opposition (this usually makes the contract unworkable if not politically non-feasible), and when contracting involves an emergency service. These "rules" can be disregarded in some cases, but they contain a good deal of wisdom that can provide guidance.

CHAPTER 1 ∿∿∿∿∿∿∿∿∿∿∿∿∿∿

The Scope and Practice of Contracting Out

Contracting out in the public sector is a topic now receiving a good deal of attention. Contracting out is a basically straightforward concept: it simply means that government agencies can provide services to the public by employing private firms, nonprofit organizations, or even other governments. These firms operate under contract with the city, state agency, or other government. Governments have been contracting out for decades—for instance, the Pentagon to Lockheed and General Dynamics for military hardware, state agencies to nonprofit firms and hospitals for human services, and cities to engineers for design and construction of streets. Despite its familiarity and simplicity, contracting out is still something of an enigma. Contracting out is well known by the governments that use it, yet it is often poorly explained, researched, and managed. Contracting out can save enormous amounts of money, but often it wastes large sums. Contracting out has been used for many years but is now suddenly a popular topic, gaining the attention of politicians, interest groups, and citizens. Oddly, contracting out for one service may be controversial, while in the same city or state or at the federal level, another service will be routinely contracted out.

Privatization

Some of the contradictions and controversies surrounding contracting out arise from emotional reactions to privatization. Privatization—which includes such activities as selling off government assets and deregulating private activities—is a highly controversial subject. Some of the emotional reaction to privatization may have spread to contracting out. Contracting out for services such as engineering or legal personnel is traditional for most agencies and precedes by many years the current trend toward privatization. However, as one of the forms of privatization (by far the commonest in the United States), contracting out may be receiving more attention, favorable and unfavorable, than would be the case were it not associated with privatization. For this reason, a brief analysis of privatization will help place contracting out in a broader perspective.

Privatization includes all activities that would decrease government activity, either by reducing government's total scope or by merely replacing public functions with private activity. Basically, the privatization movement is an effort (1) to reduce public expenditures, (2) to reform public expenditures by making them more efficient and effective, and (3) to turn more public services over to private operation.

Interest in privatization for its own sake may be limited to a few academicians, intellectuals, and laissez-faire economists. However, the concerns of these individuals have become linked with the growing discontent over the results of government spending. Many people, not all traditional conservatives, are convinced that government spends too much money. Others may be not as sure that too much money is being spent but do feel that they get too little value for their tax dollar. The result is that a large group of individuals want either more economy (less spending) or more effectiveness (better results). A smaller group want both economy and efficiency and also privatization as an end in itself.

While there is no precise agreement on what privatization is, one view holds that privatization at the local level has three components: public asset divestiture (the sale of government property), private financing of infrastructures (public facilities such as buildings and projects), and private provision of services (contracting out) (Seader, 1986).

Sale of assets (divestiture) can involve sales of citywide parking or bus transit systems or, at the national level, sale of student loan portfolios to private parties who collect debts effectively. Divestiture in other countries (where it is called denationalization) is more common than in the United States (Savas, 1987).

The use of private financing for public facilities is becoming increasingly popular. Chapter Ten presents an instance of how a New York City skating rink was privately constructed when the city could not finish the job. A more common reason for privatization is that private financing is often available for facilities the public agency cannot provide; examples are the waste conversion plants in Westchester County (New York) and Baltimore (Maryland) and the waste treatment plants in Chandler (Arizona) and Auburn (Alabama). Construction of these facilities often includes a contract to manage and operate them.

The third component of this view of privatization is contracting out, which is the subject of this book.

Savas (1982) has another, more comprehensive analysis of privatization. His view includes four elements: load shedding; restoration of competition; fees and charges; and alternative service delivery systems. Contracting out is the major example of alternative delivery systems.

Load shedding is the most basic element of privatization. Basically, the government stops providing some services and lets private parties provide such services if there is any citizen demand for them. Day-care centers are one example. Many private firms now provide day care for children of employees. Savas (1982) argues that the family can make decisions on day care more effectively than can government. Government agencies require higher standards for private day-care facilities (requiring higher-quality care than the children receive in their own homes), with the result that these standards work against private day care and thus reduce the total number of facilities.

Other examples of load shedding include traditional services, such as volunteer fire departments, or more unusual arrangements, such as the Guardian Angels (a group of youths who act as a nonpaid adjunct of police departments). Almost any service limited to specific geographical areas (such as snow removal in large condominium projects) or conferring individual benefits (such as garbage removal) can be load shed.

Restoring competition in the provision of public services is the second part of Savas's analysis. In Minneapolis both private and city contractors provide refuse collection services in different areas of the city. After some years, the city collection service was able to reduce its cost to that of the private collector. This shows that public agencies can provide services as cheaply as private firms but that it takes strenuous effort. Competition provides the incentive for this effort. Kansas City and Montreal have also created systems using competing public and private refuse collection, an arrangement that ensures lower prices and potentially better service. Both cities create separate zones for each collector, private and public, and compare results for both price and quality (Savas, 1982).

Competition usually provides a yardstick for measuring the quality and cost of public services so that local or state officials can see how efficiently a service can be provided. Although competing suppliers have been used for some services (such as residential refuse collection), this approach has not extended much beyond such usage. While most public services cannot be measured as precisely as can refuse collection, it is still necessary that the public be provided with information about what such services should cost.

Fees and user charges, Savas's third component, have been used for many years but have become more popular when the government is short of money, as in California after Proposition 13. Between 1957 and 1977, the share of all state and local revenue (excluding grants) derived from user charges increased from 12.7 to 18.6 percent (Coleman, 1980). User fees have traditionally been limited to such things as school lunches, parking, water, or water and sewer utilities but now include police and fire protection, refuse collection, and, particularly in California, "development exactions." These are charges levied on developers for not only the curbs and streetlights in their development but also the school, park, and fire station that will serve the area.

There are good economic reasons for user charges (Savas, 1982). They allow citizens to register a preference for certain functions rather than, as often happens, having the agency provide the service out of general tax revenue. Peak period transit charges or refuse collection charges are examples of user charges. User charges also effectively regulate usage through economic means, as in the case of charges for extra police services or extra garbage pickups. Finally, fees can increase equity by forcing users of a facility such as a parking lot or junior college to pay all or part of the cost, rather than taxing all residents.

The final part of Savas's analysis includes a number of arrangements for providing public services that, in effect, reduce the scope of government action. Franchising, grants and vouchers, contracting out, self-help, and citizen volunteering are the most widely cited of such arrangements. Franchising involves selecting a private firm to provide public services and awarding that firm monopoly privileges on such services as private local bus lines or refuse pickup (thereby replacing a public monopoly for a private one). In some cases, multiple franchises, such as for taxi service, can maintain competition.

Sometimes the government agency can use grants to encourage private organizations or business firms to provide a service they would not otherwise supply. Many cities or counties provide grants to local symphony orchestras or performing arts groups. These grants finance artistic events not otherwise possible, generally at lower cost than a municipal performing arts group or orchestra. The idea is to encourage private production of the service, which consumers can then purchase, rather than starting or continuing public programs. Vouchers are similar to grants but subsidize the consumer rather than the producer, thus expanding competition. Food stamps are an example of a voucher system.

Volunteering and self-help rely on the individual to provide services that would otherwise be paid for by the government agency. Volunteers check books in and out of local libraries, care for animals at zoos, lead museum tours, and fight fires. Self-help involves individual provision of public services. Examples include neighborhood crime watches and patrols (which supplement police services), returning cans and bottles to recycling centers, and parent carpools to public schools.

Contracting out, the commonest form of privatization, transfers government services to private hands while leaving the formal responsibility with the government. This reduces the scope of government somewhat, although government still decides whether to offer the service.

Contracting Out in Government

Local Government. Local governments have probably the widest and best-known range of services under contract, probably because they provide a wide variety of services that directly affect citizens and that are well suited to contracting. A 1985 survey by the International City Management Association (ICMA) (1986) indicates the range and frequency of contracts for cities.

Cities contract out a surprisingly wide variety of programs, ranging from library operations (12 percent of cities contract out this program) to tree trimming (30 percent). Services can be impersonal, such as utility billing (13 percent), or potentially controversial, such as crime prevention and patrol (10 percent). Some services are quite technical, such as data processing (24 percent), while others are basically nontechnical, such as parking lot and garage operation (13 percent). Some services are almost universally contracted out, such as vehicle towing (78 percent), while others are rarely contracted, such as traffic control (2 percent) or secretarial services (4 percent). A 1982 survey by the ICMA (see Tables 1 and 2) shows those services most and least often contracted out.

This survey is consistent with other studies. Another study of cities under 50,000 population found that the most common services contracted out were street construction, architectural

Table 1. City and County Services Most Often Contracted Out.

| Service | Percentage of Governments Contracting Out Service | | |
	For Profit	Nonprofit (or Other)	Total
Vehicle towing	78	0	78
Day care	33	40	73
Cultural programs	7	45	52
Hospital operation	25	25	50
Legal services	48	2	50
Drug/alcohol treatment	6	42	48
Mental health facilities	6	41	47
Paratransit system operation	22	22	44

Source: Adapted from Shulman, 1982, pp. 2–6.

Table 2. City and County Services Least Often Contracted Out.

| Service | Percentage of Governments Contracting Out Service | | |
	For Profit	Nonprofit (or Other)	Total
Traffic control	1	1	2
Secretarial	4	0	4
Police/fire communication	1	3	4
Fire prevention/suppression	1	4	5
Meter maintenance/collection	5	0	5
Sanitary inspection	1	5	6
Personnel services	5	1	6
Building code inspection	6	1	7

Source: Adapted from Shulman, 1982, pp. 8–9.

and engineering consulting services, legal counsel, building repair, and waste collection. The services least contracted out were building inspection, park maintenance, leaf collection, police services, and police communication (Florestano and Gordon, 1980).

Tables 1 and 2 not only display the wide range of services that are contracted out but also suggest some significant patterns. To a large degree, heavily contracted services are not highly sensitive and do not involve the essential political culture of the city. Vehicle towing, day care, and hospitals, for example (see Table 1), are functions that many cities or counties prefer not to operate themselves but that are not particularly politically sensitive. In addition to not being politically sensitive, some of the programs in Table 1 are also highly technical, such as legal services. Others involve potentially high start-up costs or are highly specialized, such as mental health facilities and paratransit systems.

On the other hand, services that are rarely contracted out (Table 2) do involve such sensitive services as law enforcement and fire protection. These are historically the services that tend to define the "culture" of a city or, to a lesser degree, a county. It is not surprising, then, that governments are not eager to contract out traffic control, fire fighting and prevention, or even inspections for sanitation and building code.

In contrast to police, fire, and inspection services, however, some rarely contracted out services are not easily explained. Meter maintenance and collection is often a thankless job that, one would assume, cities should be glad to give to someone else ("Contracting Out . . . ," 1986).

Federal Government. Although no one knows what portion of federal programs are contracted out, the total is very large. In 1984, $146 billion in defense contracts alone was procured from private sources (Comptroller General, 1986b). This, of course, does not include additional billions of dollars spent on contracting out domestic programs.

For thirty years, the federal executive branch has officially relied on private enterprise to supply products and services. This policy was originally designed to eliminate competition with private enterprise. Now determinations of whether commercial activities should be done in-house or under private contract are based on efficiency and economy considerations. All federal agencies, except Department of Defense (DOD) and a few other departments, are required since 1976 to make comprehensive studies of their activities. If private cooperation is 10 percent cheaper, the service must be contracted out (Kettler, 1986). It is arguable how faithfully these studies are made in every case, but it is clear that the federal government is committed to contracting out.

The result is that more people work for federal contractors than for the government itself. For example, in 1980 the Department of Health and Welfare (DHW) had 157,000 employees, but 750,000 more individuals worked under contracts to DHW (Sharkansky, 1980). Thus, in many cases, the contractor "tail" wags the federal program "dog."

Federal contracts are usually designed to meet staff shortfalls, which are often caused by personnel ceilings, shortages of time to complete tasks, shortages of expertise among current staff, and the need for an "outside" viewpoint. These contracts are of several types: fixed price (not subject to adjustment), cost-reimbursement (there are several kinds, all of which usually have a maximum fee), time and materials, letter (authorization to begin work immediately), and indefinite delivery (when time of delivery or amount of work is unknown) (Collett, 1981).

Most federal contracts are handled well, follow policy guidelines, and cause no controversy—they are "squeaky clean." However, with so much of the government's business done under contract, abuses occur. Solicitations for bids are "wired" for preselected winners. Undesirable bidders are "sandbagged" by being asked (off the record) to make changes that will put them out of the running, or desirable candidates will be told how to strengthen contracts. Agency staff work with favored contractors to develop "sweetheart" solicitations that only the favored firm can meet. "Good old boy (girl)" personal service contracts are written. (These individual hires, not controlled by procurement regulations, are the most common source of media exposés. The personal hire for administrative/political purposes has been raised to an art form at all levels of government.) Multiple orders to sole-source contractors also can be used to avoid competition, although this technique is often properly used to avoid bidding expense for unique products (Collett, 1981).

Contractors, in turn, abuse the process by creating minority-owned companies that only nominally have minorities in charge, by switching overhead charges to the best agency or contract, by listing top staff on solicitations but replacing them with less qualified personnel quickly in a "bait and switch" operation, and, of course, by participating in such agency abuses as the "sweetheart" contracts noted above (Collett, 1981).

The pressures on the government contracting officer are substantial. The contracting officer, who can actually obligate the government, is responsible for seeing that the government's best interests are served. "Best interest" does not merely mean acquiring goods and services at the lowest price. It means processing change orders, monitoring some contracts, binding the government, and selecting the contractor. The process is hazy and ill defined, since the contracting officer works as a team member (Cooper, 1980). Other organizational constraints are involved, such as the military's desire to maintain readiness at all times. There are subtle twists to the contracting process that are not illegal but rather irregular. These include habitually underestimating jobs to ensure that the contract is signed, constant political infighting over whether contracts should be in a specific state or congressional district, small changes that rule out bidders (for example, no contractors more than fifty miles from Washington), and, for a variety of reasons, excessive overhead payments (Cooper, 1980). The contracting officer is at the intersection of both very technical and highly political forces.

Most of the well-known examples of federal contracting are from DOD military acquisition; this is where most horror stories about such abuses as $500 hammers originate. However, given the volume of contracts and the precautions taken by procurement officers, military acquisition contracting out is probably at least as good as, if not better than, that done in civilian departments.

Several examples of government contracting issues will illustrate the issues that can arise. In one case, the Defense Logistics Agency (DLA) ruled out the low bidder, the Pines Corporation, because of a history of nonperformance on other contracts. The company appealed to members of Congress, including New York Senator D'Amato, who asked the General Accounting Office (GAO) to investigate. The GAO found no abuse of authority by DLA but did find irregularities in the computer tracking system that determined contractor delinquency rates. DLA agreed to correct the system (Comptroller General, 1986a).

In another case, the Air Force ruled that one piston-ring supplier could not be a subcontractor (the contractor wanted to use the supplier, since it produced more cheaply) because the ring had not been tested and thus the supplier was not an approved source. Representative Mazzoli requested a GAO review, and GAO reported that the Air Force decision was proper but that it might be desirable to have more than one source of piston rings (Comptroller General, 1986d).

Both of these cases suggest that when contractors do not get a contract, political influence, a time-tested method, can be used to reverse the decision. This may have been ultimately a good strategy, because both cases turned up minor irregularities in the contract system, although the suppliers did not benefit in these specific cases.

In a third case, the San Antonio Air Logistics Command (SA-ALC) reduced a backlog of open purchase orders (orders in process but not yet awarded to a contractor) from 20,000 to 12,000. The GAO investigated and found no evidence that excessive prices were paid or procurement shortcuts were taken, although over $200,000 of extra overtime was worked. Ironically, the backlog developed partially because SA-ALC buyers slowed purchases to get better prices because of the horror stories about overpriced spare parts (Comptroller General, 1986e).

In these three cases, no serious improprieties were found, although problems of unmonitored computer systems, single-source contractors, and excessive overtime surfaced. These problems are the natural result of a procurement system that involves huge volumes of money ($146 billion in 1984) and where there is an emphasis on meeting defense procurement or civilian program goals rather than cost efficiency and desire to not waste resources on reviewing low-dollar contracts (Comptroller General, 1986c).

Outside DOD, contracting out does not always move smoothly, either. The requirement for cost studies to compare in-house and contractor prices for all services is followed spasmodically. The National Aeronautics and Space Administration (NASA) does not, as a matter of policy, make the required studies but does contract out, making it unclear when it is cheaper to contract out (Comptroller General, 1985b). It is also unclear how regularly other agencies consider contracting out. At the other extreme, State Department embassies entered into sham contracts with employee organizations to avoid personnel ceilings and to avoid using local contractors (Comptroller General, 1986b). The Department of Energy embraced contracting out so vigorously that even basic management and policy functions were contracted, a violation of policy that GAO noted in a report to Congress (Comptroller General, 1979). (These Energy Department shortcomings are detailed in the Resources section at the end of the book as a case study of contracting failure.)

The examples in this section were taken from cases in which the GAO was asked to investigate and therefore are not representative, although abuses are not uncommon. Cases of effective contracting out go largely unreported, although there are exceptions. One study of twenty contracts examined whether contractors increase their contract costs in succeeding years and so wipe out the original contracting out savings. The study found that, while costs did increase, seventeen of the contracts still saved money (Comptroller General, 1985a).

Expansion in federal contracting may be near at hand. There is interest in introducing more competition to the Postal Service by allowing nonprofit and community groups to distribute nonprofit mail directly to mailboxes, thereby reducing subsidy costs, and to franchise rural routes as well as processing and some delivery services. This is an attempt to reduce postal payroll costs, which have outstripped productivity gains (Crutcher, 1984).

The Federal Aviation Administration (FAA), trying to privatize air traffic control services, began a three-year pilot program with small airport control towers serving primarily small private planes. Some airport managers liked the program. However, FAA put the scheme on hold because of tower liability insurance rate increases (due to a Labor Department ruling requiring larger contractors to pay higher FAA salaries to controllers) and to doubts about future appropriations ("Is FAA Privatization . . . ," 1986).

The Reagan administration is avidly in favor of more privatization, and efforts to contract out will no doubt proceed until 1989 and possibly later. The privatization movement is not, however, associated with one administration; it began with President Eisenhower, although its rapid expansion occurred during the Carter administration. Federal privatization is likely to increase, regardless of which party is in power, since powerful forces to cut costs will likewise continue.

State Government. States have been heavily involved in contracting out for years in such traditional areas as highway building and for such services as janitorial maintenance. There has been an increase in state interest in all types of privatization, particularly alternative delivery systems. Contracting is the most common alternative system.

Two states are using private partnerships for employment training. Ohio and Connecticut have contracted with American Works to place welfare recipients in unsubsidized jobs. The company operates the program in Dayton and Cleveland (Ohio) and in the Hartford–New Britain area (Connecticut).

Health care is another area for which states commonly use private contractors. Nineteen states contract with health maintenance organizations for Medicaid. Another thirty-five states contract with private fiscal agents to operate and manage Medicaid (Chi, 1986).

Many states have now contracted with private firms to build and sometimes operate jails and correctional facilities. Others are considering such a move. There are over thirty privately constructed detention facilities for juveniles and illegal aliens across the country. In another related area, many states contract out prison industry activity. (Chapter Two gives more details on prison and correction facility contracting out.)

Most states contract out heavily, but there is no central listing of individual contracts, even for individual states. California, for example, contracts out janitorial services and grounds maintenance in state buildings whenever it is less expensive to do so. The state has for many years contracted elevator maintenance and minor building alterations. The California Employment Development Department uses private security guard services to secure its buildings, having switched from the state police to save money (Rehfuss, 1986).

States vary greatly in the degree of contracting and the degree to which they report it. In Minnesota, for example, most contracts were for transportation (2,178 for $454 million), followed by economic security (1,720) and energy and economic development (694). In 1982 Virginia had most contracts for individual and family services (including health care), while social services and welfare were the most common contracts in Wisconsin (Chi, 1986). If California and the other aforementioned states are typical, states are contracting out in as many ways as they have programs.

Most states have some sort of rules regarding contracting out. California requires that contracts over $10,000 be reviewed for legality by the General Services Department; that competitive bidding for contracts be used whenever possible; that postcontract evaluations be completed and filed for future reference; and that quarterly reports on consulting activity be made (Auditor General, 1986). Other states have similar regulations, although the degree to which they are followed no doubt varies.

Benefits from Contracting Out

There are several reasons why governments contract out to private firms, nonprofit firms, or other government agencies.

Cost-Effectiveness. In most cases, contracting out is done because it is seen as more cost-effective. A 1981 survey of eighty-seven California local governments (thirty-nine cities, nineteen counties, seventeen school districts, and twelve special districts) showed that sixty of them reported that ''reduced cost of labor, material, or overhead'' was an advantage to contracting out. Only fifteen reported that ''increased costs'' were a disadvantage to contracting out. One city official explained: ''Our city's experience has been that the private sector can provide this particular service [refuse collection] more efficiently and economically than the city'' (California Tax Foundation, 1981, p. 9).

In the same report, fifty of the same eighty-seven officials also replied that another advantage of contracting out was the avoidance of start-up costs in providing a service. These two advantages, lower overall costs and avoiding start-up costs, are the generally accepted reasons for contracting out. The next question, of course, is how or in what ways contractors provide public services more cheaply.

Some attribute these reduced rates to the efficiency of private contractors, without explaining why these contractors can do the job more cheaply. Others credit competition, rather than a municipal monopoly, for driving costs down (Savas, 1982). The desire to survive and make a profit is given as another reason (Poole, 1980). But these reasons do not explain just how private costs are reduced.

The reasons for reduced costs primarily involve ways that private employers use their labor force. One important study compared eight services in twenty cities in the Los Angeles area (Stevens, 1984). For seven of the eight services (paving, refuse collection, tree maintenance, ground maintenance, signal maintenance, janitorial services, and street cleaning), private contracting was significantly cheaper; in one (payroll preparation), costs were about the same. The report indicated that, contrary to the conventional wisdom, private employers pay their employees as much as public employers, both in salary and fringe benefits. The private employers in the study

- used less labor
- had about 5 percent less absenteeism
- made managers responsible for equipment as well as labor
- used younger workers
- used more part-time labor
- terminated more employees (which is probably why there is less absenteeism)
- used more capital equipment

This may be the best study to date. It specifically pinpoints how savings are achieved by contracting out. Unquestionably, savings through contracting out to the private sector can be substantial (over 50 percent in some services). There are other savings as well as in labor, although no actual tests have pinpointed these.

Economies of scale reduce costs. Thus, a private contractor serving a wider geographical area than one municipality (or even small state), or serving a larger number of units in the same area, will normally have lower costs than any single government. Larger units can spread costs over more production units than can a smaller unit. For example, the cost of management may be the same no matter what the size of the unit.

Contractors who are large-scale producers can purchase state-of-the-art equipment and materials at a lower price than can small units of government and can use them more effectively over a larger number of units. Contractors can thus not only more readily afford new technology and labor-saving devices but can also use them more efficiently. This is probably why Prince George's County (see Case Study 1 in the Resources) selected a private corporation to manage and operate its central data service, although there were also handsome savings reported.

Most municipal governments have labor-intensive services such as law enforcement, recreation, and refuse collection. This labor intensiveness is a major advantage to contractors when trying to supply a public service at lower cost than the public agency. The desire to keep costs down drives contractors to seek labor-saving devices much more avidly than do many municipalities. Obviously, where cities compete directly with private contractors, such as in Montreal or Minneapolis, the same pressure to keep costs down affects the city government.

Avoiding start-up expenses is another reason why contracting out is popular. This is true for newly incorporated cities or special districts as well as for any new or expanded programs that any government, new or old, may undertake. In Los Angeles County, many cities incorporating after the mid 1950s chose to contract with Los Angeles County for a range of services from police protection to building permit and inspection services. This arrangement allowed these new cities to avoid the heavy costs of staffing new departments, erecting new buildings, and purchasing new equipment.

Contracting out costs for municipalities are often lower than they seem to be, especially when compared to the real costs for city services. Private contractors pay taxes on the profits they make (or hope to make) from providing the service. If the costs of public and private service are similar, taxes paid may make the contractor less expensive. This advantage is complicated by the fact that the taxes paid may not go to the city but to the state and federal governments, since few cities levy an income tax. Most contractors do pay local business license taxes.

Government costs may also be higher than realized, because all the costs of fringe benefits and other hidden municipal costs are not shown. Budgeted amounts for the public works department, for example, are by no means the total costs of that department. Health benefits for employees are frequently found in a different budget. So are pension funds, particularly if there are unfunded pension liabilities. Accrued vacation time is rarely reported or even estimated, even though vacation accruals are usually a legal liability, paid if the employee resigns or retires. Finally, financial, legal, and top-level administrative costs are rarely distributed among operating departments. This is a particular problem in small government units, which generally have unsophisticated accounting systems. In such cases, comparison of a private contract proposal (which includes all costs) with city provision of the service (which may not include all costs) works in favor of the city.

On the other hand, however, private contracts may be less expensive for all the wrong reasons. Corruption exists in the form of illegal contracts and payoffs (Hanrahan, 1983). There may be implicit agreement that the government wink at lowered performance levels as a way of allowing a contractor to make money on a low bid. One Wisconsin director of a nursing home for the retarded complained about a contractor's laundry service:

> Their work on the whole is almost entirely unacceptable. I'm sure that most of us as private citizens wouldn't tolerate for one minute sending our laundry out and getting it back like this without

> complaining and demanding immediate remedial
> action. Many of the items sent to the laundry
> are never returned. . . . Laundry received in the
> cottage is often not for that cottage and must
> be resorted. It isn't at all unusual to find laundry
> from such places as Lake Geneva Bunny Club,
> Marriot Inn, Holiday Inn, and so on. Laundry
> comes back wet and mildewy-smelly [Sharkansky,
> 1980, p. 119].

Sometimes private costs are low because local officials want to reduce service without openly admitting it. Reductions in service are often disguised as "more efficient" private contracts. In this case, it would be more ethical for the local unit to simply shed part of its load and let private operators pick it up if demand exists.

Flexibility. Contracting out also has the advantage of ensuring flexibility in adjusting to changes in service demands. The 1981 study of eighty-five California local governments indicated that sixty-six of the units regarded "availability of special equipment and skilled personnel" as a major advantage to contracting out. Indeed, this was the most common reason, cited even more often than reduced costs. Special districts, such as flood control and school districts, noted this reason in over 80 percent of the cases (California Tax Foundation, 1981).

Local governments frequently must change policy directions quickly. One reason, not now as evident as in the recent past, was desire of the government to make itself eligible for federal funds through changed organizational structures or revised funding patterns. This was particularly true in the field of human resources, such as manpower training and mental health facility construction (Marlin, 1984). There are many other reasons for changing policy, one of which is the need to respond quickly to citizen demands. Private contractors are more flexible. They are not bound to follow civil service rules and regulations in hiring, promoting, or disciplining employees. This reduces costs as well as increasing flexibility, since private employees can be more easily transferred and reassigned to more effective roles.

Private employees can also be rewarded more quickly for good performance—a "plus" for morale in these organizations. Civil service rules often penalize better employees as well as management. Many governments contract out simply to avoid these rules.

As concerns federal grants, the use of private contractors has a further advantage because their accounting systems are generally closer to national standards than are those of public systems. Thus, private contractors can more easily develop national cost comparisons useful for federal granting agencies (Marlin, 1984).

Peak loads can overwhelm small cities or government agencies, while these same loads can be more easily absorbed by large suppliers or contractors. Larger providers can more readily reschedule crews and provide back-up crews. Even if private firms are not formally under contract, they may still be able to absorb peak load under an emergency arrangement. While local governments are likely to pay a high price for the luxury of falling back on private contracts for peak-load assistance, such assistance may still be cheaper than having the public agency overstaff in anticipation of crises. Contracts can be devised that let private suppliers routinely provide excess peak-load capacity on call.

Responsiveness and Control. One of the major reasons for contracting out is to maximize local options. Local jurisdictions frequently do not wish to be burdened with a large staff, for this can limit the attention they can give to new problems or changed situations. A large street-cleaning crew, for example, may take time to adjust to new responsibilities for tree and ground maintenance. The crew represents a fixed investment that can only be slowly redirected. Many cities, particularly new cities, prefer not to limit their options in determining which programs to operate. They elect to keep few employees and to offer municipal service, if demanded by the public, through contracting out. A local official commented: "The fewer government employees, the fewer personnel problems. It is easier to change contractors than to change employees" (California Tax Foundation, 1981, p. 9). To this official, responsiveness to changing circumstances, citizen complaints, or council initiatives is jeopardized more by the public employee system than by contracting outside. As this view becomes more widespread, the inclination to contract out will increase.

Cities that avoid providing a full range of services often do so because they consider it too expensive. Many times, however, the question of saving money is secondary. In this case, cities prefer to keep their policy options as open as possible. They regard a large number of city services as a hindrance to the true function of a municipality, which is to make policy decisions about the nature of the city. To these cities, a city is a means of providing (arranging for) services rather than of producing them. A service is provided when a basic policy decision is made to make the service available to the public. Producing this service can be done by government, citizens, private nonprofit groups, or private firms. Less municipal production (that is, fewer services produced by the city government) means more time to evaluate where and how services should be provided.

The Future of Contracting Out: One View

Poole (1980), the author of *Cutting Back City Hall,* paints a scenario of Cabana Beach, a hypothetical southern California city, which, by contracting out all services over the years, was able to face the twenty-first century with only three employees: a city manager, a city attorney, and a secretary. Their job consisted of overseeing contracts from a leased city hall. They were considering the final logical action—selling the city sewers and streets. The situation of the council and three employees trying to evaluate and monitor hundreds of contracts, answer citizen calls, and, not least of all, answer letters from all over the country asking how they can operate with only three employees is unenviable, to say the least. Although the idea of only three employees operating a city is a bit farfetched, it is true that more government functions can be contracted out. Future directions may not be toward cities with three employees but toward cities, and other governments, that provide fewer services themselves.

Summary

Contracting out is increasing at all levels of government. Contracting is seen as more cost-effective for financially hard-pressed governments. It avoids start-up costs for services, provides more flexibility in adjusting to changes in service demands, and maximizes control in the hands of public officials who do not want to supervise a large staff. Contracting is also increasing partly because of the interest in privatization, since contracting out is the oldest and best known form of privatization.

Local governments contract out a surprisingly large number of services. The most common contracts are technical, such as for legal services, or noncontroversial, such as for vehicle towing. The least common are sensitive, such as police patrol. At the state level, as in localities, traditional services have been contracted out for years, but states are now venturing into more sensitive contracts—for example, in employment training, health care, and correctional facilities.

CHAPTER 2 ᴖᴖᴖᴖᴖᴖᴖᴖᴖᴖᴖᴖᴖᴖᴖᴖᴖ

Trends and Innovations in Contracting Out

Contracting out is not only increasing in usage, but it is expanding into new areas. Not very many years ago, these areas would have been unthinkable. Fiscal stress as well as the other reasons mentioned in Chapter One have caused governments at all levels to look for alternatives to traditional ways of providing services. As necessity is the mother of invention, so fiscal stress appears to be the mother of government innovation. Table 3 indicates, at the local level (where comparative statistics are most easily available), that reliance on contracting out with private parties increased substantially in the ten years between 1972 and 1982. All functions, from waste disposal to hospitals, were increasingly contracted out to private parties. This clearly demonstrates that cities are increasing the number of contracts with private firms, both for traditional services (such as recreational facilities, which increased eightfold), and for less conventional services (such as drug/alcohol treatment, which doubled) (Henderson, 1986). Increases in contracting out are not limited to local government. Federal contracts increased 10 percent between 1983 and 1984, with most of the increase occurring in defense spending (Congressional Budget Office, 1987).

This chapter examines new governmental functions where contracting out is already being or will be used. Three new developments will be examined: contracting out for social services; contracting out for prison operation; and contracting with private parties for financing, construction, and operation of public works facilities.

Table 3. Percentage of All City Contracts—
Public (Intergovernmental), Nonprofit, and Private—
Given to Private Contractors for Selected Services (1972–1982).

Function	1972	1982
Solid waste disposal	44	46
Recreational facilities	4	33
Personnel services	8	73
Hospitals	38	61
Snowplowing	30	85
Traffic control	4	20
Drug/alcohol treatment	7	15
Insect control	8	33
Housing	5	23

Source: Adapted from Henderson, 1986, p. 24.

Note: Slightly different names of activities in each survey were used.

Contracting Out for Social Services

Contracting out for social (human) services illustrates nicely the diversity in contracting out. Social services are somewhat different from traditional services delivered to citizens in that they involve very personal services delivered directly to individuals. Most are intimately related to the physical well-being of the recipient and, in many cases, are directly connected to the quality of life, even to living or dying.

However, although they involve crucial individual relationships with clients and require high levels of commitment of the provider, these services still are subject to the impersonal management processes of a normally contracted service. Table 4 shows that individual human service programs are contracted out from 31 percent (child welfare) to 78 percent (day care) of the cases. Except for the operation of hospitals, nonprofit organizations predominate in these services—a major characteristic of human service programs.

Programs such as those shown in Table 4 are provided by cities and counties having a wide range of organizational structures and are contracted in several ways. Often the function is a state program (as are mental health programs) and must be provided under state policies dictating frequency and level of service. The county or perhaps the largest city in the urban area may be responsible. Often the agency responsible for the service provides it under contract to other agencies or under intergovernmental agreements calling for area- or countywide services by the largest unit of government. Conversely, the program may not be mandated at all, and local units may choose to provide the service.

Often human services are provided according to intergovernmental agreements (which are, in some cases, functionally equivalent to contracts) and by nonprofit organizations. Occasionally, neighborhood groups provide the services, particularly for day-care and public health programs. Day-care facilities and hospitals, however, are provided privately in most cases. While surveys are not available to demonstrate the extent of human service contracting out at the state level, it is most likely as common as such contracting out at the local level (Wedel, Katz, and Wieck, 1979). Since many state government human service programs have the same functions as those at the local level, it is likely that the states contract with the same groups in the same proportion.

The reasons for contracting out for social services are somewhat different than for other types of services (Wedel, Katz, and Wieck, 1979; DeHoog, 1984; Valente and Manchester, 1984). Aside from the usual advantages of contracting out, the first reason to contract out for social services is that nonprofit organizations have substantial organizational advantages over public agencies. Nonprofit organizations, particularly charitable agencies, are often widely viewed as making the client's welfare a high priority. Because of this, they can attract higher-quality

Table 4. Human Services Delivered Using Contracts and Intergovernmental Agreements.

| | Percentage of Services Delivered by | | | |
| | Contracts | | Nonprofit | Agreements |
Service	Profit	Neighborhood	Nonprofit	Other Governments
Day-care facility operation	35	6	37	16
Child welfare programs	5	2	24	28
Programs for the elderly	4	4	29	21
Elderly/public housing operation	13	1	18	43
Hospital operation/management	30		27	25
Public health programs	8	8	27	30
Drug/alcohol treatment programs	6	6	41	30
Mental health programs/facilities	7	3	40	34

Source: Adapted from Valente and Manchester, 1984, p. 124.

Note: Figures are percentages of responding cities and counties that actually provide the service.

volunteer help than can public agencies. Contracting with a non-profit agency also commits considerable community support to a public program, because such agencies (for example, the United Fund) garner contributions from private citizens.

Contracting out also provides some additional flexibility in difficult financial times, since the contractor can absorb rapid changes in personnel requirements. Since demands for care by local units change with each state mandate, contracting preserves some flexibility (Straussman and Fairie, 1981).

Contracting out is also more natural for social services because it is generally believed that nonprofit agencies give better-quality service because they have more expertise. For example, the City of Rochester, using new federally funded programs, chose nonprofit agencies to manage community development, employment, and training programs. The choice was specifically to limit the growth of city staff (Valente and Manchester, 1984). In effect, the city chose to maintain flexibility and relied on the expertise of nonprofit organizations. In the case of services requiring strong management controls (such as hospitals), profit-making firms may have an edge (Doherty, 1985).

Contracting out for human services is widespread and heavily used in numerous cases. Philadelphia County's Children and Youth Agency contracts out 78 percent of its budget ($80 million) to private contractors for direct services. These services include nonplacement services (such as family-based services, day care, and day treatment for direct services) and placement services (such as foster home care, institutional care, and supervised independent living). The contracts are based on performance standards involving an acceptable quality level for each service and a quality assurance surveillance plan for monitoring contracts ("Handling Children . . . ," 1987).

Sacramento's (California) Department of Mental Health contracts out about half of its mental health projects to private providers. Providers include such clinical facilities as psychiatric health, skilled nursing, intermediate care, and psychiatric care as well as general hospitals and family homes. The Division of Contract Services includes the categories of (among others) children's services, outpatient services, and continuing care services. Each category involves different sets of providers. Continuing care, for example, involves five skilled nursing care contracting agencies, of which three are private for-profit contractors. These three contractors were hospitals for adult day care or outpatient services. The county employee monitoring continuing care programs indicates that these private providers are "highly professional" and that in thirteen years he has seen only about a half-dozen unprofessional acts, only one of which involved misuse of county funds (the contract was terminated) (Rehfuss, 1988).

Contracting out for social services is no panacea, however. Whitcomb (1983) argues that state and local mental health agencies have difficulty handling community-based residential services because it is a new responsibility, the budgets are large, and there is a shortage of skills. Therefore, these services are heavily contracted out. Nonprofit agencies tend to be strong in program skills but weak in business management, while proprietary providers are just the opposite. The result is that public agencies have to be ready to make emergency infusions of funds, monitor the contract very closely, and shift clients frequently if the providers reject the service as too difficult. Whitcomb argues that formal contracts based on competitive (not request-for-proposal [RFP]) proposals are necessary, that cost savings from contracts should equal at least 15 percent, and that agencies should look at contracting very carefully.

Contracting out will *not* work well unless (1) there is competition among providers, (2) the contract is closely monitored, (3) public agencies rather than the contractor certify all eligible patients, (4) there is clear contract authority, and (5) political influence is kept out of the selection of contractors (DeHoog, 1984; Straussman and Fairie, 1981). Some of these requirements are unique to social services contracting, such as the certification of eligibles. Others, such as the need for contractor competition, are common to all kinds of contracting. Social service programs have unique aspects, especially when contracted out, but they require management techniques similar to other services.

Prison and Correction Contracting

Privatization, particularly contracting, in the prison and corrections area is a rapidly growing area of interest for both contractors and public officials (National Institute of Justice, 1985). This interest, of course, is sparked by the growth of jail and prison populations and the severe overcrowding of prison facilities. Presently, the states of Massachusetts, Hawaii, Connecticut, and California are 50 percent over their prison or jail capacity ("Some States . . . ," 1987).

Prison Industries. Of three prison/corrections areas that are now contracting out, the oldest is prison industries. For over a century, the private sector has been involved, in one way or another, in prison industry activities. Prior to World War II, prison industries were common, but in 1940 the federal government outlawed interstate shipment of prisoner-made articles, and until the 1970s prison industries languished. In a 1979 pilot study, the federal government lifted this restriction for five states, and there is considerable activity and interest now in prison industries.

Private activity in prison industries occurs in one of two ways. Some firms contract with the Department of Corrections for prisoner labor. Best Western Hotels employs Arizona women in a prerelease center to make nationwide reservations for the hotel chain. In Utah a graphic arts company contracts for twenty-six inmates to work in the state's print shop. Koolmist, an air-conditioning manufacturer, contracts with the Mississippi Department of Corrections for twenty inmates to make condensing units. In Minnesota, Control Data Corporation (CDC) contracts with Stillwater State Prison for computer assembly component parts, employing from thirty-two to 145 prisoners, with 1984 sales of nearly 1 million (Chi, 1985). There are similar programs in Kansas, Iowa, and Nevada as well.

The second way that states use private sector contracting is through private operation of the prison industry. In Florida, PRIDE (Prison Rehabilitative Industries and Diversified Enterprises, Inc.) was founded as a nonprofit corporation to manage prison industries. PRIDE manages over twenty-two types of prison industries, from optical labs to print shops. PRIDE has already made money by converting a state cattle farm into a sugarcane farm.

Another nonprofit firm, Stillwater Data Processing Systems, Inc. (SDPS), operates in cooperation with CDC in Minnesota's Stillwater State Prison. After training, inmates program computer software for prison clients, including the state and several private firms. SDPS leases work space from the state but manages the company independently of the Department of Corrections. Similar programs planned for Michigan and Mississippi await final arrangements (National Institute of Justice, 1985).

There is still political opposition to expanding prison industries because (1) some industries are not profitable, (2) they compete with outside businesses, (3) they do not improve recidivism rates, and (4) they depress the outside labor market. Proponents argue that these programs combat idleness, help prepare inmates for release, and earn money to defray the costs of imprisonment and victims' rights payments. These arguments may never be settled, but it seems that private contractors will increasingly be called on to manage prison industries.

Financing Prisons and Jails. The second way the private sector is involved in the corrections/prisons area is that private firms build many state and city jails. This is a relatively new development, but it raises no particular political objections.

Historically, and still commonly, states and cities built jails and prisons, using general revenues or the receipts from bond issues. However, increases in the number of prisoners have outstripped the ability of many jurisdictions to buy space to build prisons. Prison population in the country increased one-third, or about 130,000 prisoners, from 1978 to 1982. Many states are under court order to relieve overcrowding. Yet, many states are short of money to acquire additional prison space and, where court orders are in effect, must construct prisons very quickly. These state governments are turning to private parties, usually under some sort of lease or lease-purchase arrangement. Straight leases, the least financially advantageous arrangement for governments, provide that the facility remain in private hands after the lease expires. Such leases were being used by eighteen of the fifty state correction departments in 1984. Michigan and Pennsylvania together accounted for half of all the prison beds leased in the United States, and states such as Arizona, Colorado, Indiana, and South Carolina also used straight leases. All leases were for halfway houses or community service centers, and no maximum security prisons were leased (National Institute of Justice, 1985).

Lease-purchase agreements pass building titles to the government agency after lease payments have been made over a period of years. Lease purchases are permitted in many states and are commonly used for office buildings, school buildings, and airport terminals. In the corrections area, Los Angeles County has financed a police station, splitting the lease into certificates of participation to attract more investors. Jefferson County (Colorado) also financed a correctional facility this way. Sacramento County, Philadelphia, and Portland recently built jails using lease-purchase financing. Several other states are considering the use of this financing mechanism (National Institute of Justice, 1985). The significance of leasing is that more and more jurisdictions are interested in contracts that call for the construction and operation of prison facilities.

Facilities Management. According to the newsletter *Privatization,* over thirty nationwide state detention centers for illegal aliens, juvenile offenders, and mental patients are privately owned and operated. The Texas legislature allows the state Department of Corrections to contract with private companies for the construction and operation of prison units with fewer than 500 inmates, if the company guarantees a 10 percent savings over state operation. Three other states have enacted similar laws, with a dozen more considering such legislation ("Some States . . . ," 1987).

Container Corporation of America (CCA) offered in 1985 to operate Tennessee prisons under a ninety-nine-year franchise, with a first-year fee of $200 million. The state was still considering the proposal in 1987. CCA began in Tennessee, in October 1984, with operation of a local work house for 300 male and female offenders in Hamilton County. The firm has a four-year contract at $21 per inmate per day. CCA also operates a juvenile residential treatment facility in Shelby County and nine jails in several other states.

One of these jails is a six-story facility in Panama City, Florida. Originally considered dangerously overcrowded, jail conditions are improving, and crowding has subsided since CCA has developed additional facilities. A new Panama City jail was remodeled and refurbished, and a work camp was constructed. Complaints and lawsuits by inmates and citizens have declined, and state inspections rate the CCA-operated jail as one of the state's best ("Jails . . . ," 1987).

The Federal Bureau of Prisons has a three-year contract with a private corporation, Eclectic Communications, Inc. (ECI), to house federal prisoners in La Honda, California. The sixty offenders are low security risks, and the prison is completely operated by the private firm. ECI began in 1981 with a contract for managing a program of prisoner early release to a college or university in the Santa Barbara area. Expanding to operating work-furlough programs in Santa Barbara and Los Angeles, ECI now operates thirteen correctional facilities under contract with federal agencies and the states of California, Nevada, and Virginia. Florida and Pennsylvania also have nonprofit or private firms operating private juvenile facilities (National Institute of Justice, 1985; "Contractor Provides . . . ," 1987).

The pressure to expand prison space is not limited to the United States. France has recently decided to call on private companies to build, staff, and operate new penitentiaries. Private employees are to be recruited by the private companies but trained and certified by the government. Prison guards originally favored the plan to ease overcrowding and create new jobs but now oppose the proposal. They argue that new employees would not have civil service status, that hardened criminals would remain under their control, and that private guards would have easier prisoners as well as more sophisticated equipment ("France Looks . . . ," 1986).

Private operation of prison facilities has sparked a bitter debate. Supporters of privatization see private operation as the only alternative to gaining more space and advocate preserving flexibility in prison management by using private employees. This side also argues that the need to maintain standards in order to keep contracts will counteract any inclination to cut corners, particularly since the media and unions will be observing. Finally, advocates note that, in many respects, private operation of prisons is not dissimilar to private mental hospitals or perhaps even nursing homes.

Opponents argue that the power of the state should not be turned over to private parties. They also worry that private operators will cut corners and will bring pressure to bear for harsher sentences in order to keep prisons full to maintain profit margins. The question of liability for inmate controls, such as a death in an escape attempt, probably rests with the public agency, but this is still unclear. Security concerns, as liability issues, are unresolved ("Supporters, Opponents . . . ," 1987).

Money, or public agencies' lack thereof, will probably settle the contracting out issue in favor of more privatization. Impassioned arguments in favor of the state's responsibility for the use of force (to imprison people) will probably lose to pressures to build and operate more prisons more quickly. As long as the prison population continues to expand rapidly, pressure to build and operate prisons and correctional facilities will increase, and the private sector, under contract, will often provide that service. If private contracts that are presently under way, such as in Tennessee and California, are successful, the pressure to contract more out will increase.

Financing and Operating Public Infrastructure

America's infrastructure (that is, public works facilities) is falling apart. It will take many billions of dollars to restore our streets, roads, bridges, sewage treatment plants, and water purification plants. The huge capital investments made in the past have undergirded much of the economic growth since World War II, but these tunnels, bridges, and sewage systems are aging. In addition, population growth and environmental concerns, such as for clean water, will create further need for public works projects in the coming years.

Public works projects needed in the immediately foreseeable future may total several trillion dollars. Repairing and building new wastewater plants alone may have a yearly nationwide price tag of $6 to $9 billion in the 1990s (Sullivan and Marietta, 1987). Another estimate is that wastewater treatment plant construction, renovation, operation, maintenance, and upgrading to meet federal clean water standards will total over $100 billion by the year 2000 (Quinn and Olstein, 1985). To meet these estimated needs, Congress has authorized over $40 billion since 1972, but federal money for treatment plants is dwindling; the federal grant share of local plant construction costs has declined to about 33 percent and soon will convert to loans only (Johnson and Heilman, 1987).

Wastewater plants are only one public works need. According to another survey, mass transportation systems, roads, streetlights, and bridges are in the worst condition. Municipal buildings, correctional facilities, and sewage and solid waste treatment plants are also in poor condition. Cities and counties are planning to double their expenditures on these public works (infrastructure) projects, with 60 percent of the respondents intending to double their current level of expenditures and nearly a quarter of respondents intending to triple expenditures (Touche Ross, 1985). One estimate claims that 82 percent of the nation's bridges need repair, at a cost of $27 billion, and water supply/treatment facilities will cost over $100 billion in the next two decades ("Infrastructure Privatization . . . ," 1986).

As an example, consider the staggering needs of a single state, New Jersey. Forty-five hundred of its 6,000 bridges need repair. The state must build 237 wastewater treatment plants within the next decade, but can only build twenty-four with current levels of federal aid. The Port of New York and New Jersey will have infrastructure needs of $40 billion during the next decade. To meet these challenges, however, New Jersey can only commit $20 million in 1983 (Touche Ross, 1984).

Infrastructure Needs and Contracting Out. What does this construction backlog mean for contracting out? After all, contracting out primarily involves operating the projects after construction. The answer is that the most likely way to reduce the backlog of public works projects is through privatization. This involves private financing, design, construction, *and* operation of a number of facilities. Operation of facilities will be, de facto, contracted out as part of a privatization plan that finances, builds, and operates plants. Contracting out in many cases, then, will not be a formal decision about the best way to operate the facility but will be only a part of the overall decision to privatize the plant. In many cases, the city or county simply enters into a contract with the private party to build and finance the plant for a number of years. Private sources will be increasingly used to provide public services.

Historically, public works facilities were financed by bonds issued by local governments. The facilities were designed under one contract, built under another contract, and operated (rarely) under a third contract. Changes now are occurring. First, there is a tendency for contracts to be combined. With private financing (a second change), there may be a single contract for financing, design, construction, and operation. Such a combination reduces the time, energy, and paperwork required by four separate operations, and this is one reason why privatization can reduce costs.

The classic example of such an arrangement is a service contract where the private party formally contracts with the municipality for a service such as sewage treatment. The private party finances, designs, constructs, and operates the facility. The municipality merely determines how much of the service is needed and when it is needed and sets service standards (Pestle, 1987). The service is contracted out, but as part of a much larger package in which financing is the major consideration.

Privatization Arrangements. Privatization arrangements are not yet commonplace. An International City Management Association survey indicated that about 3 percent of local governments have chosen privatization as the means of financing capital aspects. Most of these (64 percent) were for solid waste facilities (Valente, 1987). However, another survey reports that 38 percent of respondents planned to privatize facilities in the next two years. Respondents indicated that demand for services and

taxpayer resistance to tax increases were the two issues that heightened their interest in privatization. Local officials also reported that the primary advantages of privatizing facilities were cost savings, risk sharing (for example, of construction delays), and shorter implementation time (Touche Ross, 1987).

Although the total number of local governments that have privatized a public works facility is small, there are some notable success stories. One study reviewed the experience of sixteen cities across the nation that considered privatizing wastewater treatment plants during the early and mid 1980s. Eight cities eventually chose privatization, which in this case involved private ownership and operation of the plant, with the city paying a fee for the services. In most cases, the financing was public, with proceeds from a tax-exempt municipal bond issue loaned to a private sector party, such as a limited partnership between the municipality and the owner-operator.

The size of the eight cities and the cost of their wastewater plants ranged from 404,000, for a $20 million plant, to 6,800, for a $5 million plant (the cities were not identified). The final decision to contract out was usually based on economics, followed by the speed with which the project could be completed. The major reasons that the remaining cities did not privatize were reluctance to lose control over the plant and its employees as well as uncertainty over buy-back provisions (Johnson and Heilman, 1987).

This account does not mention contracting out. Practically, the question of whether to contract out was completely subsumed by the basic question of financing and construction. This is not to say that political questions, partly involving control over employees, were not important—five of the six municipalities that did not privatize mentioned political issues as a factor in their decision. What happens with privatization is that operation of the plant seems considerably less important than financing questions: Contracting out is incidental to the primary arrangements of financing.

Scottsdale (Arizona) recently completed a 20,000-acre-foot water treatment facility that will deliver Colorado River water to the city. Scottsdale formed a partnership with three private parties, one to build the plant, one to be project engineer during construction, and one to operate the plant. The city was the limited partner; the private parties were the general partner. Scottsdale and the general partners will both share in the value of the plant after the end of the agreement. The city pays a monthly water bill, varying with the volume of water used, to the partnership. Financing was done by industrial development bonds under the provisions of the 1984 Federal Tax Code. Under the 1986 Tax Reform Act, there is a limit on the number of industrial development bonds that can be issued by any state, and depreciation schedules have been changed. Privatized financing for Scottsdale-type arrangements are thus more difficult now (Sullivan and Marietta, 1987; "New Facility . . . ," 1987).

Westchester County (New York) privatized the design, development, construction, and operation of a refuse-to-energy-disposal plant that serves a population of 860,000. Refuse is burned, and the energy generated is sold to Consolidated Edison. The county pays the contractor a fixed rate per ton (now $18.72) for disposing of the refuse, plus an additional charge if Consolidated Edison pays the contractor less than six cents per kilowatt hour (the additional charge totaled $12 million in 1986).

The plant was built with a combination of public and private financing totaling $50 million of contractor equity, $157 million of industrial revenue bonds, and $28 million of New York State Environmental Quality Bonds. The developer assumed all risks and responsibility, guaranteeing the construction and operation of the plant during a twenty-year contract that will expire in 2005. The county guaranteed sufficient refuse, based on agreements with thirty-five municipalities to deliver their refuse to the plant, plus the refuse from the county. Again, the issue of contracting out was settled once the arrangements for financing were completed, and the new project's employees work for the contractor ("Westchester's Privatized . . . ," 1987).

Baltimore, acting through the Northeast Maryland Waste Disposal Authority, is privatizing its solid waste composting facility. A private contractor is constructing and operating the plant, which is financed by private equity contributions and public revenue bonds. The facility will compact 210 tons of wet sludge into seventy tons of dry compost daily, with Baltimore paying a fee for each wet ton of sludge composted. The contractor will provide full staffing, staff training, and labor relations for employees in the new plant. At the end of the twenty-year contract, the authority can either purchase the facility, operate it itself under private ownership, or demolish it and use the land ("First 'Sludge' . . . ," 1987).

Two Texas cities, Irving and College Station, used privatization to provide for additional water supply. College Station designed a water tower with city engineers, and a private contractor financed the construction. The city agreed to purchase a minimum amount of water at a guaranteed price for the balance of the contract. The contractor operates the facility, delivering water on demand. At the end of the contract, College Station can extend the contract or buy the tower for a small fee.

Irving's contract is virtually identical, although the contractor drilled wells rather than constructing a water tower. Both cities cite preservation of municipal bonding capacity for other purposes as a major advantage of the arrangement, since the contractor arranged private financing ("Two Successful . . . ," 1987).

Despite the success of several privatized arrangements, public ownership is likely to remain the dominant form of financing infrastructure needs, at least for waste and wastewater plants. Tax-exempt debt is available, and public officials want to maintain control over water-related projects. Where debt limits or tax ceilings exist, cities can use tax-exempt leasing even under the 1986 Tax Reform Law, although doing so is more expensive than bond financing. In some cases, however, private financing is required, and private funds, both tax-exempt debt and equity financing, will generally be available. Advantages of privatizing include faster construction, use of advanced technology, and "more flexibility in hiring and staffing plants than municipalities" (Sullivan and Marietta, 1987, p. 62).

The key issue in privatizing public works projects, whether they are water-related or not, is that the financial arrangements almost always involve private operation of the completed facility. Operation of the facility is, in effect, contracting out, determined solely by initial considerations of financing, construction, and design decisions. Governments over the upcoming years must upgrade old facilities and build new ones to meet the needs of an expanding population. If these governments privatize in order to do so, the number of facilities with private rather than public employees will increase. This may be a substantial change in the way public works facilities are operated, depending only on what percentage of new infrastructures is privatized. If privatization occurs, the effect will be the same as a major increase in contracting out.

Summary

Contracting out is not only increasing, it is also expanding into entirely new areas or into hitherto infrequently contracted areas, and much more aggressively. Three such areas are social services, prisons and corrections, and financing and operating public infrastructure.

Nonprofit contractors and, to a lesser degree, other governments have traditionally dominated the human and social service areas. Nonprofits are credited with great client commitment and with having more flexibility and expertise than government. Currently, however, private firms are moving into the social services.

Prison and corrections contracting is becoming extensive. Many contractors are involved either in managing prison industries or in contracting for prison labor, while there has been great recent interest in having private contractors build prisons and operate jails and detention centers for juveniles and nonfelons.

Financing and operating public works projects is a recent phenomenon. It particularly concerns wastewater and sewage plants but also includes roads, bridges, and other public works. Governments increasingly see contracting as the only way to quickly construct new facilities without the need for infusions of public money.

CHAPTER 3 ⟿⟿⟿⟿⟿⟿⟿⟿⟿⟿

When and When Not
to Contract Out

What services are generally contracted out? Under what circumstances? To whom, and why? For most managers in the public sector who are wrestling with the basic contracting out decision, these questions are of most concern. The answers vary substantially: some are clear and seem to be based on effective experience in specific cases; others are not well substantiated. Some agencies look hard and carefully for the best outside contractor, whether private or governmental. Others simply look for any available contractor.

No one, without careful analysis, should judge why contracting decisions are made. Second, contracting out is a relatively new process for most cities. It is true that in some places contracting out has been going on for a long period of time, as in the Lakewood plan in Los Angeles County, where the county has provided a wide range of municipal services to a large number of cities since 1954 (see Case Study 2 in the Resources). However, cities in Los Angeles County tend to depend on the county for most services and thus have not experimented with a range of service providers.

Third, little is written about the basic question of when to contract out. What has been written has been presented in a fragmented way, often through occasional professional literature such as Management Information Service reports to city managers who are members of the International City Management Association. These reports often deal with technical issues rather than broad strategy concerns. The least helpful literature (but often most common) is polemic tracts about either (1) how cities can save considerable money and delay the rampant growth of government by contracting out or (2) how contracting out plays into the hands of unscrupulous businesses who underpay their employees and care only for profit. The result is that managers and political leaders have Hobson's choice: They can choose to avoid most information, or they can choose to review a good deal of bad or irrelevant material.

The purpose of this chapter is to review the common arguments for and against contracting out, compare them to the available information about contracting out, and suggest some rules of thumb for making preliminary decisions on whether to contract out specific services.

Contract Out When It Reduces Costs

The basic reason to contract out public services is to save money. Money is frequently, if not always, saved when services are contracted out. A study of twenty Department of Defense contracts between 1978 and 1981 showed savings in seventeen of the contracts (Comptroller General, 1985b).

There are many reasons why contracting out can be cheaper than having the government provide the service itself, even though the private firm retains a profit. As noted in the first chapter, private firms use their work force more effectively (Stevens, 1984). They often achieve economies of scale by distributing equipment and personnel over a wider area and using technologically advanced equipment. These firms can, if necessary, pay higher salaries to attract key people, avoid civil service rules that increase the cost of labor, and use part-time employees. Savings do not always occur, but they happen frequently enough to make cost saving a major reason to contract out.

The federal Office of Management and Budget estimated savings of $3.6 billion dollars in the five years from 1982 to 1987 if all federal agencies contracted out all services such as janitorial, laundry, or keypunching that cost comparisons showed could be done more cheaply by private parties (Comptroller General, 1981). Monroe County (Rochester, New York) purchased social services from private groups at a per-case cost of $328, compared to $476 per case internally (Straussman and Fairie, 1981). San Jose (California) contracted with a private vendor to collect parking citations, partly because the court system had not been following up on delinquent citations. The city's first-year revenue increase was $300,000, even after paying the vendor $160,000 (League of California Cities, 1981).

Actual costs are not often documented, and to some degree, contracting out to save money is an act of faith, as is reflected in the following comment by a California local official:

> Often contracting with the private sector is less expensive than with other government agencies but without technical skills to monitor the contracts, one must trust the contractor to perform satisfactorily. When a city is burned once or twice by private contractors the tendency is to go back to other government agency contracts or do the work by force account [California Tax Foundation, 1981, p. 5].

One case where actual savings have been demonstrated is in residential refuse collection. Several large cities, including Minneapolis, Montreal, and Phoenix, have competitive systems in which city services compete with private firms. In five of the six cities reviewed, the annual cost per household for contract firms is from $7 to $22 less than municipal collection. In Minneapolis, city collection is extremely competitive with private collectors (Savas, 1977).

Other than this example, there are few examples of actual savings other than informed commentary asserting that contract services are indeed cheaper (or are not cheaper) than government operation. One study of small cities showed that only 40 percent found contracting out prices cheaper than city provision, while 34 percent indicated that contracting was more expensive (Florestano and Gordon, 1980). Lafayette (California) retained a private maintenance firm to provide all public maintenance functions, including supervision of all employees or subcontractors as the main contractor. This arrangement, under a carefully written contract with a specific work program, saved the city 16 percent in 1977–78 (Roy Jorgenson Associates, 1981).

In California, Governor Deukmejian argued that contracting out surveyor jobs for road construction in the Transportation Department was cheaper than using state employees. The union representing the employees filed suit to block contracting out, armed with internal department memoranda and a report by the legislative analyst stating that contracting out was not cheaper ("Contracting Out . . . ," 1982). The real reason may have been the governor's desire to keep total work-force levels down rather than to save money, since the former was more politically embarrassing. Here, contracting out became a political issue rather than a careful analysis of costs—not the first time this has happened. When good cost information is not available, other factors weigh more heavily in the contracting out decision.

The reasons why contracting out may be cheaper than using city forces vary widely, from avoiding start-up costs to achieving economies of scale. Whatever the reasons, careful estimates have to be made on the costs of the existing service. These cost studies are all too frequently nonexistent or else do not include many costs, such as imputed rent for city buildings. (Most of these points will be covered later in this book.)

Contract Out Services Only
When They Can Be Monitored

Government agencies ultimately have the responsibility for the services that they arrange or authorize, even if they do not actually produce them. Therefore, the agency basically has only two alternatives: It must either do the work itself or have others do it. When others do the work, as in contracting out, the government unit must then be sure that the service is being handled properly. In other words, governments either have to perform the task themselves or monitor others who may perform it.

Because of the political, if not legal, responsibility for the service, a basic rule of thumb for deciding when to contract out is to choose only programs that can be effectively monitored. If a program cannot be monitored, such as hospital management or drug/alcohol treatment clinics, it should be operated using government employees so that there will be public accountability. A better solution, of course, may be to contract out the service and monitor it properly.

Monitoring services properly is easier to say than to do. The fact that contract monitoring is often ineffective does not mean that agencies should not try to monitor, but rather that if they cannot do an effective job of monitoring the contract, the service perhaps ought to be provided by the government.

One of the reasons for difficulties in monitoring is that providing a service and monitoring the service require quite different skills. One California city manager indicated that public works supervisors are accustomed to supervising crews for maintenance or minor construction projects but are not used to reviewing work done by private contractors (Aleshire, interview with author, Oct. 1986). If so, perhaps we should not be surprised that an agency can effectively monitor drug and alcohol clinics or hospital operation programs but be unable to operate them. Conversely, policy communications and building inspection programs may be well operated by the agency, but it may not be able to monitor private contractors who provide these services.

Some services by their very nature are difficult to measure and evaluate. Law enforcement services, such as fire suppression and prevention or police traffic control and crime control, are probably the best examples. While there are some measures for evaluating the effectiveness of these services, the measures are not applied widely or with any consistency. If the programs were to be conducted under contract, it would be very difficult to agree on performance standards and even more difficult to apply them. This is probably one major reason that relatively few cities contract out these types of services.

Observers commonly identify monitoring of services as the Achilles' heel of the contracting out process. The California Tax Foundation's 1981 survey indicates that there are two major problems with contracting out: contractor unreliability and the difficulty in monitoring contracts (California Tax Foundation, 1981). These two problems may be but two sides of the same coin, since unreliable contractors may simply be contractors who anticipate weak monitoring.

In one study of public works contracts, Tribbett (1983) notes that such contracts are difficult to monitor and evaluate. This is somewhat surprising, since public works contracts usually involve more specific measures of performance, such as signals maintained, street-miles swept, or miles of lane lines painted. However, Tribbett's views are echoed by Roy Jorgensen Associates (1981), a firm specializing in highway maintenance contracts. The firm argues that viable street maintenance contracts require that the agency (1) have a measurable work program, (2) make a contractual fund commitment to the program, and (3) inspect for quality and timeliness. Jorgensen and associates note that a major disadvantage of contracting out (at least in less developed foreign countries) is the inability of agencies to monitor and manage contracts.

A study of social service contracts in Michigan revealed that little performance evaluation took place (DeHoog, 1984). Instead, agencies monitored expenditures, checked the contractors' determinations of eligibility, and reviewed contractors' self-reports but made few field visits. In short, the agencies narrowly concentrated on compliance with the contract rather than reviewing actual performance of the contractor.

The Government Finance Officers Association (GFOA) notes that rigorous monitoring should include a way to assess productivity to ensure that the contractor provides quality service to the government (Kelley, 1984). The GFOA notes that when the contract is signed, the local agency's work has just begun. Unfortunately, many governments assume that the problem is solved at this point. GFOA also notes that because managing a contract is so different from operating a program, it is difficult to estimate the costs of contract compliance.

The federal government requires that a contractor's successful bid be 10 percent lower than the cost of government operation, presumably to allow for a margin of error and also to allow for monitoring costs, which can be substantial. Indeed, Levinson (1976) indicates that an argument against contracting out is that the savings from outside contracts can be consumed by monitoring costs.

By now, the point should be clear. Monitoring contractor compliance with the contract is (1) an important part of the contracting out process, (2) potentially time consuming and expensive, and (3) often done poorly. A number of problems arise if the contract cannot be effectively monitored. These problems are as broad as basic quality control and as narrow as technical compliance with the letter of the contract. For all these reasons, it is better not to contract out services if they cannot be properly monitored.

Contract Out When Complex or
Technical Services Are Needed

A common reason for contracting out is for the agency to obtain complex, technical, and technologically advanced services. These are some of the oldest, and also the best, justifications for contracting out. If the agency did not use outside contractors, or consultants (as they are often known), staffs would have to be expanded considerably for intermittent and nonroutine work.

Scarce Skills. Contracting out for scarce skills is routinely done at all levels of government and by all types of government agencies as a way of contracting for expertise. Data-processing systems are a good example. Every unit using a complex management information system contracts with private companies for installation, if not operation, of the system. This is what happened in Prince George's County (see Case Study 1 in the Resources), which employed a data-processing system with a central mainframe computer. Prior to the development of this arrangement, other computer-based systems were developed, such as a computer-aided dispatch system for the police and fire departments. This was a complex system designed to improve and speed the assignment of emergency personnel and was installed by outside consultants. As in many similar cases across the country, the system was much too expensive to retain data-processing specialists on the staff, and thus contracting out was the only answer. Outside consultants may be asked to train permanent staff, or, as in the case of Prince George's County, may be retained to operate the facility in order to assimilate continuing technological data-processing advances.

Data processing is only one of the many instances where government agencies contract out to obtain scarce skills. Most small and several large cities and counties routinely use private contractors for plan checking. All building permits requiring special review of construction plans are sent to the contractor, and the cost is normally assessed as part of the building fee. Since plans requiring complex checking occur irregularly, this arrangement avoids increasing city or county staffs for less than full-time work. Conversely, the contractor can distribute the efforts of professional plan checkers over many government agencies.

Legal services are frequently contracted out. Everyone may want a personal attorney, but this does not mean that the personal attorney has to be a full-time agency employee. Attorneys can be retained for specific uses, for special circumstances, or for continuing consultation on a part-time basis. Table 2 showed that half of reporting cities contract out legal services. Given the costs of fringe benefits, secretaries, and office space, contracting out is probably cheaper than retaining full-time attorneys, except for the largest cities.

Other examples include social services such as day-care facilities, child welfare programs, management and operation of public housing, hospital management, and mental health programs. Some of these services were listed in Table 2, but even those services not shown are contracted out about 30 percent of the time, often to nonprofit groups. Including these services in this section is not strictly accurate, since the skills involved are not scarce. It is not difficult for government agencies to hire people with these skills. However, when human service recipients involve large numbers of heterogeneous individuals, a common practice is to use private or nonprofit providers.

At the state level, using outside providers is quite common. At the local level, public employees are used for distributing welfare or making eligibility determinations, but human service programs (including everything from alcohol treatment to mental health) are provided by private groups. There is a general belief that private agencies provide better service, partly because they have more expertise with a wider range of services. Since many human services are not widely supported by all citizens, there is little pressure to have government employees provide the services themselves. For these reasons, contracting out is likely to increase in this area.

One-Time Help. Contracting out for one-time or intermittent help is probably the most common reason for contracting out. At the local level, engineers develop the road plans for local public works street projects, while architects design public buildings. At the state level, engineering staffs often design state highways or bridges, but construction is contracted out.

For specific problems ranging from data processing to centralized purchasing, outside consultants are widely used. This is partly because the agency could not afford to retain these consultants on their staffs but also because outside opinion is needed to lend legitimacy to internal recommendations.

Another common use of consultants involves the use of certified public accountant firms for annual audits of financial accounts. Since these firms are used every year, their use is not, strictly speaking, one time. However, outside reviews by specially trained accountants are necessary for certifying the financial health of government agencies. Another example is bond counsel for bond issues. With the advent of creative government financing, the assistance of investment houses such as Dean Witter or Smith Barney is required. Indeed, there seems to be no end to the ways government can use one-time consultants, from contracts for planning recreation events with payment based on attendance to employment of planning consultants to prepare and update city master plans.

These last two examples occurred in California, largely because of the limitations imposed by Proposition 13 on local property taxation. These limitations caused cities and counties to seek ways to save money, and the result, in these cases, was to use contracting out for services that previously had been provided by city staff. In these two examples, money is saved, with no loss of local control or quality of services. This demonstrates that contracting out for one-time help is a viable alternative to retaining large in-house staffs.

Capturing Technological Advances. Contracting out is sometimes a means of capturing technological advances, ranging from minor advances, such as labor-saving fire equipment, to major advances, such as weapon systems acquired by Department of Defense contracts with major aerospace firms.

The billion-dollar aerospace industry exists on government defense contracts. The process is fueled by the Pentagon's attempts to take advantage of technological advances by contracting with these firms. The contracts frequently are bid at and approved for unrealistically low amounts. This is partly because a total cost estimate might be rejected by Congress as too high, but it is also owing to hopes that the pressure to meet the low bid might force technological advances that would keep the costs down. There seems to be little evidence that this contracting out practice actually fosters identifiable technological advances, but it is a major argument for contracting out.

The argument that aerospace expenditures stimulate new technology was used to justify the National Space Agency's 1960s drive to put a man on the moon. The technological advances were to benefit the general public, as did the resulting new and improved glues. There may be few analogies to this federal effort at the state and local levels, although it is commonly assumed that private contractors will search relentlessly for ways to reduce their costs and to make additional profits. Private contractors also have more incentive to use labor-saving devices, such as one-man-loadable garbage trucks.

It is profitable for contractors to obtain expensive labor-saving or technologically advanced equipment when they have the ability to spread its use over a wider number of clients or a wider geographical area. Examples are fire equipment for reaching tall buildings or equipment for conveying workers to the tops of trees for tree trimming or to tall streetlights for bulb removal or maintenance work. Most small agencies simply must contract with private firms or larger government agencies to have access to such equipment.

In 1971 a new organization, Public Technology, Inc., was created to adapt new technology to the needs of local governments. Cities and counties could contract with the nonprofit firm for information on technological advances—ranging from the reuse of asphalt pavements to developing traffic control systems that are lightning resistant—that are applicable to local units. Clearly, contracting out was, in these cases, the only way to obtain or share information on technological breakthroughs by individual units.

Contract Out to Establish Benchmark Costs

A common argument for contracting out is to establish a cost basis for comparing government provision of the service with private contractors. The Government Finance Officers Association states that "the need to compare the costs of public and private delivery of a service" provides one reason to contract out (Kelley, 1984, p. 96).

Savas (1982, p. 90) notes that contracting a portion of the work offers a yardstick for comparison; the cost is visible in the contract price. This occurs in competitive garbage collection systems, where both public and private collection systems compete. Analysts at the Urban Institute also argue that contracting out provides benchmarks for comparison (Fisk, Kiesling, and Muller, 1978). Poole (1980) offers garbage collection in Minneapolis as an example.

Few if any studies deal directly with benchmarks provided by contracting out. While the process of putting government services out to bid does establish some sort of a benchmark for costs, it is doubtful that the reason for contracting out is simply to compare costs.

The garbage collection study cited by Poole (1980) examined

the effect of competition between public and private municipal refuse collection systems. Competitive systems in six large cities usually resulted in much lower private costs per ton of garbage collected, except in Minneapolis, where determined city efforts drove city costs down to those of private collectors. These competitive systems had a number of advantages over all-municipal or all-contract systems. One of the advantages was that by retaining some municipal service, the city had a yardstick against which to measure private performance. Conversely, by retaining some contract collection, the city had a yardstick to measure performance of its own collection (Savas, 1982).

It is an important advantage to have a benchmark against which municipal costs can be measured, and this is certainly a legitimate reason for contracting out. Creating such a benchmark is not as simple as it may seem, however. First, true benchmark costs are not the costs of one bid on a contract; they are the actual costs revealed through subsequent bids after some years of experience. Second, true comparisons involve comprehensive government agency costs, including any costs of letting, awarding, and monitoring the contract. Until government accounting systems can provide these internal costs, there can be no real comparison. Finally, there is little proof that many cities have developed and are using true benchmark costs. (See Chapter Five for some measures that could be used as benchmarks.)

Contract Out to Avoid Management and Policy Constraints

Some cities contract out as many services as they possibly can. They resist providing services because they are convinced that, for a number of reasons, managing a large work force is a bad idea. This may be because these cities have found contracting out less expensive, or it may be for other reasons. For many new cities, there is a desire to concentrate on immediate problems without the distraction of having to manage programs and staff departments. For many cities, there is a belief (often unspoken and sometimes not even understood) that the role of the city or other governmental unit is to concentrate on major policy issues, not manage services.

This last point is often the real reason that some agencies contract out many programs, even if the official reason is to save money. After all, cities do not exist to provide services. (There are few agencies other than cities who contract out most or many of their services.) Cities exist to meet the needs and desires of residents. If there is little citizen demand for services, contracting out is perfectly acceptable.

Are many cities contracting out all or most city services? Probably not, with the exception of those cities in Los Angeles County using the Lakewood plan (see Case Study 2 in the Resources). In any case, the Lakewood plan proves that cities need not personally provide all services themselves to satisfy their citizens.

The fact is that some cities choose to contract more services than others, and not always just because it is less expensive. Why? As a case in point, consider the comments of the city manager of Garden Grove, California. He describes the city's test for programs, designed to minimize the work force and to ensure that city services are done by others, if possible.

1. Can this service be purchased from another jurisdiction?
2. Can the city enter into a joint management agreement with one or more other jurisdictions to provide the service?
3. Can the city participate with an existing special-purpose government agency or special district in providing the service?
4. Can the city buy the service from a private firm—a private nonprofit agency or a private individual?
5. Can a new service provider be created? (Powers, 1980, p. 4)

This test has resulted in the use by the city of contractors (such as nonprofit corporations) to operate cultural programs, contracts with private firms (for example, to handle custodial services), and joint agreements with other agencies (such as the county library).

Cost reduction does not necessarily explain every effort to contract out services by cities such as Garden Grove, even though Powers (1980) suggests in his article that this is the case.

For such cities, providing services may instead deflect city attention from policymaking to program management. Policymaking requires one approach; program management, another. Policymaking means responding to citizen complaints, making long-range civic plans, and/or acting as a sounding board for the community. Program management is simply providing services. Most cities have no trouble doing both, but some cities seem to focus all their energy on policymaking.

Some managerial problems are eased by contracting out most services. For new cities, attention to intense political problems and institution-building activities are often far more important than developing a city staff. Political leaders may demand that management attention be devoted to the former issues, and thus it is simpler to contract out, either to private parties or other government agencies. Staff time can then be devoted to policy issues.

Another nonfinancial reason for contracting out is to prevent top management from being stretched too thin. When policymaking activities become heavy, agencies must choose between adding additional management staff and maintaining programs or reducing the management job. One way is to contract out, thereby releasing management from some responsibilities. Of course, the additional time that properly monitoring contracts would consume must be factored in.

A final reason for contracting out many programs is that it prevents managers from fighting program "fires" and ignoring long-term strategic planning. Large staffs require supervision, and civil service rules and limits make it difficult to manage and divert attention to people problems. Supervision time subsumes long-range planning time, illustrating Gresham's Law of Planning—that trivia drive out planning. Likewise, decision makers can have their attention diverted from policy matters to administrative issues. Their attention span is limited, and routine matters quickly fill up an agenda.

A major problem is the existence of large in-house staffs. Commitments to services, and the large staffs thus involved, are time consuming. In addition, large staffs increase political pressures from below. The staff members, most of whom vote in local elections, become a potential political factor. The fewer the employees, the more flexible the city staff will be to new initiatives from elected officials. The council can demand that top management pay more attention to broader issues than the delivery of services.

By far, the majority of cities contract out relatively few services, and of those that contract out, many do so for financial considerations. But those cities, or other government agencies, concerned with top-level policies rather than services (for whatever reasons) might do well to consider contracting out more services.

Contracting Out for Political or Other Reasons

There are a number of miscellaneous situations in which contracting out can be of considerable use, either temporarily or on a long-term basis.

Occasionally, functions must be added rapidly—for example, when a new area is annexed. Contracting out can provide an arrangement that requires no sudden purchase of equipment or additional personnel, and the service can be produced quickly by contractors. This was the case in the State of Michigan when social service programs under Title XX federal grants were enacted (DeHoog, 1984). In other cases, such as refuse collection, private parties may already have been providing the service. At a later date, decisions can be made about whether the contract should become a permanent solution.

Another reason to contract out is to pass off controversial programs, such as welfare or health, to other jurisdictions. Allowing other agencies to provide the service may reduce conflict (National Association of Counties, 1977). For example, restaurant inspections may be less controversial if county, rather than city, inspectors enter eating establishments.

Do Not Contract Out to Disguise
Service Cuts as Cost Savings

Nothing is more destructive to good management than to contract out services with the unstated understanding that the contract provides for declines in the level of service. This does not officially happen very often, but unofficially, this may happen by not monitoring the contract, by making slipshod estimates of cost, or by requiring lower standards in the contract. This may occur when policymakers mistakenly assume that contracting out will automatically reduce costs and do not take into account service levels. Lower performance is not the difficulty; rather, the problem lies in disguising reductions in service as cost savings brought about by contracting out.

Such behavior is not unethical, but it is highly deceptive and dulls management sensibilities to actual cost issues. Cost comparisons between contractor and government services then become difficult to make, and evaluation becomes meaningless. It is far better simply to state that service levels may (or will) decline.

Do Not Contract Out If
There Is Strong Employee Resistance

Contracting out in the face of strong employee resistance is often unwise. In many cases, employee resistance may be politically more expensive to elected officials and may outweigh any monetary savings of contracting out. This is not to say that employee or union opposition is necessarily justified; rather, officials must pay attention to vocal political opposition. Wise managers are aware of this necessity. For example, a Benton Harbor (Michigan) city manager was dismissed for suggesting contracting out city services, an action that would have involved layoffs of most city employees (DeHoog, 1984).

The International City Management Association (ICMA) survey discussed in Chapter One mentions that employee and union resistance was frequently cited as the key reason for dropping the contracting out alternative (Shulman, 1982). The prospect of employee layoffs is sure to engender concern, if not outright opposition. This concern may spread beyond the department whose services are to be contracted out, and morale throughout the organization may suffer. If union opposition occurs, it will appear in areas as diverse as labor-management relations and political campaigns. Attrition rather than layoffs is often a better strategy. It is possible to require contractors to employ displaced employees, or employees can be reassigned or retrained within the agency itself (Shulman, 1982).

Do Not Contract Out Emergency Services

Most local officials indicate that emergency services would be the last programs to be contracted out. Emergency services generally include police and fire services (such as fire suppression and inspection, police traffic enforcement, and police patrol) and police services (such as vice, narcotics, juvenile, and detective). These services are the very essence of a local jurisdiction, and contracting them out would be to surrender the very reason for its existence (Rubin, 1983).

This reluctance to contract out does not extend to related services such as police or fire communication or data-processing systems, and it does not seem to apply to ambulance services, emergency medical services, or vehicle towing (Shulman, 1982). A number of cities do contract these services out and apparently suffer no ill results. The ICMA survey shows that 10 percent of the 1,659 reporting cities contracted out crime prevention/ patrol, although half of these contracts were with neighborhood groups. Even so, 3 percent contracted these services to profit-making groups. Five percent more used intergovernmental agreements, probably for arrangements similar to the Los Angeles County Lakewood plan, whereby the county provides all types of police services to cities. Five percent of cities reported that they contract out fire prevention/suppression, although to profit groups only 1 percent of the time (Shulman, 1982).

Some cities, then, do contract even those services closest to their raison d'être. Why, then, should some cities or government agencies be reluctant to contract out emergency services? Sometimes it is fear of political furor, sometimes wariness of the political power of fire and police groups, sometimes fear of loss of control over a volatile area, sometimes resistance to change. In any case, the conventional wisdom opposes contracting out in such areas. A good rule of thumb is to assume that emergency services are not likely to be contracted out.

Summary

Government agencies should consider contracting out if they (1) can save money, (2) are willing to effectively monitor contracts, (3) know how to capture technological advances and use specialized services, (4) want to set benchmark costs figures, and (5) seek to reduce management and political leader time spent in delivering services. However, agencies should be very wary of contracting out if they (1) expect employee resistance, (2) are considering contracting out emergency services, or (3) are trying to save money by cutting service levels through contracting.

PART II ∽∽∽∽∽∽∽∽∽∽∽∽∽∽∽∽∽∽

The Contracting Out Process: A Step-by-Step Guide

Part Two covers the technical part of this book, from the manager's initial feasibility study through monitoring the contractor's work after the contract has begun.

Chapter Four deals with activities that take place, from the initial consideration of contracting through the signing of the contract. The first step is an internal feasibility study to identify contractable services and establish performance measures. The next step is to solicit and review bids. The manager must then decide whether to base the award on formal invitations to bid (ITBs), which involve sealed bids and public openings. The ITB process is normally used when the contract can be clearly defined. The other way of arriving at contracts is through requests for proposals (RFPs). RFPs are usually used for personal services, sole-source suppliers, or emergency procedures. They involve negotiations among the parties prior to signing a contract. The processes for awarding contracts differ for RFPs and ITBs, although success with either method requires competition among contractors, which is often hard to achieve.

Chapter Five involves monitoring the contract once the contractor has begun to provide the service. Monitoring is an important aspect of contracting out because it is often the only way that effective performance can be ensured. Weak or ineffective contracts are usually not monitored enough, while effective monitoring ensures that good contracts receive the credit they deserve. Monitoring involves three basic issues: First, there is the cost, which varies from ''no official cost'' to over 10 percent of the contract. Second, there is the question of who should monitor contracts—those line officials closest to the service, or a more removed (and presumably more detached) individual. Finally, there is the question of how the methods of monitoring, inspection, complaint, performance standards, and reports are to be used.

Chapter Six presents some common contract provisions intended to prevent various problems that have plagued contracting out. These provisions include avoiding contract interruptions when the contractor cannot continue, penalties for failure to perform, the ability of the contractee to change service levels, response to emergencies, and preventing a contractor from bidding deliberately low to win a contract and then inflating later bids. The chapter ends with a discussion of the costs of these provisions.

CHAPTER 4 ∿∿∿∿∿∿∿∿∿∿∿∿∿∿∿∿

Conducting Feasibility Studies, Preparing Contracts, and Selecting Contractors

The steps in the first part of the contracting out process are feasibility studies, contract preparation, and contractor selection. Each step deserves separate attention.

A careful feasibility study as well as a general policy review of contracting out services should precede the preparation of any contract. Such a study makes possible a well-written contract, which is of great assistance in preventing later contractor difficulties. Well-written contracts eliminate questions such as "What level of service was actually specified?" or "Who actually authorizes payment for the contract?" or "Under what circumstances can either party insist on renegotiation?" Proper contractor selection eliminates contractors who may perform poorly or who are unsuited for the contract.

These three preliminary steps—feasibility studies, comprehensive contract preparation, and careful contractor selection—are the keys to a successful contracting out experience.

Laying the Groundwork: Analyzing Existing Services

Identifying Activities. The first step in the long process that ends in the selection of a contractor begins with identifying those activities that might be contracted out. This involves carefully examining what services your government agency actually provides, breaking them into even more specific activities, and identifying the measures that mark effective performance for each activity.

Some call this a service inventory (Wesemann, 1981), while others refer to it as a survey of existing services (Marlin, 1984). In any case, this activity is simply a comprehensive evaluation of everything the agency does, both in direct services to citizens and in support services for these direct services. The significance of such an inventory is that it provides a careful analysis of the services before even preliminary decisions are made about contracting. Sometimes only a portion of the total services or activities can be contracted out; sometimes all should be contracted out; sometimes none should be contracted out. Careful inventories make possible these differentiations among activities.

These inventories have an additional advantage, since decisions to contract out are often made suddenly, for impulsive or political reasons. When this occurs, there will have been at least some study of the governmental unit's activities and the consequences anticipated.

Examples of activities include

Local government sidewalks: Patching, root cutting, replacement, installation
State highway/freeway patrol: Dispatching, helicopter patrol, radar monitoring (not citations), vehicle maintenance, accident investigation
Federal public building maintenance: Window washing, floor waxing, carpet care, restroom cleaning, painting

Some of these activities are commonly contracted out, while others rarely are. They are listed only to illustrate some of the activities in an inventory. An inventory ensures that every activity performed by the agency is identified. Should the service be contracted out, no activity will be overlooked when a contract is prepared.

Once identified, performance indicators for each activity should be listed. These indicators essentially show how the service can be measured and serve as the basis for the actual contract, identifying what the unit is buying and how it will be measured. If the service is not contracted out, the indicators can be used as (1) performance indicators for internal management purposes, (2) cost-control items if the agency has a very sophisticated accounting system, or (3) performance data in budget presentations.

In addition to a list of activities and their performance measures, the inventory might include for each activity (1) the resources consumed (employees, supplies, expenses), (2) a description of the inventory, (3) the volume of quality indicators, and (4) the unique circumstances surrounding the activity. Most organizations do not have such an inventory, and many top managers do not know enough about their agency to create such a list. The inventory then becomes a management device for top management to ensure that program managers are indeed familiar with their programs.

Performance Measures. Performance measures, or specifications, can be direct measures of the volume or amount of the service produced. An example would be freeway-miles built. Since direct measures cannot always be identified, indirect measures, such as hours spent auditing, are used. Indirect measures emphasize the process being used and are most common when consultants for personal services are used. Table 5 illustrates some typical measures.

Direct measures are by far better than indirect measures. They emphasize the actual performance, or output, of the service. Taxpayers are paying for inspections, vaccinations, and the number of displays, not the qualifications of those operating the program. Showing more than one direct measure focuses attention on multiple goals of the organization by showing that building inspectors are judged both by quantity (inspections) and quality (the speed of responses).

Another advantage of direct measures is that they can be made into very specific levels of service. For example, a building inspection specification may be that 90 percent of all inspection requests received by 9 A.M. should be made that same day; a data-processing operation should be down no more than 5 percent of working hours; and under private custodial services, all carpets shall be shampooed every three months.

Table 5. Typical Measures of Performance.

Service	Direct Measures	Indirect Measures
Public health	Vaccinations Visitors Counseling sessions Patient satisfaction	Nurse training Hours open Number of doctors Equipment quality
Data processing	Items entered into computer Programs written Down time	Operator training Staff experience Number of analysts
Building inspection	Number of inspections Response time Reinspections	Number of inspectors Inspector experience Complaints
Museums	Number of displays Number of visitors Square feet of display space	Number of docents Facility condition Staff training

Source: Adapted from Marlin, 1984, pp. 46–47.

Ideally, all measures would be direct. Unfortunately, in most situations the best that can be done is to insist that direct measures be used whenever possible. There are several reasons why direct measures are not always available. First, in many cases the output cannot be specified, as in the case of lawsuits if the legal unit is simply responding to outside suits. Sometimes the activities are unpredictable, such as snowplowing or responding to ambulance calls. Occasionally, contractors will not bid on certain direct measures for which they do not wish to be held responsible, such as drug addicts cured or percentage of contraband seized. In these cases, the agency will have to rely on indirect measures or not contract out the service. Finally, the quality of services may be so important that only indirect measures are appropriate, such as with technical appraisers or specialized trial lawyers.

Deciding Which Services to Contract Out

Now the inventory is complete. Which services, if any, should be contracted out? Or, if there is pressure to contract out, which services should be eliminated as possibilities for contracting?

General Rules. The following are general considerations affecting contracting out that the wise manager and legislative body will consider even before making a general feasibility study:

1. Do state or local laws prohibit private contracts?
2. Do intergovernmental regulations limit the use of grants or shared revenues for contract services?
3. Do personnel issues limit contracting?
4. Do labor relations contracts limit contracting?
5. Will displaced employees who remain with the agency seriously affect agency operations because they must be retrained, because they ''bump'' other employees, or because their morale and that of other employees declines?
6. Will employee unions seriously resist contracting out?
7. Do existing employees have the training and experience to monitor and evaluate contracts?

8. Is the legislative body supportive?
9. Is the community supportive?
10. Can corruption or the appearance of corruption be avoided?
11. Are there contractors available who are likely to bid?
12. Is the real reason for contracting out strong enough to carry the proposal through the often difficult and extended process of contracting out?
    (See Wesemann, 1981, pp. 31–35; and Valente and Manchester, 1984, p. 8.)

The above policy considerations are not necessarily related to the technical virtue of contracting out but rather are important in evaluating the political, legal, and financial merits of the case. Many of these considerations are highly politically charged and thus should be dealt with prior to a lengthy (or even a relatively limited) feasibility study. These political or personnel questions are more important at the local level because employees usually have more political weight than at other levels. While not technical, some of these issues will require more thought than others (Meyer and Morgan, 1979).

The last question, concerning the real motives behind contracting out, is worthy of mention. Not all contracting out proposals are based on abstract merit. Many revolve around considerations of politics (for example, reducing the number of government employees at all costs). Some involve simply management convenience if not actual pique (for example, eliminating an unwanted union).

Legitimate reasons for contracting out involve cost, the likelihood of superior private performance, and other reasons mentioned in Chapter Three. All other reasons are essentially invalid, or at least unlikely to save money or improve efficiency.

Feasibility Studies. Once the preliminary review has been completed, the actual feasibility study is relatively simple, although some discretion is involved. The final study revolves around cost. It is largely a comparison of agency costs with an estimate of contractor costs.

The contractor's costs must be estimated, but this need not be a shot in the dark. Most agencies simply select several contractors offering the service and request estimates for their costs of providing the service. There is normally no reason for contractors to be untruthful or to hedge the estimates. The estimates can be taken as approximations of the bids that will be made if a formal bid is requested. There are some cautions to be observed, however.

First, the contractor's estimate is not a bid and is likely, if anything, to be a bit low. After all, it is to the contractor's advantage to move deliberations closer to a decision to contract out.

Second, requesting quotations can be a delicate operation. It should be done in such a way that (1) it is clear that no promises of a contract are made, (2) no hint of improprieties is possible or can be raised, (3) no favoritism toward any contractor over another exists or can legitimately be raised, and (4) every contractor asked to quote prices has complete information on the service to be provided in order to obtain accurate estimates. The best way to accomplish these aims is to ask for quotes openly, if not publicly, with the endorsement of the legislative body.

The next step is to obtain agency costs for the service (see Los Angeles County, 1984). This is not as difficult as is sometimes claimed, if one keeps in mind that the process is a management decision, not a cost accountant's plaything. The simplest and best approach is to identify all avoidable costs, both direct and indirect. Direct costs are obvious: They are those costs directly attributed to the service, such as salary, benefits, and expenses related to the service. Indirect costs are such items as departmental administration and, in a large agency, divisional and systemwide expenses, such as rent, utilities, and insurance. It may be hard to accurately estimate indirect costs and some direct costs, such as employee shares of the pension plan, but that is the job of the finance division. The basic issue is to include only avoidable costs. Administrative costs, for example, may be legitimately charged to the program, but if they cannot be avoided, they should not be counted.

Agency costs associated with a contracted service (such as monitoring, letting bids, and preparing documents) should be included if they are net additional costs. This is not always the case. The County of Los Angeles, for example, does most contract monitoring by management staff as part of their other duties.

A sample calculation of avoidable and unavoidable costs, compared to a private estimate, is provided in Table 6. While the example is hypothetical, it closely resembles a sample problem in the Los Angeles County *Contract Manual* (Los Angeles County, 1984, sec. 40.03).

Table 6. City Park Grounds-Maintenance Cost Calculation.

Facts: There are six park grounds-keeper positions and one supervisor. One of the positions is vacant and will not be filled. Contract maintenance will be done by management staff, but a part-time secretarial position will be eliminated.

Analysis:

Cost Item	Full Cost	Avoidable Cost
Budgeted salaries (6 grounds keepers @ $20,000, 1 supervisor @ $25,000, PT secretary @ $5,000)	$150,000	$150,000
Service level adjustment (unfilled position)	(20,000)	(20,000)
Budget at established service level	125,000	125,000
Vacancy rate adjustment (6%)	(5,000)	(5,000)
(Adjustment depends on agency experience) Estimated actual avoidable salaries	120,000	120,000
Add: Employee benefits @ 25%	30,000	30,000
Direct supplies and services	10,000	10,000
Total direct	160,000	160,000
Indirect costs: Department overhead (12%)	19,200	11,200
Citywide overhead (14%)	22,400	—
Total direct and indirect	$201,600	$171,200

Estimated avoidable costs	$171,200	
Contractor cost (informal quotes)	$164,000	
	$ 7,200	(contract is cost-effective)

Table 6 shows that contracting out is cheaper than city operation. The savings are less than 10 percent, however, which makes the choice marginal, particularly when the agency does not include monitoring costs and when the contractor bids are only estimates. The city should probably not contract out under these conditions.

At any rate, the feasibility study is now done, and assuming that a decision is made to contract out the service, the bidding process can now begin.

Soliciting and Reviewing Bids. There are two ways the bidding process can be done (see Marlin, 1984; Chapters Seven and Eight). One is by a formal invitation to bid (ITB), which involves the careful legal process of formal bidding announcements, sealed bids, public openings, and so on. ITBs are used, or should always be used, when the service can be defined precisely. The other process, requests for proposals (RFPs), is used in situations where the service cannot be easily defined or for personal services.

Invitations to Bid (ITBs)

The ITB process contains only a few basic steps, although each step must be done very carefully to avoid mistakes that could invalidate the contract.

The first step is to prepare the invitations to bid. This is a job for attorneys, although managers should be generally aware of the elements in an ITB. The legal notice should include such things as where the bids should be delivered, when and where the bids will be opened, specifications for the proposed service, location where the formal bid proposal with all bidding details can be obtained, the name of the unit, and the statement that all bids may be rejected.

The bid proposal form that bidders will fill out should include such things as bidder instructions, terms and provisions, service specifications, place for the official bid and price, information about bonds or deposits that may be required, statements about bidder qualifications, provisions for disqualification, and reporting and payment provisions.

For the agency manager, the most important part of these documents concerns the service specifications, which must be quite specific. For example, a contract for grounds maintenance has to indicate how often each area is to be mowed, what the height of cut grass is to be, where the cut grass is to be disposed of, when the lawn is to be fertilized, how often it is to be aerated, and so on. Exhibit 1 is an excerpt from a bidder's document from the City of Phoenix for a custodial contract and specifies instructions for certain areas to be cleaned; these instructions take precedence over more general instructions listed earlier. This proposal excerpt was only a tiny part of the entire specifications section and shows that tedious detail, even to specifying the most insignificant items, is necessary to ensure that the expected work is done.

Exhibit 1. Some Specifications of a Custodial Contract.

Employee lunchrooms, kitchens, lounges, conference room, lobbies, hallways:
  Clean chairs with damp cloth: Daily
  Clean ledges and countertops with damp cloth: Daily
  Empty wastebaskets (change liners as necessary): Daily
  Clean tables: Daily
  Vacuum carpet thoroughly: Daily
  Damp mop: Daily
  Clean sink: Daily
  Damp clean exterior of trash containers: Daily

Source: Adapted from Marlin, 1984, p. 62.

After the bid proposal is completed, it is advisable to hold a prebid conference for potential contractors. All bidders who obtained bid proposals are invited to attend this meeting, the purpose of which is to clarify instructions, answer questions, interpret the bid specifications, and anticipate potential problems. This conference may include an actual walk-through of the site or project from or at which the contract will be performed.

The staff who will deal with the successful contractor should be introduced to bidders, who should all attend the same conference. In potentially troublesome situations, the media and all top officials perhaps should be included (Wesemann, 1981). This conference is so important that managers should consider making it mandatory. At minimum, it should be announced in the bid document so there is no excuse for contractors not attending.

In addition to the prebid conference, the agency may want to consider prequalifying bidders. This is particularly helpful if many bidders appear to be financially weak and hence likely to go bankrupt or otherwise be unable to perform during the span of their contract. Prequalification tests must be uniformly applied to all contractors and cannot be arbitrary or capricious. They can be based on past performance on other contracts or on proof of financial responsibility. Prequalification data include site visits to the contractor's office, credit reports from banks, references from previous employers, or even data submitted by the bidder.

It is customary to protect the agency by requiring bidders to put up bonds. A bid bond is designed to guarantee performance after the contract is awarded and generally should only be enough to pay for the cost of rebidding the contract if the bidder does not honor the bid. High bid bonds only serve to discourage bidding and usually only cover actual costs, such as office supplies, that were consumed in bidding.

A performance bond helps ensure that the contract is completed satisfactorily. It is usually from 10 to 100 percent of the contract value. The bond should be geared to the type of contract. A contract for custodial services may not present major problems if other contractors or the agency itself can step in. Conversely, data-processing services may be irreplaceable for some time. The bond should vary according to the risk, because high bonds tend to keep out small but potentially effective bidders. Even for financially well-established firms, a high performance bond may cause the contractor to add the interest charge to the bid.

Occasionally, government agencies require contractors to provide liability waivers to relieve the jurisdiction for liability on projects. This is not always a good idea. As is true with high-performance bonds, liability waivers tend to eliminate small contractors, while large contractors tend to add it to the cost of the project or contract. In addition, liability waivers may not always be enforceable (Wesemann, 1981).

After opening the bid, the final step is awarding the contract. Although most proposals give the agency the right to accept the bidder's proposal immediately, most jurisdictions take some time to evaluate the final bids. Conversely, the agency should have reserved the right to reject all, so adequate time should be taken to look at the bids. In Los Angeles County, a task force composed of the personnel director, administrative officer, purchasing agent, county counsel, and the auditor-controller reviews all contracts over $5 million. Some such team should examine each bid—either a team of experts, such as those who were responsible for preparing the contract, or a different, less interested group, such as citizens who evaluate a number of contracts.

Marlin (1984) suggests that the team include someone from the department that awards the contract (presumably the purchasing department), someone from the using department (for instance, parks, mental health, or police), someone from the legal department, a person who can evaluate if the bids are responsive (probably from the using department), and someone who can compare and evaluate costs precisely. These team members may only have to be phoned or have to review the bid documents individually, but they should be part of a formal group.

This team evaluates the bid (1) to determine if it is in compliance with the requirements (for example, that a performance bond and all required documents were included), (2) to examine the qualifications of the bidders to ensure that all are "responsible" bidders (nonresponsible bidders may be rejected), (3) to identify the best bid (presumably the lowest, if all bidders are responsible), and (4) to prepare a formal recommendation to the individual awarding the contract.

The work of this team is important, particularly now that cities have greater antitrust liability. In a 1982 lawsuit, the Supreme Court held that the City of Boulder (Colorado) was not exempt from federal antitrust activities merely because of home rule provisions (*Community Communication Corporation* v. *City of Boulder*, 1982). The case involved a cable television franchisee who was prohibited from expanding service to an unserved portion of the city. The decision underlined the vulnerability of local officials to potential antitrust action. Some time-honored practices, such as spreading the city's insurance among all brokers or bank deposits among all banks, may now be illegal. The same rule applies to specifications that, by design or not, require the use of certain vendors' equipment.

Marlin (1984, pp. 66–67) lists a number of procedures that can help in avoiding potential antitrust actions, as follows:

1. Devise and apply purely objective standards for all contractor procedures.
2. Pay particular attention to contractor procedures when they affect prequalification of bidders.
3. When developing the specifications, use only contractors who will not bid on the contract.
4. Put the entire procurement process in writing and publicize it.
5. Do not contact vendors or providers informally during the bid or negotiation process.
6. Keep formal records of compliance with the bidding and procurement process.
7. Stay in close contact with good legal counsel at all times.

These rules are little more than common sense. However, applying them faithfully will make unintentional errors much less common and intentional dishonesty much more difficult.

Requests for Proposals (RFPs)

Requests for proposals are the second major way of arriving at contracts. An RFP is a shorthand method of describing negotiated bids, whereby the contract is entered into after both parties have discussed terms, provisions, costs, and other elements of the contract. There is no formal bidding process. RFPs are most common when contracting for consulting or other personal services, such as architects or engineers, than for such services as building maintenance or data processing. The major concern in using an RFP is for the quality of the product. In an ITB, the concern is primarily cost. ITBs focus on minimum qualifications, while RFPs focus on the evaluation process for potential bidders.

In addition to personal service contracts, RFPs are commonly used for (1) experimental programs, such as an unusual drug-testing program or a new process for treating sewage disposal at the treatment plant; (2) sole-source suppliers who have special products such as computer software programs or special patents; and (3) emergencies when there is insufficient time for bidding. It is probably wise to justify decisions in writing whenever the RFP process is used in lieu of the more formal ITB process.

The same or a similar group of agency personnel who review ITB proposals should direct the RFP process. This includes all actions from the earliest review of services to the final award of the contract. The bidding process begins with the feasibility study and definition of the scope of services and proceeds to the identification of a possible list of providers. The team searches out possible bidders, ensures that a list of prequalified bidders is current, and encourages the formal provision of proposals by providers or individuals on the list.

The actual RFP proposal is basically a simple offer for bidders to propose a service for a given price, although there are variations, as in the case of a given price with the bidder offering a level or type of service for that price.

The RFP should contain certain basic provisions. It should be written to ensure equal treatment to all parties and to avoid the faintest hint of collusion. It should also provide for postbid variations, so that negotiations can proceed between the provider and agency over quantities, cost, and quality after a successful provider has been identified.

Other items in an RFP are similar to those in an ITB. The specifications, assuming the service can be precisely defined, should include service and staffing levels, performance bonds, service event schedules (dates that training sessions will be held, dates that software programs will be completed), performance reporting schedules, and a place where potential conflicts of interest can be identified.

The RFP should request price quotations. It should also specify criteria for selecting a provider and the weights to be applied to each criteria (see Table 7), an explanation of the RFP

Table 7. Weights for Evaluating a Proposal.

Criteria	Score (hypothetical)	Weight	Weighted Score
Firm or contractor qualifications:			
Experience	1	20%	.20
Qualifications of persons to be assigned	3	30	.90
Technical value of proposal:			
Meets or exceeds specifications	3	20	.60
Ability to clearly present plans	2	10	.20
Fees:			
Cost compared to other bids	4	20	.80
Total		100%	2.70

Source: Adapted from Marlin, 1984, p. 78.

Note: 1 = low 2 = fair 3 = good 4 = superior

document itself, and an explanation that the contract is to be negotiated. In addition to the RFP itself, a record should be kept of all contractors who make proposals.

Equally important is the contractor response to the RFP. It should be required by the RFP to include (1) vendor qualifications; (2) vendor experience on similar or equivalent jobs; (3) information about costs, charges, and fees; and (4) information about the quote and a statement that the quote is not an offer the agency can take but that negotiations will occur.

After the responses are received, the original team reviews the proposals. The team narrows the list of contractors to a final few by reviewing the proposals, usually by applying some formal evaluation system similar to that in Table 7.

When the list has been narrowed, the team (or in some cases, an individual) negotiates with the finalists (individually and confidentially) over the contract. These negotiations may include visits to the contractor's office or to other job sites of the contractor and lead to the final choice of a contractor. In preparation for the award, the team may want to develop a draft contract so that all parties can review it prior to signing. During these negotiations, a list of proceedings should be maintained to support subsequent proceedings.

The final step is drawing up the formal legal contract with the successful contractor. The contents of this contract will vary with state and local laws and so should be drafted by competent legal counsel. The substantive content should be somewhat similar to that of actual bid awards, including reporting requirements, contractor fees and payment schedules, specifications for performing the service, termination dates, and penalties for inadequate performance (or incentives for high performance).

There are two ways of taking cost into account when making contract awards under RFP procedures. One is to factor costs formally into the award criteria (as in Table 7). The other is to adopt a two-step bidding process. If this is done, the first submission is for technical qualifications, and approved contractors may then submit contract proposals. The lowest bid is then chosen (Meyer and Morgan, 1979). In this method, contractors submit both technical qualifications and sealed formal bids for the projects. Once the favored contractors are selected, their sealed bids are opened, and the lowest offer is accepted (Marlin, 1984).

Many professional individuals and their firms do not like to compete on the basis of money. They wish to be selected for their professional qualifications, and until fairly recently, professional organizations frowned on competitive pricing competition as "unprofessional." However, in 1978 the Supreme Court struck down codes of ethics prohibiting pricing competition as an antitrust violation, and this decision has opened the door to more competition on the basis of price (Slawsky and De-Marco, 1980).

A major criticism against the RFP process is that it is inherently judgmental and highly subject to corruption (Wesemann, 1981; AFSCME, 1983). This is why the procedures briefly summarized here should be carefully gone over by the agency's legal counsel. The issue is not only actual corruption but also the appearance of it, since this destroys the agency's public support. Negotiated bids are inherently subject to public suspicion of government, which is all the more reason to deal as openly and formally as possible, whether the bidding process is negotiated or formally bid.

Another problem is that negotiation may result in higher costs than formal bidding because professional persons, such as engineers or architects, will not compete with each other. This is less common in recent years, particularly since the Supreme Court ruling in 1978, but it still occurs. Many jurisdictions are not taking advantage of some of the more sophisticated bidding procedures that take price into account, such as the two-step procedure mentioned earlier. Conversely, some experts believe that competitive bidding does not always result in the lowest costs, because the time and expense bidding involves lead many contractors to avoid it (Wesemann, 1981).

To avoid the problems of perceived and actual corruption, Meyer and Morgan (1979) recommend a procedure similar to that used by Lakewood (Colorado), which is outlined in Exhibit 2.

Exhibit 2. Summary of Lakewood (Colorado) Procedure for Negotiating with Consultants (adapted to contractors).

---

1. Aggressively pursue potential contractors.
2. Review the entire list of possible contractors when a contract is to be let.
3. Select three firms for interviewing purposes. Have each submit a statement of qualifications for the specific contract.
4. Rank the statements.
5. Negotiate with the top-ranked firm.
6. If negotiations fail, then negotiate with the next-ranked firm, and after that, the third-ranked firm if necessary.
7. Negotiate only on
   • the contractor's desire to do business with the agency
   • professional qualifications
   • specialized experience of the contractor
   • capacity of the firm for performing the service
   • familiarity of the contractor with the work
   • past performance of similar contracts

Source: Adapted from Meyer and Morgan, 1979, pp. 13-14.

Note: Since this list is adapted from a system designed for architectural and engineering services, it may not be perfectly adaptable for direct delivery of services. For example, there may not be a wide number of potential contractors in most cities, or the agency may be required by state law to use an ITB procedure.

Attracting and Selecting a Contractor

Competition. Competition among contractors is healthy for any agency wishing to contract out, for it greatly increases the likelihood of a better and cheaper contract. Conversely, without some competition, contracting out is unlikely to be cost-effective. Competition involves more than private contractors. Other levels of government may provide services as well, and in areas such as human services, nonprofit firms are often available. Citizen or neighborhood groups also may provide competition. At the local level, neighborhood groups deliver the service in 8 percent of all cultural/arts programs, 6 percent of all day-care facilities, and 5 percent of crime prevention programs and general recreation programs (Valente and Manchester, 1984).

The idea of competition also extends to city forces. In several cities, city departments formally compete with outside groups. In San Diego County (California), employees bid to provide services in geographical areas for landfill operations and mental health. Phoenix (Arizona) uses this system for a range of services from street sweeping to custodial services. Finally, several large cities, such as Minneapolis, Kansas City, New Orleans, and Oklahoma City, have city crews compete with private firms for refuse collection in specific areas (Valente and Manchester, 1984).

Competition among suppliers of a service thus need not be limited to private contractors but extends to a wide range of possibilities. One major possibility is dividing up the service area into smaller geographical regions, such as waste disposal sections of the city, groups of buildings for janitorial work, or various sites for grounds maintenance. Contracts can be let for each area, and small contractors or other groups may be able to effectively and cheaply provide services for these areas when they would not be able to compete financially for an entire service. There is less risk of overall service disruption with several competitors, for the other contractors can usually expand to cover the area. Subdividing service areas in this way was how Minneapolis Sanitation Division employees were able to compete with private firms, eventually matching their prices (Savas, 1977).

However, these possibilities have to be cultivated, for they do not occur automatically when the agency wants to consider contracting out a service. A conscious decision is required plus some additional work in devising and evaluating service districts. Likewise, many potential vendors, such as nonprofit groups, have to be encouraged to consider bidding. Aggressive advertising is required, and it has to be well in advance of the actual contract proposal so that smaller or newer firms or organizations can consider making offers.

Most additional competition comes from encouraging and enticing small contractors into bidding. Small contractors are usually cheaper, although they may be somewhat more risky than large, well-financed contractors. In general, large contractors are somewhat more professional, require less supervision, and are more likely to be flexible about contract modifications. Advertising announcements are more likely to attract the large contractor, and many small contractors have to be contacted personally through a contractors' association handbook or the telephone book's yellow pages (Wesemann, 1981).

Agencies in metropolitan areas are most likely to benefit from competition among suppliers, because there are more people and hence more suppliers. Wesemann (1981) argues that being in a metropolitan area generally means that suppliers will be available. He suggests that those who doubt this should consult the local phone book yellow pages. If at least five potential suppliers cannot be located after looking under all headings, the city will probably have little competition for contract services. Agencies in a metropolitan area have more competition not only because there are more suppliers but also because (1) they have less distance to travel; (2) there is less "home-town parochialism" (at least for cities) working against out-of-town contractors; and (3) there are more intergovernmental providers as well as private contractors.

Agencies in less populated areas who wish to contract out sometimes benefit from weaker union opposition to contracting out, from some increased interest in providing services by local contractors who regard municipal contracts as good advertising and sometimes as a civic duty (this advantage may be limited to cities), and from generally lower wage and overhead costs of contractors (Wesemann, 1981).

Contractor Aversion to Government Work. Many contractors are not interested in government work, even when they might well be successful. Since businessmen are extremely pragmatic when it comes to their pocketbooks, this aversion usually has little to do with ideology but more to do with government agency behavior. Some government actions simply repel contractors or make them raise their bids to cover the extra expenses. Excessive bid or performance bonds or demands for liability waivers can cause contractors, particularly small ones, to incur heavy expenses. These high bonds may seem to protect the agency at low cost, but often they serve little purpose, since the agency can often only recoup specific expenses, such as the cost of rebidding the contract.

A similar problem is the difficulty of contracting with the agency. Lengthy bidding documents and extensive reporting requirements make agency business seem formidable if not more costly.

If some government agencies were private credit customers, their credit would be cut off, since they often fail to pay on time, and their payments are often unpredictable. Most contractors usually operate on borrowed money, so this type of financial behavior can cause them either not to bid or to inflate their estimates.

Wesemann (1981) notes that many contractors dislike dealing with municipalities because they fear that they will be pressured to "pay off" local officials. A similar fear of contractors is of becoming a "political football" because of public controversies over the contract, even if no illegal activities are involved.

There may be good reasons for these deterrents to contractor interest in government contracting. What is an excessive bid bond to a contractor may be a reasonable requirement to the contracting agent. Agencies cannot always control disbursements if they are made by someone not in their agency. Political conflict over contracting out may not be avoidable. Fear of "payoffs" may not exist. But if contractors believe that these situations exist or may exist, the result is largely the same. For this reason, agencies with control over their operations should review bond totals, payment procedures, and the amount of information they require from bidders to be sure they are not inadvertently reducing competition.

Summary

There are three basic steps in the first stages of contracting out. The initial service inventory becomes the basis for a feasibility study. After a positive feasibility study, the contract is prepared and then becomes the basis for contractor bids. Finally, the contractor is chosen.

If care is taken at every step of the way as these three events proceed, the odds are great that a successful contracting relationship will take place, that the agency will have a workable contract, and that the work specifications will make the contractor's task (and rewards) clear. However, only careful periodic review of the contractor's work performance ensures final satisfaction with the service. The next chapter on monitoring covers the evaluation aspect of contracting out.

CHAPTER 5 ∽∾∽∾∽∾∽∾∽∾∽∾∽∾∽∾

Monitoring the Contract
and Measuring Performance

Both parties have signed the contract, the contractor has posted the performance bond, and his workers are now ready to begin maintaining the building, mowing the grass, or operating the data-processing center. The highly visible part of contracting out is finished. The agency's work, however, is just starting.

Now begins the important, but less glamorous, work of ensuring that the contractor completes his tasks effectively, responsively, and according to schedule. This monitoring job continues through the life of the contract and into succeeding contracts. When agency director, attorney, and legislative body have long since turned their attention to other matters, some contract agent will still be reviewing the contractor's reports, listening to citizen complaints, and making inspections of the contractor's progress.

The monitoring and performance measurement phase of contract administration contributes significantly to the success of the contracting out process. Much of the criticism of contracting out by unions and employee groups is based on shoddy or nonexistent contract monitoring (AFSCME, 1983; AFSCME, n.d.). No amount of careful contract preparation or detailed specifications will ensure adequate performance by the contractor: Actual performance must be monitored carefully.

In many respects, contract monitoring is no different than supervision of services provided by the agency itself. The same sort of inspection, attention to citizen complaints, and evaluation of performance reports should take place whether the service is provided in-house or is contracted out. The same standards should be applied and the same level of citizen or user satisfaction should be demanded. Monitoring does not assume that the contractor is untrustworthy—only that he or she is human. Contractor employees, like agency employees, are fallible. Misunderstandings over the contract occur. Close monitoring can prevent small difficulties from becoming major problems.

Monitoring has two basic parts (see Meyer and Morgan, 1979). The first is to ensure that legal obligations in the contract are fulfilled, for it is obvious that the contractor must be held to the legal provisions of the contract. The second part is to ensure that acceptable levels of service are provided, which is at least as important as ensuring legal compliance with the contract. It is difficult to specify every possible item or provision, however, and it is also hard to foresee every contingency. When bottlenecks or contingencies occur, it is the contract agent who must propose contract revisions that will take care of the unforeseen problem in the next contract.

Many observers insist that the difficulty of monitoring fully matches its importance. Tribbett (1983) surveyed California municipal public works directors. His respondents considered the difficulty of monitoring and evaluating contracts to be the second most important disadvantage to contracting, after the issue of emergency responses by the contractor. A survey of special districts, school districts, cities, and counties found "difficulty in monitoring contracts" the most commonly cited disadvantage to contracting out, just ahead of "unreliability of contractor" (California Tax Foundation, 1981, p. 9). One respondent commented: "Private contracting requires more supervision, inspection, and work measurement, and more costly detailed specification writing" (p. 5).

Whitcomb (1983), writing about social service residential care contracting, remarks that agencies often pay little attention to monitoring. Finally, one city manager, long experienced with contracting in two states, commented that cities manage their contracts poorly, relying on complaints rather than careful inspection. He suggested that one reason for this is that skills in providing city services are of little use in monitoring a contract (Aleshire, interview with author, Oct. 1986).

The lack of inspection or careful review of contractors is probably a natural extension of the kind of reviews that agencies give their in-house services. Few public works directors carefully check the routes of municipal refuse collection trucks, measure the number of spills not cleaned, or count the lids left lying beside garbage cans. Few state agency managers observe precisely the number of times each month that wall panelings are cleaned by janitors. Few national park supervisors examine the precise number of times soap and toilet paper are installed in campground restrooms. How then do these managers know what levels of service are being provided? Often, they do not. They wait for complaints, assuming that lack of complaints means that the service is being performed adequately. Lack of complaints is commonly accepted as a good indication of general satisfaction. Excessive faith in complaints is not limited to those who know no better. Sophisticated directors know that the service may be good or not, based on some professional standard such as times per month cleaned, but that this service level will not be important if there are complaints. Difficulties arise when users complain, and complainants will not be convinced by demonstrations of high professional standards. Why worry about detailed and painstaking monitoring if the citizen cares little? Thus, officials often simply rely on complaints.

Not surprisingly, the same standard is applied to contracted out services. If complaints are the way in-house public services are judged, complaints are the basis on which contractors will be judged. But there are better ways to monitor contracts.

Monitoring remains largely a mystery. Most books, monographs, or papers attest to its importance but say little about just how it is accomplished. Who monitors—or who should monitor? What are the methods used in monitoring—and how often do they occur? What is a good monitoring program? What kinds of measures can be used to actually verify performance? How much does monitoring a contract cost? These and other questions are covered in this chapter.

What Is Monitoring and How Is It Done?

There are several methods of monitoring contracts, including reviewing contractor reports, taking citizen surveys or interviews, relying on citizen complaints, and making inspections or observations.

Contractor Reports. A contractor report is the way a contractor reports progress to date, explains costs, describes problems in providing the service, and certifies that the service is meeting the specifications of the contract. It is her statement of work completed and stands as the formal statement of compliance with the contract. Of course, the report must be verified independently by the contract manager, but until challenged, it normally is the offical work completion document. More than one report should be required, of course. There normally will be a stream of different reports over the duration of the contract.

A complete report includes the following information:

- Work progress to date (streets swept, areas cleaned, and so forth)
- Comparisons of work to date with the contract schedule
- Expenditures to date
- Forecasts of work and expenses for the entire contractual period, based on experience to date
- Reports of user satisfaction (particularly if complaints are handled by the contractor)
- Levels of service provided
- Narrative accounts of matters such as (1) necessary adjustments to the contract, (2) problems encountered in meeting the contract, and (3) explanations of variations in performance

Special reports will be necessary from time to time. In many cases, narrative accounts will be a separate report. Certainly, whenever a special deviation occurs, a special report should be demanded by the agency if the deviation does not automatically trigger a required report. This kind of special report should also include a specific plan to remedy the problem or to bring performance back to contractual levels.

Reports are only as good as the attention paid to them. The contract manager should review them carefully, comparing the information in them with that obtained from other forms of monitoring. Sometimes mere cursory review of the report is as far as monitoring goes. One social services contractor told the Massachusetts Taxpayers Foundation, "I could be running a zoo here and they wouldn't care as long as I filled in the little blocks on the form" (AFSCME, n.d., p. 33).

Inspections and Observations. Inspection and observation of contractor performance are the traditional methods for determining adherence to the contract. The type of inspection varies greatly depending on the nature of the service. Wesemann (1981) believes that for certain functions, such as rubbish disposal, inspections based on complaints only are sufficient. Janitorial services might be handled the same way. Many services, such as lawn maintenance, require only inspection upon completion. For services such as nursing homes, surprise inspections may be necessary. In other cases, such as tax parcel assessing, inspection of a certain percentage of units is required. Some services, such as paratransit system operation, may require periodic samples of all units (vehicle condition, in this case).

Monitoring must be flexible, and the contractor must be willing to perform some duties at times when the agency is ready. Contract data-processing systems should not be down for servicing on days when special payrolls or billing activity are required. Swimming pools should not be closed for maintenance on warm summer weekends. In such cases, the contract agent must be familiar enough with the contractor's schedule to avoid these scheduling embarrassments.

Marlin (1984) divides observations or inspections into two classes: simultaneous and subsequent. Simultaneous observations are on-site inspections while the contractor is working. The contractor may or may not be aware of the inspection. Evaluations of the contractor's performance usually have some sort of rating scale or form to note problems or quality of service. For refuse disposal problems, the number of missed spills and lids left off could be noted. In addition, note of matters such as noise level and amount of property damage could be made.

Subsequent observations include inspection and reviews after the work is complete. As noted earlier, building maintenance might operate on a complaint basis, depending on the building users to notice deficiencies. However, building maintenance could also be reviewed by counting the number of wastebaskets not emptied, the quality of the floor buffing (on some scale), or the number of ashtrays uncleaned (see Marlin, 1984).

Both subsequent and simultaneous observations often use a scorecard rating system that compares actual performance to some standard or measure, such as dirty ashtrays or unlidded refuse containers. (Scorecard rating systems are discussed later in this chapter.)

Complaints. Relying on citizen complaints is a common method of contract monitoring. When the contract involves internal operations (such as a data-processing operation) rather than citizen services, complaints from the using department or group of employees serve the same purpose.

Complaints are almost always a basic part of contract monitoring, although in many places, such as the County of Los Angeles, they are used as only one source of information. The Los Angeles County Manual says "customer complaints should seldom be used as the sole basis to reject a service or deduct money from the contractor but can be used to support the findings developed from using the other surveillance methods" (Los Angeles County, 1984, sec. 50.03). The County of Los Angeles may consider complaints only one source of information, but it insists, nevertheless, that the complaint be documented and that special training be provided for those who take complaints. Agencies vary greatly on the degree of formality with which they treat complaints, whether or not they are the primary or a secondary monitoring method. Some agencies have formal complaint logs and tracking systems, while others have much more informal complaint processes.

Complaints may be directed to either the agency or contractor. If they go to the contractor first, she usually transmits them to the agency, while immediately (hopefully) following them up. The agency contract manager then follows up on the complaint. The advantage of this process is that the contractor can immediately address the complaint and that this also provides more immediate contractor feedback on the service quality.

If the complaints go first to the agency, they are relayed to the contractor, who then resolves them. The advantage of this method is that the agency has better information about how fast and how well the contractor responds to complaints.

Combined methods allow the contractor or the agency to take the complaints, with the contractor resolving the complaint as soon as he hears about it, either directly or from the agency. Later reports from the contractor will list the complaints he handled, while the agency checks the complaints they received to ensure that the contractor took action (see Marlin, 1984).

When a service affects a particular group of citizens directly or there is great citizen interest, it may be useful to establish and publicize a phone number (or even a desk) for complaint calls.

Sometimes surveys of citizen satisfaction are used. (This technique will be covered as part of the later discussion on effectiveness.)

Usage of Monitoring Types. Reports, inspection and observation, and complaints are probably the best-known types of monitoring. (Another widely used method, performance measures, will be discussed later.) Several surveys have been taken to determine the relative frequency of monitoring techniques. Tribbett (1983) surveyed thirty-six California public works departments about contracting out in 1982, and Meyer and Morgan (1979) analyzed responses of 184 Arkansas, Louisiana, Oklahoma, and Texas cities over 10,000 in population. The results are shown in Table 8.

While the results are not strictly comparable, Tribbett's study is limited to public works functions, and his results represent the number of public works departments that rated inspections as the method of evaluation most frequently used. Meyer

Table 8. Most Common Methods of
Monitoring or Evaluating Programs.

| | Frequency | |
Method	Tribbett (Most frequent method used by respondents)	Meyer and Morgan (Percentage of respondents using given method)
Periodic inspections	48.6	61.4
Citizen complaints		65.2
Level of citizen satisfaction	5.7	
Cost-benefit analysis	11.4	46.2
Performance standards	34.3	30.4

Source: Adapted from Tribbett, 1983, p. 34; Meyer and Morgan, 1979, p. 37.

and Morgan covered a wider range of cities and functions and asked respondents if they used a given technique. They then tallied all cities that used a given method. The results are interesting. Only about one-third of the cities use performance standards for monitoring programs, and only about three-fifths periodically inspect services. In Tribbett's sample, over 80 percent of the cities used either periodic inspections or performance standards as the most frequent method of evaluation.

Cost-benefit analysis is not defined in the Meyer and Morgan study. Tribbett (1983, p. 14) refers to the relative minor usage of cost-benefit analysis in his survey as "indicating that cities have done little cost accounting, . . . thus making it almost impossible to perform a cost comparison." He apparently considers cost-benefit analysis as a means of judging whether contracts are cost-effective, not necessarily how they can be monitored. It is not completely clear how cost-benefit analysis is a means of monitoring.

Monitoring contractor performance raises several interesting issues, particularly the question of why it is often not taken more seriously. An equally interesting question involves who, or which person, is to do the monitoring.

Who Monitors Contractors?

Organizations use several arrangements for assigning individuals to contract. There may be central contract managers for one or more contracts. These managers usually rely on line personnel in the department closest to the contract for detailed information on contractor performance. Monitoring a contract may be assigned to someone in the line department. There may be a central contract manager with a specially assigned field officer. Or contract monitoring may simply be one of several duties assigned to management or supervisory employees.

The *Contract Development Manual* of the County of Los Angeles (1984, secs. 40.03.42, 50.05) indicates that "primary responsibility for monitoring lies with the central contracting/monitoring staff with some line administrative help" but also notes that several departments have created contracting units for developing new contracts and monitoring existing ones. It is clear that monitoring responsibility is shared among central and operating department personnel. Hayes (1984) refers to the field manager as the person who has primary responsibility for periodically monitoring the contract. The field manager is normally on the staff of a large agency. If there is no field manager, the contract manager usually monitors the contract.

A 1981 study by the California Tax Foundation indicated that department heads or administrators of local units most frequently monitored contracts, followed by lower-level staff members or project coordinators. Several agencies "evaluated by results" (the meaning was not explained). Table 9 shows the results.

In this study, some case studies of individual units were presented. The City of San Leandro, for example, (1) monitors street resurfacing and sealing contracts by ongoing inspections conducted by city personnel; (2) monitors marina maintenance landscape contracts daily and meets weekly with the contractor; (3) responds to citizen complaints; and (4) monitors contractors' liability self-insurance contract by approving disbursements. San Leandro claims that these procedures do not incur additional costs.

Table 9. Responsibility for Monitoring Contracts
in California Local Governments.

Primarily Responsible for Monitoring	Cities	Counties	School Districts	Special Districts
Department heads or other administrators	26%	41%	36%	36%
Department staff or project coordinators	22	26		22
Evaluated by results	14	9	18	23
Evaluating office performance (maintenance contracts)			12	
Top elected and appointed officials		11		

Source: Adapted from California Tax Foundation, 1981, pp. 19–23, 35–41, 51–55, 65–71.

San Joaquin County (1) inspects contracted janitorial services daily; (2) monitors the casualty insurance claims adjustment contract by constant interaction with the contractor; and (3) has the judiciary monitor the services of contract lawyers for indigents when the public defender is ruled to have a conflict of interest.

Bakersfield School District relies on user complaints to monitor the office equipment maintenance contracts. A record of service calls is made, and if there are disproportionate numbers of recalls, the company is notified. As with San Joaquin County, the district does not associate cost increases with monitoring activity.

Fresno County Metropolitan Flood District monitors its professional service contracts for engineering and for appraisal/negotiation contracts by constant interaction about professional standards. In the case of appraisal work, the contractor submits reports of time, hours, and work accomplished. On the other hand, for flood basin maintenance, the district supplements monthly inspection with reliance on adjoining property owner complaints.

Centralized monitoring keeps the administration of the contract in the hands of those who arranged and awarded the contract and who know the details of contract administration. A centralized monitor would be, for example, a member of the purchasing department or the procurement officer. Centralized monitoring also replaces contract monitoring in that it exchanges those close to the product and contractor with those more removed and thus somewhat disinterested. The major advantages of this arrangement are to (1) develop specialization in contract administration of contract managers and procurement officers, (2) maintain a more consistent posture toward contractors, and (3) reduce the chance for corruption or collusion between contractor and line official.

It seems reasonable to assume that line officials are better trained and experienced in their jobs and that they know the service or project better than contract officers. Using line officers for routine services is commonplace in state and local governments. These local officials occasionally make interpretations of the basic contract document but usually only monitor the quality of contractor services. Large, complex projects, particularly at the federal level, seem to be suited for centralized monitoring. Weakening top-level contract control apparently weakens the government's accountability for the procurement system as a whole.

The General Accounting Office (GAO) criticized in 1979 the Department of Energy for allowing program personnel to "(1) review and approve contractor cost vouchers for payment and (2) monitor the technical progress of the contractor's work" (Comptroller General, 1979, p. iii). The department even commented disapprovingly that "GAO noted a general attitude that the Department's procurement system exists primarily to facilitate the work of the line officers" (p. iv). If contracting out does not aid line officers, whom does it aid? Apparently, federal procurement is more concerned, for fiscal and legal reasons, with accountability than with actual performance. Opponents of contracting out will note that their worst fears are confirmed.

Monitoring systems that work well at one level of government or for one kind of contract apparently do poorly elsewhere. Selecting the person or persons to monitor contracts requires judgment about several issues such as (1) how complex the contract is, (2) the size and diversity of the unit of the agency,

(3) the nature of the service or project being contracted out, (4) the qualifications of the program officials, and (5) the nature of program officials' relation to the contractor.

The Cost of Monitoring Contracts

Monitoring is not cheap, although not all agencies figure in the cost (or do not monitor effectively, which, of course, reduces the cost). Even among agencies that carefully monitor contracts, there is a wide range of reported costs and practices. Most jurisdictions do not know what their costs are, and many are not particularly interested in finding out.

There are some studies of monitoring costs and also some expert guesses. A study of comparable functions under contract versus in-house operation in California cities reported monitoring costs of about 25 percent of the total contract (including contract administration costs). This same study indicated that contract costs were an average of 54 percent lower, so the costs of contracting out were about half the captured savings (Stevens, 1984). The City of Minneapolis carefully monitored the performance of a refuse disposal firm, including taking complaints and having a field foreman make spot inspections, at a cost of 3 percent of the contract (Savas, 1977). (This probably did not include administration costs.) The California local governments surveyed above in Table 9 generally reported no costs. The County of Los Angeles regards monitoring costs only when they can clearly be isolated, since in most cases monitoring "is performed by existing management staff" (Los Angeles County, 1984, sec. 40.03.40–41). This does not mean that the county regards monitoring as having no cost but that monitoring is a part of management responsibilities and cannot be eliminated by contracting out.

Federal Office of Management and Budget (OMB) guidelines call for contracting out whenever it is 10 percent cheaper than in-house operations. Much of this 10 percent is the cost of monitoring the service (Comptroller General, 1981). Wesemann (1981) suggests that private contractor informal estimates should be padded by 5 to 10 percent when calculating estimated cost of a contract, although this is not attributed specifically to monitoring. A controversial Phoenix waste collection contract cost

16 percent of the contract to monitor. This cost included other contract administration costs. Total costs were increased by a large number of complaints. Finally, only one of four city and county managers surveyed personally in 1986 could estimate monitoring costs (which he estimated as 5 percent).

Assuming that the cost of contract administration is considered separately from monitoring, a crude estimate of monitoring costs is from 5 to 10 percent of the contract cost. Accurate monitoring cost estimates would require at least rudimentary cost accounting, and most jurisdictions have no desire or intention to do such cost accounting, for several reasons. First, the desire to obtain accurate monitoring costs is probably insufficient incentive to create a cost-accounting system. Second, the effort to ascertain and compute monitoring costs is probably greater than the use that would be made of them. Since these costs are frequently buried in general management costs, they cannot be isolated and used in cost comparisons. This is Los Angeles County's position. Finally, contracting out is often an ideological issue. Facts are of little importance, and in such cases, even crude estimates of monitoring costs do not affect a decision to contract out.

Elements of a Good Monitoring Program

An effective contract monitoring program has four basic parts: (1) contractor relations, (2) contract provisions, (3) the job of the field or contract manager, and (4) citizen relations (assuming that the contract involves direct public service).

Contractor Relations. Contractor relations include the part of the monitoring process that deals with the direct relationship of the contractor to the monitoring agent (other than complaints, which are part of citizen relations). These relationships begin immediately after the contract is signed, with an initial meeting with the contractor, ideally before she begins operation. The initial meeting is particularly important if a preaward meeting was not held with all bidders. The purpose of the meeting is to go over specific contract provisions, since the contractor may not have reviewed all provisions carefully. At this meeting, agency employees who will be contract monitors can meet the contractor (see Wesemann, 1981).

Close contact with the contractor should not end with this initial meeting. Two kinds of continuous interaction are necessary. Formal contacts, involving mandatory contractor reports and complaint processing, are vital. However, informal contacts are equally important. The contractor needs to know how the agency rates his services, if his response to complaints is adequate, or whether adjustments in the contract need to be considered. Feedback on performance is as important to a contractor as to the agency employee monitoring the job. The agency must get speedy information from the contractor about problems in service delivery, since these problems affect both parties. Major problems should not wait for the next formal report, and minor problems should be dealt with quickly lest they be overlooked.

The Contract. The contract itself must be written properly for an active monitoring process to occur. The most important provisions for monitoring demand specific performance standards. For example, important parts of a vehicle maintenance contract are provisions on how quickly engine repairs are to be completed, when vehicles are to receive preventive maintenance, and the quality of interior care. These provisions provide the basis for evaluating contractor performance and are a standard to which both parties are committed.

Another part of the contract involves penalties for nonperformance. Penalties vary from severe (jeopardizing the contract) to minor (calling for warning or possible minor payment deductions). A major penalty for refuse disposal might be missing pickups several times, while a minor violation might be exceeding the number of garbage spills per 100 pickups. If penalties are not outlined specifically in the contract, they cannot be enforced at all, which makes monitoring impossible.

The Contract Manager's Job. The field or program contract manager needs specific guidelines so that the monitoring process is consistent, effective, and equitable to the contractor. Hayes (1984) provides a list of the activities that each contract manager should perform.

1. Inspect work and correct unsatisfactory work.
2. Ensure that required permits are acquired.

3. Monitor work performance to ensure conformance to budget and work schedule.
4. Review work performance to ensure comformance to safety rules.
5. Review contractor invoices for accuracy and completeness.
6. If the contract is fixed price, decide if the percentage of billing is equal to the percentage of work completed.
7. Verify any withholding of contractor funds.
8. Compare equipment charges for rentals, labor, and material with contract provisions and any change notices.
9. Compare invoice labor rates with the contract.
10. Verify that services were delivered, material delivered, laborers worked, and equipment used.
11. Initiate any necessary changes in the scope of contract (change orders).

However, contract monitors need more than a list of actions to take. A common complaint of top managers is that contract monitors tend to have been supervisors in the city service who were replaced by the outside contract, and that these managers are unprepared for monitoring responsibilities. These monitors require training, for monitoring contractors is not the same as supervising laborers. Some specific contract knowledge that field monitors need can be obtained from a headquarters contract manager, but in many cases the manager in the field is the only monitor the agency has. She needs a great deal of information about the contract, the performance standards, the processing of contractor reports, and the handling of citizen complaints. Formal training is the best way to provide her with this experience, if the agency is serious about monitoring.

Citizen Relationships. There are basically two ways that citizens can formally be brought into the contracting process (assuming the service directly affects citizens). The first is to have a formal citizen complaint system in place. The citizen should know where to send complaints, the contractor should know her responsibilities if she is to receive complaints, and the contract monitor must see that complaints get processed speedily and that citizens are notified of actions taken. Since many jurisdictions rely primarily on complaints for service monitoring, it is all the more important to be sure that the system works effectively.

Citizens are also important in judging the effectiveness of a program whenever that program or service is judged by citizen surveys. The book *How Effective Are Your Community Services* (Hatry, Fisk, and Winnie, 1977) provides a wide range of ways to monitor services but relies most heavily on citizen surveys. The book, aimed at municipal services, is applicable as well to those services provided under contract. For example, library services can be judged on general user satisfaction, convenience, speed of service, or service and helpfulness, all of which can be determined by user surveys. These surveys can be used to judge contractor performance (12 percent of all municipalities contract out library services, usually to nonprofit organizations), with agreements about surveys written into the contract. Many large organizations have their own libraries, and the principles of citizen surveys can be translated easily into user surveys.

If desired, citizens, working as volunteers, can also be used to formally monitor the performance of contractors. Whatever the method, it is important to have citizen satisfaction as part of the monitoring process. Exhibit 3 summarizes the elements of a complete monitoring system.

Performance Standards, Efficiency, and Effectiveness

Most experts claim that the best way to monitor programs is to establish definite performance standards in the contract and then inspect or spot check often enough to ensure that these standards are maintained by the contractor. Such a set of standards provides a definite means for judging contractors. From the contractor's view, standards provide a guideline for calibrating bids and also provide potential protection from arbitrary monitoring by agency officials.

Unfortunately, the majority of contracts do not have clear standards. Most contracts are reasonably specific about such items as penalties to be levied, contractor payments to be made, and dates of tasks to be completed. Specific standards about

Exhibit 3. Elements of a Complete Monitoring Program.

Contractor relations
  Initial meeting with contractor after bid award
  Continuous monitor-contractor interaction
  Formal and informal contractor feedback from monitor
The contract
  Specific performance standards
  Penalties for nonperformance spelled out
The contract manager
  Comprehensive list of duties
  Training programs for contract managers
Citizen relations
  Formal complaint system
  Citizen surveys

---

exactly what constitutes adequate performance are often missing. When these are present, they are generally limited to input measures—that is, the resources to be consumed in providing the service (such as the number and type of aids for a nursing home).

Input measures establish how professional a contractor's staff may be or how well staffed the service is. They may indicate that the equipment is modern, or they may be as specific as the quality of the street asphalt or the computer software program. Good standards, however, must specify actual performance. The question is rarely how well qualified the staff is but how well the end product satisfies the user. Measures such as the number of registered engineers on a street maintenance contract or the registered nurses per shift in a nursing home can only be crude predictors of actual performance. If agencies had better measures of outputs (such as the number of projects designed or patient health after treatment), they could rely less on substitute measures of inputs or resources consumed.

Because many performance standards do not specify actual results but only input measures, it is often impossible to demand actual contractor performance. All that can be demanded is adherence to the contract. This is a poor substitute for performance, but it is no worse than when the agency performs the work itself and uses the same type of standards. The fault lies with the agency (or, in some cases, the state of knowledge), not the contractor. The agency is not monitoring effectiveness or actual accomplishment but only effort and legal conformity.

Measures of effectiveness involve actual outputs or the impacts of the service on the user or the public. In the case of engineering, these measures might involve projects designed or number of streets paved. In the case of nursing homes, such measures might include the average length of stay (although this might be an invitation to treat patients too hurriedly). These examples reflect measures of actual outputs.

Impacts on users are usually more important than agency outputs but are often difficult or impossible to measure. Such impacts might, in the case of street repair, be the smoothness of the paving as well as citizen satisfaction with the project; for nursing homes, patient satisfaction; for police patrol, reductions in the crime rate; for defense procurement, reductions in the average time to fill orders.

Efficiency is another criterion that should be considered. Efficiency is the ratio between inputs and outputs. Keeping the amount of time of delivery equal, procurement of airplane parts at an average lower cost demonstrates an increase in efficiency. The same number of arrests with fewer patrol officers demonstrates efficiency (if the policemen are not making more arrests for jaywalking rather than for burglaries).

Efficiency and effectiveness are two major criteria for judging performance of public functions, whether this judgment is performed in-house or by contractors. When combined with contractual performance standards, the contractor can be judged on legal conformance with the contract (standards), on effectiveness (are the correct outputs, such as a reduced crime rate, being produced?) and efficiency (are the outputs being produced cost-effectively?).

In the case of efficiency and effectiveness, the contractor can only be judged in comparison with previous agency operations (for example, is the service being performed more effectively and efficiently than before?).

Exhibit 4 lists some sample performance, efficiency, and effectiveness measures for recreation and library programs. Park maintenance has a performance standard calling for weekly mowing. The efficiency measure is cost per acre mowed, and the effectiveness measure is citizen satisfaction, probably determined by citizen or facility user surveys. The contractor, of course, is only legally required to meet the performance standard, which should be included in the contract.

Efficiency and effectiveness measures can be used on a comparative basis. The contractor's performance on them can be compared to similar scores when the agency was providing the service. If the contractor is meeting performance standards but the measures of effectiveness and efficiency are lower than in the past, the standard may need to be revised. If some time has elapsed since agency operation of the service, the contractor's scores can be compared on a year-to-year basis. If scores are declining over time, even though performance standards are being met, perhaps the contract should require that effectiveness ratings be consistent over years or should provide incentives for exceeding previous effectiveness scores.

Changes in efficiency scores may indicate the contract provisions for performance should be adjusted up or down, or that

Exhibit 4. Performance, Efficiency, and Effectiveness Measures.

Service	Performance Standard	Efficiency Measure	Effectiveness Measure
Recreation:			
Park maintenance	Weekly mowing	Cost per acre mowed	Citizen satisfaction
Facilities	Minimum staff Hours of operation	Cost per hour of operation	Citizen usage
Recreation services	Number of programs	Cost per program	Citizen usage
Library:			
Circulation	Hours of operation	Cost per volume circulated	Client usage
Reference	Speed of response to questions	Cost per request	Percentage of requests handled satisfactorily
General:	Staff qualifications	Cost per user	User/citizen satisfaction

a lower bid can be expected in the future. If inflation is a factor, dividing the unit cost each year by the consumer price index will give true costs. For example, the following computation indicates that the hypothetical price per unit was actually lower in 1986 than in 1985:

	1985	1986
Cost per unit	120	126
Consumer price index	105	112
Adjusted unit cost	114	113

There are two recent changes in measuring effectiveness that are increasingly being used by cities. Visual ratings of services, such as garbage collection and street sweeping, are sometimes used for measuring effectiveness. Likewise, citizen surveys to determine satisfaction with the program or service are occasionally used. Kansas City (Missouri) conducts citizen interviews about refuse collection and other services as part of the contract monitoring process. Newark (New Jersey) has conducted mail and telephone resident surveys, and Savannah (Georgia) regularly surveys citizens (Marlin, 1984). DeKalb (Illinois) also surveyed citizens about municipal services (Center for Governmental Studies, 1985).

The principle of visual rating systems and citizen surveys can be translated directly to other levels of government, since similar types of services exist. These surveys might be called user surveys, but the intent to measure effectiveness is the same. Since user satisfaction is part of the informal evaluation of many programs, this would simply formalize the process. Visual rating systems apply directly to certain programs at every level of government, such as janitorial services.

Exhibit 5 shows how visual rating systems work, in this case in Charlotte, South Carolina. Community inspectors select the blocks randomly, assigning a 0 (very clean) to 5 (very dirty) rating. The exhibit shows that the city objective of a 2 or lower rating was met that year. Visual rating guides are normally based on pictures taken of streets or sites, with given pictures corresponding to a 1, 2, or 3 rating to guide the raters.

Exhibit 5. Street Cleaning Ratings, Charlotte, South Carolina (1980).

Objective: Maintain the cleanliness of all paved streets so that a random sample of streets in any zone on a given day has an average rating of at least 2 (on a five-point scale where 0 indicates "very clean" and 4 indicates "very littered"), with at least 80 percent of the sample blocks in the section rating 1 or better. Rating will be made by community development inspectors.

	May	June	*Cumulative Ratings*		
			Five-month	*Eight-month*	*Twelve-month*
Average cleanliness rating of all paved dedicated city streets (based on a random sample)	1.12	1.09	1.26	1.25	1.26
Percent of sample streets receiving a rating of 1 or better	79	74	56	61	63

Objective Resolution Statement: State whether or not the visual rating objective for city streets is being met. If not, explain why not: "This objective has been met. The average street rating for the year is 1.26, which meets the objective of maintaining an average of 2. Sixty-three percent of all streets surveyed rated a 1 or better for the year."

Source: Adapted from City of Charlotte, 1980, p. 106.

Citizen or user surveys for use in monitoring programs fall into four categories (see Marlin, 1984). One technique, interactive cable systems, is rarely if ever used. The other three methods are mailed questionnaires, telephone surveys, and interviews (either in the home or in some common location). The use of these survey methods was popularized in *How Effective Are Your Community Services* (Hatry, Fisk, and Winnie, 1977). The methods for using these techniques are widely known and can be found in many sources.

Mailed surveys may be the most accurate reflection of real citizen views, since individuals complete the surveys privately. Such surveys are relatively inexpensive but have a low return rate. Conversely, telephone interviews reach many people but are more expensive than mailed surveys. Also, people cannot always be reached by phone, and those with phones may not be representative of the population. Home interviews can replace telephone interviews, but home interviews are extremely expensive. Multiple citizen interviews in malls or supermarkets are possible, but the group may not be representative. The use of citizen surveys still poses many difficulties.

In summary, contracting out a service does not relieve the agency of responsibility for evaluating performance. It is not enough to insist that the contractor adhere to the performance standards in the contract. A well-managed agency will evaluate efficiency and effectiveness, comparing them over time. Visual ratings and citizen surveys are two relatively new ways to accomplish evaluation.

Summary

This chapter outlined the basic steps of the important, but often neglected, job of contract monitoring. While most agencies pay some attention to monitoring, it is often minimal. Serious monitoring is often disregarded on the assumption that complaints from citizens and users will ensure performance.

In an ideal system, monitors would be selected from the field and program level, where the greatest expertise lies, and would avoid collusion or excessive sympathy for the contractor. These monitors would be experienced in the program area and would also be well trained in overseeing contractor performance. They would carefully use citizen complaints to supplement visual site inspections that compare contractor performance to standards in the contract. The standards would be checked for variance weekly or monthly. The periodic checks would measure efficiency and effectiveness over time, as well as simply ascertaining adherence to the contract.

Not many agencies achieve this ideal system. Most probably do not even try very hard to approach it, for many reasons. Some agencies simply do not care, some do not find it cost-effective, some dislike monitoring for ideological reasons, and some simply are unaware of the importance of monitoring. But other agencies monitor their contractors and reap the benefits of tighter quality control, more cost awareness, and a reduced likelihood of contract abuse by agency and contractor alike. To the extent that effective monitoring becomes more common, contracting out is likely to gain more support from its current critics.

CHAPTER 6 ∽∽∽∽∽∽∽∽∽∽∽∽∽∽∽∽

Keeping Control
and Dealing with
Performance Problems

Many agencies are reluctant to contract out because they feel uneasy about the possibility of losing control of the service. Once the contract is awarded, they feel the contractor has control of the service. In fact, although service provision is ultimately in the hands of the agency, the contractor has a contract for a given period of time and may have the primary control over service quality.

Officials spend a good deal of time worrying about these prospects. Most of the concern comes from agencies that have not done much, if any, contracting and thus have less familiarity with the process. Sometimes the concern arises from doubts about the contractor, who may be the only supplier in an area, or who may be relatively inexperienced.

These concerns about performance should be distinguished from concerns about the quality of the service. Concerns about keeping control revolve around the inability of the agency to respond to contractor failure to perform services, not specifically about the ability to monitor and to determine how the contractor may be deficient. The issue is how the agency responds to the contractor's failure to perform adequately, not how the agency makes such a determination. (This latter issue involves how the agency monitors performance, which was covered in Chapter Five.) Questions of control also involve alternate service delivery systems. The agency will approach the contractor's failure to perform differently if it can make other arrangements for the service than if it cannot or has not provided for alternatives.

Many unforeseen events can befall contractors, regardless of their intentions. Strikes occur, bankruptcies happen, suppliers fail to deliver, and sometimes, for no apparent reason, service simply is not acceptable. Unfortunately, when this happens the agency may have terminated its own employees and may feel completely helpless. Concerns about such possibilities often explain why many government agencies choose not to contract out.

In actuality, performance failures rarely occur. Most contractors perform effectively and to agency satisfaction. Furthermore, there are arrangements and provisions that can be made to provide protection against contractor failure to perform. However, for purposes of discussion in the following cases, it is assumed that the agency is relying entirely on the contractor and has no capacity to provide the services.

Contract Interruptions

Contract interruptions arise when the contractor cannot continue to provide the service. Contractor bankruptcy (rare) or strikes against the contractor are examples of contract interruptions. In these cases, the agency, without a staff or without alternative, faces a situation where the service is completely interrupted.

There are contract provisions that will shield the agency from such problems. The most obvious are provisions that require the contractor to post a performance bond sufficient for the agency to replace the services, either by adding its own staff or by hiring another contractor. Another approach is to purchase (or have the contractor purchase) interruption insurance whenever it is available. The intent in both cases is to protect against financial difficulties arising from contract interruption. The problem is that money alone will not create providers if none exist. Creating and finding providers require planning for contract interruption contingencies far in advance of the contract provision so that a performance bond or insurance may be secured.

Agencies should consider three alternatives to complete dependence on the contractor: (1) the use of contingency contracts with other providers, (2) partial contracting (dividing the contract among competing contractors), and (3) competing themselves with the contractor (dividing the contract between the contractor and the agency itself).

Contingency contracts bind a secondary contractor to provide services in the event that the primary contractor for the agency cannot or does not perform. A common contingency contract for cities might be with the county, with the agreement being that under specified conditions and within a certain period of time, the county will provide given services (such as police protection by the sheriff's department). The contract could also be with other private contractors, assuming that competing contractors are available.

Another technique is to use partial contracts, whereby the service is divided into portions, usually geographical, and different contractors are used. Marlin (1984) notes that partial contracting involves an agency or city decision to perform a portion of the service using their own staff. When partialing occurs, failure by any one contractor can be met simply by having a competing contractor expand operations to the unserved area. One example of this occurred in Montreal, where by 1980 about thirty-eight private contractors provided refuse collection services along with city collection (Savas, 1977). Another example is when a small agency or contractor provides janitorial work in various agency buildings, which would enable it to cover at least part of the cleaning area in which another contractor does not perform.

Another way to establish partial contracting is to divide the work into functions or type of work. Usually the most routine or easily managed portion is contracted out, since vigorous competition for such "easy" jobs will produce the lowest bids (Marlin, 1984). The agency retains staff for the remaining functions as well as the capacity to perform all the work should contract interruption occur. This is criticized as "creaming" the contract (by opponents of contracting), but the ultimate issue is to reduce costs. If contractors can do so, it should not matter which part of a job they perform. An alternative is to divide the contract among competing contractors, although care has to be taken to contract out equally profitable portions to ensure competitive bidding. When private contractors compete in this manner, total costs are often driven down substantially, although monitoring the contract to ensure quality can become a problem.

The final way of avoiding dependence on contractors is to have city forces share the contract with private contractors. This technique, common in large cities for refuse collection services, provides an excellent way to establish benchmark prices for the provision of services, enabling agencies to check on how much more efficient (or inefficient) private contractors are than city forces. Minneapolis has, over the years, driven municipal costs down to private collector rates (Savas, 1977). Having municipal forces available for expansion into any gap left by private service interruption considerably reduces the threat of such interruption.

These three options—contingency contracts, partial contracting, or agency sharing—do not happen simply because the agency is concerned about contract interruption; they must be arranged. Agencies may have to create competition where none exists, using various means such as frequently bidding contracts to attract attention, approaching firms that normally do not provide the service, or negotiating with large or small government agencies to provide services on a contingency basis.

Another way to protect the agency from contractor difficulties is to develop dispute resolution techniques similar to labor-management grievance arbitration. A neutral third party resolves disagreements over whether the contract is being followed, with both parties agreeing to abide by the decision. Seader (1986, p. 5) notes, "The contract should have . . . simple and straightforward dispute resolution procedures so that the service or facility does not get interrupted while the parties argue over whose fault problems are."

Failure to Perform Adequately

Enforcing a contract when the contractor fails to perform adequately should be a simple task, but it is not always. If the agency has no alternative but to contract through the contractor currently used, threats to reduce payments or suspend the contract can be hollow. Again, the problem is not determining whether the contractor is performing adequately but, after such a determination is made, being in a position to take action. Dilatory contractors are apt to perform more diligently when the agency has an actual alternative.

To protect the agency, certain legal provisions should be included into the contract that provide for performance bonds for poor performance and for the right of the agency to reduce or suspend payments for contractor failure to meet standards. Most contracts for contracting out have such clauses, but they may be worth little if the agency, lacking alternate providers, is reluctant to enforce the contract. Thus the task of the agency, after inserting these clauses into the contract, is to make sure that alternatives exist.

The major alternatives are similar to those for contract interruption. In order of preference, there should be (1) a competing private contractor who is providing adequate service in other areas or on other contracts for the agency; (2) another government agency that can, under a contingency contract, assign part of its work force to the job; (3) an agency force providing the service in some of the areas that can expand its coverage to the area with poor service; (4) other private contractors (perhaps inexperienced) who would be willing to provide the service; and (5) agency staff who are assigned to monitoring the contract and who can, through overtime or other arrangements, provide the service until other arrangements can be made.

Of course, if any one of these five alternatives is actually available, the agency will not be as concerned about contractor performance. Control of the contracting out process depends on having alternatives. Alternatives are usually a real possibility only if the arrangements are made before the agency commits itself to one contractor. Of the five alternatives listed above, all require some previous arrangements—they will not arise spontaneously when needed. For example, the second alternative requires reliance on another government agency. Preliminary discussion and commitments are needed if any emergency support is to be available. As in the case of contract interruption, the alternatives must be arranged before the contract is signed.

Changing Service Levels

The ability of an agency to change contract service levels during a contract period can also be important. If the agency cannot demand such modifications, it has lost some control over the service. Changed service levels become necessary, for example, after a new budget is approved but while a multiyear service contract is still in place. The agency may need to reduce service levels as part of an overall retrenchment effort. Perhaps priorities have changed, and the service under contract is to be reduced. Normally, reductions in service levels are resisted by contractors because they generally mean lower profits or at least more inconvenience, while increases presumably mean greater profits. In either case the contractor may not be willing to change levels, either because it is inconvenient or because he is operating at optimum profitability.

The question of service levels is usually handled in the contract itself. Unlike service interruption or failure to perform, the alternative of competing contractors or contingency contracts is probably not very useful. The service is acceptable, but changes in levels are desired. No one wants to substitute another contractor or other agency; they simply wish to have the contractor be more flexible.

There are three general legal provisions that should be considered to ensure that levels of service can be changed. The two most important are (1) a contract provision to allow the agency to terminate the contract if a grant or subsidy ends and (2) a provision giving the agency power to change contract levels at its option.

It is important for the agency to be able to terminate contracts on short notice, because it is not uncommon for the particular service to be dependent on grants or subsidies from another level of government. Reductions in service levels due to grant or subsidy cutbacks are probably more common than actual terminations, since the level of federal grant support to state and local governments has been reduced steadily since 1975. In such cases, the agency needs the power not only to terminate the contract but also to change levels of service at its option, precisely as if it were using public employees for the program (National Association of Counties, 1977).

One method is to have contracts specify desired levels of services. Using street sweeping as an example, the contract would specify that streets be swept weekly, biweekly, or monthly, with one month's notice required for any change and no change more often than once a year. Another example would be janitorial contracts that call for maintenance of buildings every day and walls washed every month, with up to three changes per year in the schedule for these tasks. Contractors may well be able to adjust to such provisions, whereas they would not bid on a contract that merely said that the city reserves the right to modify or terminate contract provisions.

Normally, sharp reductions in a service are uncommon when the agency itself provides the service. Such reductions should be equally uncommon when the service is contracted out, but the city can hardly guarantee to contractors something that it could not guarantee if it were providing the service itself. Reductions (or, rarely, increases) are occasionally part of public sector life, and the contractor should take this into account.

If the agency insists on such provisions to protect itself against cutbacks or changed priorities, it will quickly find that contract costs rise in all but the most competitive situations. The contractor faces uncertainty during the life of the contract and will attempt to protect against this by hedging with a higher bid. Specifying alternative levels of contracts, as suggested earlier, may reduce the uncertainty somewhat, and likewise the bid, but the net result is still likely to be a higher-priced contract. What the agency has done is pay a premium for the privilege of changing service levels when it desires.

Emergency Response

Emergencies seem to occur when they are least expected and when the agency is least prepared for them. Snowstorms blow in when road maintenance employees are assigned to other duties. Potholes occur when half the street repair crew is on vacation. A second fire breaks out when the fire-fighting crew is at the first one. The software packages are delayed just before the new computer system is to print the first payroll checks.

In the first two of these situations, the emergency can be met by reassigning workers to the emergency, even if it means disrupted schedules for other work. Emergencies, by their very nature, demand that other projects be dropped immediately to solve the crisis. However, what if there are no employees to reassign?

This situation arises when cities contract out those functions (such as street work) that are fairly labor-intensive. When cities provide the service, the laborers assigned to street striping, patching, and general maintenance double as emergency teams. This is not the case when the workers are private employees under contract. They have no responsibility for emergency response unless it is specifically written into the contract. Kelley (1984) relates cases of unwary and rash cities that contracted out the public works and maintenance functions and bitterly regretted this during the first snowstorm. In any event, lack of contractor responsiveness is often considered a major drawback to contracting out. Tribbett (1983), in a survey of California public works directors, notes that emergency response was the major drawback to contracting out. One consultant (Roy Jorgensen Associates, 1981, p. 81) comments, "There is no ability to handle emergencies," and that this is one of the major arguments against contracting out. However, he goes on to assert that this fear is largely unfounded, based on his U.S. and Brazilian experience, and that contracts can simply treat emergency responses as extra work items.

Emergencies in the public works area often occur, as noted above. However, most local officials think of the uniformed services—such as police and fire services—when they think of a major emergency. No doubt a major reason why many jurisdictions are reluctant to contract out police and fire services is that they fear that any kind of service interruption will endanger the safety of residents.

It is difficult to evaluate this concern. Certainly, municipal provision of police and fire services has not prevented job actions by those employees against their municipal employers, although most of these job actions have been "sickouts." In these cases, employees are still available for major fires or crime outbreaks. One can argue that most police and fire job actions are mostly inconvenient and pose no major threat to public safety. Similarly, there is no evidence that contracted out emergency services are subject to job interruptions. Part of the reason for this lack of evidence is that few cities have contracted out basic police and fire services to private contractors; the ICMA study shows that only 1 to 3 percent of cities do so (Shulman, 1982).

Poole (1980) notes major exceptions to this rule of not contracting out emergency services, including Lexington (Kentucky), which hired a company to patrol high-crime housing areas; St. Petersburg (Florida), which hired a private security guard for its parks; Houston (Texas), which has a private force for its city hall area; and many cities that hire private security forces for their airports. For fire protection, Scottsdale (Arizona), several districts in that area, and much of the unincorporated area are served by Rural Metro, a private company in existence for over thirty years. Elk Grove (Illinois) and Hall County (Georgia) have similar arrangements. No service interruptions have been reported, although the contracts were in many cases controversial, and the quality of police and fire service during transitional periods probably suffered.

In any case, there is little clear evidence that (1) contracting out public works services makes cities vulnerable to emergencies such as snowstorms that could not be handled because the contractor was unresponsive, or (2) contracting out emergency services such as police and fire has resulted in any service interruptions.

Agencies that are nevertheless concerned about maintaining capacity for emergency response after contracting out should consider several alternatives. At a minimum, the contract should have a clause calling for the contractor to respond to emergencies (as defined in the contract). This may increase the cost of the contract or cause some or all contractors to withdraw. In such cases, the agency must contract with other government agencies or provide the service itself. If the agency prefers private contracts but cannot get adequate emergency response provisions, it will have to make one or more of the following arrangements: (1) develop contingency contracts with other providers; (2) let partial contracts to several contractors on the assumption that at least one will be able to continue operation if the others cannot; (3) provide for agency competition with the private contractor so that both city and private work forces exist, thus ensuring that one can meet emergencies; and (4) create an agency monitoring force large enough to respond to emergencies, at least on a short-term basis.

Lowballing

The final issue involved in keeping control of the contracting out process involves "lowballing." Lowballing applies to contractors' practice of bidding artificially low in order to obtain a contract. After the first contract, the contractor becomes the only party with experience in providing the service and later substantially raises bids for contracts. Since the agency is now dependent on the contractor, it is initially lowballed into a high-cost contract. The practice is known by several names, such as "buy-in" (Marlin, 1984), but the practice is the same.

Basically, lowballing involves a lack of competition: It works because no other contractor exists and the agency has become dependent on one contractor. There are little published data that indicate the frequency of lowballing, and one is inclined to dismiss the issue except for the concerns raised (without details) by several researchers (Kelley, 1984; Marlin, 1984). The best response to the threat of lowballing is to maintain competition so that an alternative to the original contractor is always present.

There are several provisions that can provide protection against lowballing and, in effect, ensure that competition exists.

One useful provision grants the agency the power to unilaterally extend the contract for an additional period of time, thus maintaining the contract while the agency seeks competitors. The prospect of a unilaterally extended contract will also cause potential lowballer contractors to present bids nearer their actual costs over time. The State of California's General Services Administration uses such provisions to prevent lowballing by its janitorial contractor.

Providing short-term contracts is another tactic that ensures competition. Assuming that there are several firms interested in the contract, a relatively short contractual period will be more likely to encourage an unsuccessful initial bidder to wait for the next opportunity. This potential competition should reduce the likelihood or effectiveness of lowballing. The disadvantage is the cost in time and effort spent in continually calling for bids on the short-term contracts. There may also be transition costs, if one contractor replaces another, as the new party becomes familiar with the contract.

Competition can come in ways other than bidding wars. Often partial contracts can be awarded, such as for refuse disposal contracts. Since two competitors share the contract, competition should be institutionalized. In some cases, the agency itself can compete for part of the service, thus maintaining the internal capacity to provide the service. Finally, intergovernmental contracts with a neighboring agency, such as a larger city or the county, may be possible.

Contractor Controls Are Not Free

Contracts that give agencies extra options at the expense of the contractor can be expensive. The various contract provisions mentioned include (1) performance bonds, (2) contract interruption insurance, (3) provision for reduced or suspended payments in case of poor performance, (4) power to terminate the contract if the supporting grant or subsidy dries up, (5) power to change the levels of service the contractor must provide, (6) power to extend the contract, and (7) rebidding the contract often (short-term contracts would provide the same protection). These provisions all make contracts less potentially profitable for a contractor and drive up bids. Picturing a contract with all these provisions stretches the imagination. Such a contract would certainly cost more than if the agency itself provided the service.

Obviously, there must be some trade-offs. Protecting the agency against all possible ways in which it might lose control over the contractor will drive contract costs up too far. Placing no such provisions in the contract may leave the agency at the mercy of a contractor who has no competition. Contracting out cannot be a risk-free option, any more than can providing the service in-house. If an agency wants to contract for a reasonable fee and yet retain control over the contracting out process, it will have to look at ways of maintaining competition, such as (1) contingency contracts, (2) partial contracting, or (3) retaining an agency work force. The ways of maintaining competition, with some of the contract provisions listed above, are shown in Exhibit 6.

Contract provisions, such as demanding emergency responses or unilaterally extending the contract, are no substitute for actual competition between private and governmental contractors. The agency that relies on formal contractual provisions instead of maintaining competition is likely to become disenchanted with contracting out, both because the agency will probably find few reliable contractors and because the lack of competition eventually drives costs up.

Summary

Agencies can keep control of contracting out by contractual provisions that prevent contract interruption: through contingency contracts with alternate providers, partial service contracts, performance bonds, insurance, and increased competition. They can avoid failure to perform by providing for reduced payments, providing for suspension of payments, and requiring performance bonds or developing contingency contracts. Governments can modify contracts by using specific contract clauses, authorizing the agency to terminate the contract if the grant or subsidy expires, or providing for a wider range of alter-

Exhibit 6. Keeping Control of the Contracting Out Process.

Issues	Solutions
Contract interruption: Contractor bankruptcy or strike against contractor leaves agency with no provider.	Develop contingency contracts with alternate providers Create partial service contracts with other contractors Obtain contractor performance bond Obtain contract interruption insurance Provide for agency competition Provide for dispute resolution
Failure to perform: Contractor fails to perform adequately while agency can neither enforce nor terminate contract.	Provide for reduced payments in contract Provide in contract for suspension of payments Provide a performance bond to include poor performance Develop contingency contracts with alternate providers Create partial service contracts with other providers
Contract prevents agency from changing service levels: Desired modifications in service levels, up or down, cannot be changed during contract life.	Use contract clauses giving agency authority to change contract levels at its option Provide contract provision allowing agency to terminate contract if subsidy or grant ends Provide for a wider range of alternative levels in the contract
Emergency response: Contractor will not or cannot respond to emergencies unforeseen in contract.	Insert clause in contract calling for emergency response at agency option Develop contingency contracts with other providers Use partial contracts with other providers Provide for agency competition in producing the service Create an agency monitoring force large enough to respond to emergencies

Exhibit 6. Keeping Control of the Contracting Out Process, Cont'd.

Issues	Solutions
Lowballing: Contractor obtains contract by artificially low bid, planning to raise bid for subsequent contracts when agency is dependent on one contractor.	Allow agency to unilaterally extend contract Rebid contract frequently to maintain private competition Use short-term contracts to maintain private competition Use partial conracting Create agency competition

nate service levels. The contracting agency can ensure emergency response by using specific clauses for extra work or by using contingency contracts, partial contracts, and agency competition. Finally, lowballing can be avoided by short-term contracts, contractual provisions allowing unilateral agency extension of the contract, or frequent rebidding of the contract. These provisions do increase the costs considerably, for they have the same effect as an insurance policy.

Arranging fall-back positions, such as arrangements with other contractors or another government agency for emergency help, is needed as much as specific contract provisions. Without the help of other contractors or governments, the right, for example, to terminate the contract is an empty threat.

Keeping control of the contracting out process requires both careful planning for alternatives and specific contractual provisions.

PART III ⚘⚘⚘⚘⚘⚘⚘⚘⚘⚘⚘⚘⚘⚘

Types of Contractors and Contracts

Part Three deals with the various types of contractors and some actual contracts and related documents. In a somewhat different way than Part Two, this part also describes some of the "nuts and bolts" of contracting out by presenting actual contracts and describing the three kinds of contractors: for-profit, nonprofit, and government.

Chapter Seven describes and contrasts the three kinds of contractors. Contracts with other governments are quite common and generally do not raise many questions. They are often entered into without the careful analysis of costs and benefits that private contracts receive, since they are seen as "safer." Intergovernmental contracts are also supported by many people because of their tendency to unify government services in the area.

Nonprofit organizations frequently contract with governments, particularly in the health and human services and in cultural and recreational programs. Nonprofit organizations are now becoming more like for-profit organizations, a case in point being private nursing homes, which operate much like nonprofit nursing homes. Nonprofit organizations tend to have strong community support, are able to attract human and financial resources fairly easily, and are perceived to have strong commitments to their clients.

Private organizations are marked by efficiency, flexibility, and management skills. These perform best in specific programs such as public works (street sweeping, rubbish collection), where a formal estimate can be obtained and the agency can specify quantifiable objectives. Frequently, private contractors are the only persons in a position to provide new or technologically advanced skills or equipment.

Chapter Eight presents four contracts generally typical of those common to local units of government and involving direct public services. These include a police intergovernmental agreement, a contract for managing an engineering department, a private fire protection agreement, and a county golf pro shop concession agreement.

Chapter Nine presents parts of two contract documents that do not involve direct public services. These are the specifications for a state department building security system with a private party and a state contract for janitorial services in a large building.

CHAPTER 7 ∽∽∽∽∽∽∽∽∽∽∽∽∽∽∽∽∽

Understanding the Major Contractors

So far in this book, contracting out has generally been discussed as though it were always or almost always done with private firms. With exceptions, such as human services contracting, where heavy use of nonprofit firms is common (see Chapter Two), the discussions have assumed that contracts were with private, profit-seeking individuals and companies. This could have been expected, given the growth of private contracting in recent years and the conventional assumption that contracting involves private firms. However, a good deal of contracting out, mostly by state and local governments, takes place with nonprofit firms and with other governments.

Contracting with other governmental units may well be more common than with private companies (no reliable figures exist). This is certainly true in health and human services (perhaps with the exception of hospital operations and day-care centers). Contracting with other governments is also more common than with private parties in the area of public safety (with the major exception of vehicle towing and also probably ambulance service). Finally, in parks and recreation and in cultural activities, intergovernmental contracting (IGC) is more common than private contracting, although nonprofit contracting is more common than either. In both public safety and recreation and in cultural service provision, of course, public work forces are the traditional and most frequent way of providing the service.

Although nonprofit organizations, outside of health and human services, are relatively unaccustomed to delivering services, there are some major exceptions. Over 20 percent of local governments used nonprofit groups to provide paratransit services, to operate cultural and arts programs, and to operate museums.

Table 10 shows some of the functions that private, nonprofit, and government contractors provide. It is clear that the use of alternate providers varies widely, depending on the particular function being considered. Cities and counties contracted with private firms in only 1 percent of the cases for fire suppression but 80 percent of the time for vehicle towing. Cities and counties in no case contracted with nonprofit firms for residential waste collection but did use these firms 35 percent of the time for museum operation. Finally, 42 percent of local governments used other governmental agencies for bus system maintenance and operation, but only 2 percent of local units contracted with other governments for vehicle towing.

Thus far, private firms, nonprofit firms, and other governments have been discussed only in terms of the services they commonly contract with local governments. It is necessary to look at each type of organization, its strengths and weaknesses, and the major reason why it is widely (or not widely) used in contracting.

Intergovernmental Contracting

Intergovernmental contracting (IGC) is a service delivery choice in which one governmental unit agrees to provide services to a contracting unit. A simple example of such a contract is when the county agrees to collect refuse for a city or cities within the county, normally billing the citizens directly. There are many permutations: The county may subcontract its refuse collection to a private contractor or may use property tax

Table 10. Local Governments Contracting for Selected Services
with Private, Nonprofit, and Government Providers.

Service	Private[a]	Nonprofit[b]	Other Governments
Public works and transportation:			
Solid waste disposal	28%	2%	31%
Residential wastewater collection	35		8
Traffic signal maintenance/installation	26	2	14
Bus system operation/maintenance	24	10	42
Paratransit system operation/maintenance	23	23	29
Streetlight operation	39	2	21
Public safety:			
Crime prevention/patrol	3	7	5
Fire prevention/suppression	1	4	9
Ambulance services	24	11	17
Vehicle towing/storage	80		2
Parks and recreation:			
Recreation services	4	18	9
Parks landscaping	9	3	5
Operation of libraries	1	11	28
Operation of museums	4	35	16
Support functions:			
Building/grounds maintenance	20	1	4
Heavy equipment vehicle maintenance	32		2
Data processing	23	2	11
Payroll preparation	10	1	3
Delinquent tax collection	10	3	20

Source: Adapted from Valente and Manchester, 1984, p. iv.

Note: Information on human services programs is in Table 4, Chapter Two.
[a] Does not include franchises with private companies, which total as much as 15 percent of the reporting localities for residential solid waste disposal.
[b] Includes contracts with neighborhood groups.

levies to recover its costs or may receive direct payments from the city or cities. These permutations and a wide range of practices make IGC complex and somewhat difficult to generalize about. In addition, there are several kinds of quasi-contractual agreements among government agencies, which serves to confuse the issue of IGC.

Varieties of Intergovernmental Agreements. These quasi-contractual arrangements are called *agreements,* a word indicating a lower degree of contractual commitment. A common quasi-contractual arrangement is an informal agreement. These are unwritten, verbal, and extralegal agreements between two or more units of local government for the performance of a particular service or services. For example, two units may agree to maintain a common boundary street, share expensive equipment, or enter mutual aid pacts for fire and police, each agreeing to aid in event of emergencies (National Association of Counties, 1977). Another quasi-contractual agreement is a service exchange. This is an informal agreement, common in rural areas, where one unit provides a service to the citizens in both areas and is compensated by the other jurisdiction, which provides an alternate service. One small rural community might informally provide police services to another in exchange for fire services. This is similar to a contract, but nothing is written and no money changes hands (National Association of Counties, 1977). Since so many local units are small and/or rural and because these kinds of arrangements are common, the amount of quasi-contracting may result in understating the amount of intergovernmental contracting.

Joint service agreements are formal agreements between two parties for joint planning, financing, and delivery of a service to the inhabitants or administrative organizations of all participating agencies. Each individual unit retains responsibility for the service and has usually elected to enter into the agreement because it can in that way obtain the service more economically. A simple example is the creation of a data-processing service bureau that serves three municipalities.

Formal service agreements or contracts are business transactions between government units, as when a county agrees to maintain a city's streets. While there may not be a formal contract, there is at least a memorandum of understanding and legislative approval by both parties, which makes the agreement legally enforceable. These service agreements are the most common way by which services are provided by one unit to the other (National Association of Counties, 1977).

Intergovernmental Contracting: An Economic Model. There are two approaches to IGC. To many (perhaps most) jurisdictions, IGC is simply one alternative way to provide services. The matter is a simple economic choice. Price is the determining factor unless some other criterion, such as convenience or availability of the service, intervenes. From this view, service delivery is a calculation to be made with the best interests of the recipient as the sole consideration. Hence, contracts are carefully examined, reviewed, and evaluated from a single point of view: whatever is in the best short-term interests of the government agency. The unit searches for alternative service delivery options and chooses the one that maximizes its benefits or reduces its costs. A newly incorporated city, for example, must provide a permit office from which citizens and contractors obtain permits and also must perform the electrical, plumbing, and carpentry inspections called for by those permits. The choice is simple: Calculate the costs of having municipal employees operate a permit office and make actual inspections and then obtain estimates of the costs of contracting for engineers to check more complex building plans. Next, estimate the costs of having another government agency (if one is available) perform the services and also obtain estimates for private parties (if private contractors are available) to perform inspection work. Then, after a careful analysis, choose the best combination of quality and price for providing building inspection services.

The same principle applies if the city already has a building department, except that actual city costs can be obtained by a cost study, which would precede the comparison of private and intergovernmental costs. The procedure is relatively simple and predictable, again assuming that other government agencies or private contractors are available and willing to provide the service.

Economic calculations are the way most units make such choices. Of course, emotional or political commitments to one or another delivery system interfere with a purely "rational" choice. One example of such an "irrational," or at least noneconomic, attitude is a political preference for using city employees for all city services. Another example is antipathy toward another governmental unit, which rules out contracting.

Intergovernmental Contracting: A Political Unification Model.
There is another view, political rather than economic in nature,
of IGC. Scholars, urban reformers, and some public officials
are concerned with finding a way of improving and rationaliz-
ing the "crazy quilt" arrangement of government services in
a particular geographical area, usually a large urban area. Contracting with the largest government in the area, usually the
county or possibly the state, is desirable because it ensures a
more uniform level of service or a higher quality of service. For
example, the county may provide services to many municipalities
at a higher or more professional level than some cities would
provide on their own. If this plan is not feasible, perhaps cities
can band together to provide common services. Perhaps one
city can purchase services from another.

The ideal of reformers is to have a simplified governmental
system, perhaps with only a few large agencies, or even a consolidated county. This is rarely politically feasible. However,
there are arrangements where many functions are provided by
one unit of government or even where most functions are provided by a few. It certainly would be advantageous, for example, to have all traffic signals synchronized on a major arterial
crossing several cities, to have all tax assessment done uniformly
by one unit, and to have sanitary inspections of all restaurants
done under one set of laws administered by one agency.

A reasonable ideal is to have areawide functions, such as
those mentioned above, provided centrally and to have purely
local functions provided by local units. Local functions might
include city park maintenance and local traffic enforcement. The
advantage of centrally provided areawide services and locally
provided local services is obvious. Centrally provided services
should be cheaper, due to economies of scale; should include
more professionally trained employees; should elevate service
levels across the geographical area; and should simplify government structure.

A view of IGC as a device for government integration
has specific effects. First, it changes the perspective of such
observers as reformers and academics. They look favorably on
intergovernmental (IG) contracts and less favorably on contracts

with private contractors, since IG contracts involve potentially more areawide governmental integration. These observers often have substantial influence on decisions to contract and tend to establish an intellectual climate highly favorable toward IG contracts. In such a climate, there is generally little concern for costs but more concern with policies leading to some sort of integration.

The second consequence of this view is to incline governmental units, particularly smaller ones, to look (1) to a larger unit of government for the service, (2) to some sort of joint agreement between governments for providing the service, or (3) to some cooperative arrangement with another government to share the function. This tendency is a good deal stronger when some larger unit of government is interested in providing the service, as is the case in Los Angeles County under the Lakewood plan (see the case study in the Resources). When arrangements for joint cooperative action exist, many agencies take the psychologically and often politically simpler route and join an existing group of governments or arrange with a larger unit to provide the service. Agencies frequently will not seriously search out private contractors, even though such contracting could be less expensive.

The Extent of Intergovernmental Contracting. As noted earlier, the amount of IGC is substantial, particularly at the local level. Cities and counties contract from 1 percent of the time in the case of secretarial and public relations and information services to 43 percent of the time for public and elderly housing. Every governmental service is offered under IG contracts, although many are infrequently delivered by this method, as Table 11 shows. In general, the services commonly purchased by IGC are those providing large-scale economies of operation, such as public housing or bus system operation, or those that require highly trained employees, such as mental health facilities. Some services are rarely contracted out to other government agencies. These services tend to be important management functions, personnel services, programs unique to the agency, or services, such as vehicle towing or fleet maintenance, that are commonly contracted to private operators.

A surprising number of government jurisdictions provide IG services. In 1973 the federal government provided flood

Table 11. Services Cities and Counties Most and Least Often
Purchased by Contract from Other Governments (1982).

Most Purchased		Least Purchased	
Operation/maintenance of		Vehicle towing and storage	2%
public/elderly housing	43%	Heavy equipment fleet	
Bus system operation/		maintenance	2
maintenance	42	General fleet maintenance	2
Sanitary inspection	36	Personnel services	2
Operation of mental health/		Secretarial services	1
retardation facilities	34	Public relations/information	1
Solid waste disposal	31		

Source: Adapted from Valente and Manchester, 1984, p. xv.

control, housing, soil conservation, and urban renewal services
to local governments. Those cities that reported receiving such
services obtained them from the federal government in 25 percent or more of the cases (Shulman, 1982).

However, most IG contracts are between localities and
sometimes between states and localities. In 1982, 52 percent of
all city service contracts involved IG contracts with the county.
That percentage was down from 59 percent ten years earlier,
since cities appear to be relying more on private contractors
(Henderson, 1986; Zimmerman, 1974). Most school district contracts involved recreational and park services, such as the use
of school facilities for recreation programs. Special district services contracts ranged widely, but by far the most common was
bus transportation by a transit authority (Shulman, 1982). IG
contracts are most common among large cities and counties in
the western United States and in cities and counties with professional managers. Since these are the places in which population changes are taking place, IGC will probably increase in
the future.

Nonprofit Contractors

One major alternative to IGC, assuming that private contractors are neither available nor satisfactory, is contracting with

nonprofit groups. Nonprofit organizations are a major provider of services to public organizations (Orlans, 1980). They provide these services most often to local government units and most often in the areas of cultural, recreational, and human services, as Table 12 shows. Nonprofit groups include neighborhood or community groups, such as the "commute clubs of the Golden Gate Transit District" (Armington and Ellis, 1984), as well as such diverse groups as the United Way, Friends of the Library, the Sierra Club, the Oregon Museum of Science and Industry, and Sutter Community Hospitals (Sacramento), to name only a few.

There is a slight tendency for larger governments of cities over 250,000 in population to rely on contracting with nonprofit organizations. This is the case with day-care facilities, mental health programs, and programs for the elderly. This is probably because nonprofit organizations large enough to operate such programs are found in larger cities or counties. Conversely, smaller units are slightly more likely to contract with private hospitals.

Nonprofit organizations commonly provide cultural and arts programs and staff museums, usually using volunteers. Public agency work forces play a lesser role in these services, and private contractors are rarely involved.

Nonprofit organizations are often very successful in producing services under contract. They are deeply committed to the program or service, often having been created because of member interest. The Humane Society, for example, exists because of a commitment to animals—and what better organization could maintain and operate the animal shelter?

There are several reasons why nonprofit organizations are effective in producing services, all of which are related to these organizations' program commitments. In many cases, the organizations are small. While this may pose some financial questions (see Whitcomb, 1983), it also gives such groups a substantial amount of flexibility. Employees are usually not limited by a civil service or position classification system typical of government agencies and thus can perform a variety of services.

There are other organizational advantages nonprofit agencies possess. Because of their flexibility and program commitments

Table 12. Services for Which Over 10 Percent of Cities and
Counties Contract with Nonprofit Organizations.

Service	Percentage
Cultural/arts programs	47
Drug/alcohol treatment programs	45
Mental health programs/facilities	43
Day-care facilities	43
Museum operation	35
Programs for the elderly	33
Public health programs	29
Hospital management/operation	28
Child welfare programs	26
Paratransit system operation	23
Animal shelter operation	19
Public/elderly housing	19
Recreational services	18
Recreational facilities operation	12
Emergency medical service	11
Ambulance service	11
Bus system operation/maintenance	10

Source: Adapted from Valente and Manchester, 1984, p. xv.

Note: Nonprofit groups include contracts with neighborhood groups.

as well as a history of service, these agencies frequently enjoy
general community support. For example, having the Friends
of the Library or the local historical society operate a library
or a museum seems appropriate, almost to be expected, as compared to having them run by some private for-profit organizations, which would strike most people as somewhat unusual.

This level of public regard gives nonprofit organizations
another organizational advantage: the ability to attract volunteer
help. Many Americans donate their time to philanthropic and
community services, and it often seems that nonprofit organizations attact more than their share of volunteers. If they manage
the operation of cultural, artistic, or human service programs,
nonprofit firms are also in a good position to use their network
of supporters, many of whom work as volunteers. These supporters, particularly if they are well off, make substantial contributions to the museum or library. Community support can
be widespread, as the yearly United Fund drive indicates.

Along with these organizational advantages come some weaknesses. There often is little competition among nonprofit organizations to provide services, primarily because there is only one local Friends of the Library or historical society. The only competition may come from public work forces. Perhaps competition from private firms could be developed by the use of subsidies to cover expected operating losses. However, subsidies are used in only 13 to 18 percent of the cases and have not resulted in many private firms providing the services. Furthermore, in urban areas where many human service nonprofit organizations exist, there still may be little direct competition, because each organization provides a slightly different service. This can lead to fragmentation of services rather than direct competition.

Another weakness of nonprofit organizations lies in their financial instability, as suggested in the discussion of human services in Chapter Two. Nonprofit organizations are somewhat more likely to be underfinanced or to manage programs less cost-effectively than private organizations (Whitcomb, 1983; Valente and Manchester, 1984). Much of this is due to size: Nonprofit organizations are often small, and smaller organizations of all types are more financially unstable than larger organizations. Of course, small private firms have similar problems and have been known to go bankrupt while attempting to fulfill a contract. Even so, financial strength and strong management are generally perceived as not being the strong suit of nonprofit organizations.

An actual example will help illustrate some of these points about nonprofit organizations. Housing Opportunities of McKeesport, Pennsylvania, is a nonprofit corporation formed in 1975 to help people acquire or maintain home ownership and renew older, declining neighborhoods (Armington and Ellis, 1984). Housing Opportunities is guided by a fifteen-member board of bankers, builders, consumers, lawyers, and accountants. Expenditures totaled $430,000 in 1983–84 and the firm supported twelve full-time staff, six part-time employees, and twenty-five volunteers. Housing Opportunities is heavily involved in counseling delinquent homeowners and first-time homeowners not eligible for conventional mortgage financing. The delinquent counseling program is so successful that it is used by banks and savings and loans in servicing delinquent accounts.

Another activity is research and counseling, which involves marketing these two counseling programs to other nonprofit organizations. The final major project of Housing Opportunities is home remodeling and construction. These activities are conducted through a for-profit subsidiary that channels its profits to Housing Opportunities. Housing Opportunities, originally financed 98 percent by private contributions, now earns 60 percent of its revenues from the sale of services.

Housing Opportunities, rather than receiving city contracts, competes with the McKeesport Housing Authority's scattered site program. The public agency located public housing residents in scattered housing throughout the city, selecting the worst buildings (which are nonetheless structurally sound) for rehabilitation and rental for public housing. Housing Opportunities also selects the worst sites but rehabilitates housing for sale to owners. It can acquire and rehabilitate about 45 percent more cheaply than the Housing Authority, at least partly because the federal Davis-Bacon minimum wage rates do not apply to the use of private money.

Housing Opportunities has a unique program of providing zero-interest second mortgages to buyers, payable only when the property is sold. If the property is sold for less than the amount purchased, Housing Authority assumes the loss and guarantees to the homeowner one-quarter of the balance after the first mortgage is repaid. The city also benefits because the homeowner pays property taxes. Housing Opportunities claims that the annual cost of its housing is only 40 percent of total local and federal public housing costs.

The use of volunteers, the flexibility, and the commitment of Housing Opportunities demonstrate why nonprofit organizations are often so effective, even in this case when they are not providing services under contract.

Profit-Seeking Organizations

Housing Opportunities' subsidiary was created as a private, profit-seeking company, at least in part to help fund nonprofit Housing Opportunities. This shows that there is often only a slight difference between nonprofit organizations and their private counterparts, the difference being whether an operating surplus is called profit or a reserve for program support.

There may seem only a slight financial difference between for-profit and nonprofit organizations, but in principle, and generally in practice, there are substantial differences. To examine the differences, we should first examine Table 13, which indicates those services for which nonprofit firms contractually perform services for over 30 percent of cities and counties. The frequency of contracting indicated in this table ranges from 80 percent in the case of vehicle towing to 30 percent for the operation and management of hospitals.

Several of these services are public works services (waste disposal, streetlights, and tree trimming). In addition, many other similar services such as street repair, solid waste disposal, and traffic signal maintenance, also were contracted to private companies in over 20 percent of all cases. For several reasons, public works services lend themselves to contracting. First, they require only moderately skilled employees. Private employers have lower wage and fringe benefits than government, partly because they are less unionized and because relatively rapid turnover keeps private rates at the low end of the scale. Second, there are usually several firms offering these services, and thus more competition for contracts occurs. Third, the services are tangible (so many trees trimmed or lights maintained), and governments may have more confidence that they can easily measure contractor performance. Finally, some public works services, such as tree trimming, require expensive capital items that any particular jurisdiction might underutilize but that contractors can spread over contracts with several localities (Valente and Manchester, 1984).

As also seen in Table 13, local governments frequently contract with nonprofit firms or individuals for internal support services such as legal aid and vehicle maintenance and fleet management. There are plenty of suppliers available for these services because these services duplicate private activities, thus ensuring competition. Legal aid is most common in smaller cities, where a full-time attorney may not be needed and where

Table 13. Local Government Services Provided in Over 30 Percent
of All Cases by Contracting with For-Profit Organizations.

Service	Cities and Counties Contracting
Vehicle towing and storage	80%
Legal services	49
Commercial solid waste collection	44
Streetlight operation	39
Day-care facility operation	35
Residential solid waste collection	35
Heavy equipment maintenance/management	32
Emergency vehicle maintenance/management	31
Tree trimming/planting	31
Operation/management of hospitals	30

Source: Adapted from Valente and Manchester, 1984, p. xv.

Note: Services almost always contracted out (such as street construction or engineering services) were not included in this survey.

there are many attorneys to choose from. To a large degree, this also applies to vehicle fleet maintenance and management, although in this case the private contractor may be able to spread the cost of specialized equipment over more vehicles.

Private firms are commonly used to operate and manage hospitals, particularly in larger cities and counties. These private operators—often specialized management firms—tend to have stronger internal controls, better billing and accounting procedures, and more effective procedures for claiming reimbursements. This may not improve care much, but it could strengthen the hospital's financial status. Private organizations also commonly provide day care under contract, usually in smaller cities and counties (Valente and Manchester, 1984).

The specific services covered in Table 13 and the reasons for their popularity underscore the reasons for the increasing use of for-profit contractors. Basically, they can usually provide the services at lower cost than the public agency. This is particularly true in areas requiring less skilled employees, where tighter supervision of workers and control of wages and fringe benefits can make an important difference. These lower personnel costs were verified by the Ecodata study discussed in Chapter One (Stevens, 1984), which showed significantly lower costs with private contracts. The functions studied were primarily public works functions (such as tree trimming, street sweeping, and so on) for which relatively unskilled laborers are commonly used.

There is tremendous pressure for private firms to be as efficient as possible, which results in lower costs to the contracting agency. Most firms face substantial competition unless they have a very specialized service. Even if their service is very specialized, they will likely face competition in that service area. This pressure forces them to lower costs wherever and whenever possible. Thus, private firms invest in labor-saving, technologically sophisticated equipment, not because they are enamored with technology, but because they are anxious to avoid labor costs. Of course, once such equipment is acquired, it can be used for many activities or contracts at a lower rate than government units can use it, since it would otherwise sit idle for long periods.

For-profit firms generally have stronger management skills, particularly larger firms, because cost control is very important to them. That is why they are efficient, even aggressive, in billing and collections, which makes them effective in functions such as hospital administration. For-profit firms (and nonprofit firms, for that matter) are more flexible in using their work forces. They can readily adjust to varied work times. This flexibility is largely a function of using more unskilled, temporary, and part-time labor, which also makes these firms useful for short-term situations where temporary employees are sought.

These qualities of for-profit companies also make them vulnerable to charges that they are concerned with profit rather than service, a frequent complaint of associations of employees such as the American Federation of State, County, and Municipal Employees (AFSCME, 1983). Their focus on predictability and performance under specific conditions, a function of emphasis on cost control, also subjects them to the criticism of not responding well to emergencies.

It is dangerous to overgeneralize about for-profit firms, since they vary greatly in size, experience, amount of competition, and quality of management. Small firms all too often do not show management strength and have often gone bankrupt after receiving contracts. Often the owner is more skilled in performing the service than in managing his organization, with predictable service quality shortcomings. However, AFSCME's criticism of contracting out suggests that management shortcomings are as common in large national for-profit service firms as in small local firms (AFSCME, 1983).

Not only is it unwise to generalize about differences in for-profit firms, it is also dangerous to consider them as greatly different from nonprofit firms. Nonprofit organizations have an image of commitment to quality and concern for clients, which contrasts to the image of for-profit firms as efficient and powerful. Yet, most functions have at least a few nonprofit providers, in services dominated by for-profit organizations, and vice versa. A nonprofit firm conveys an image of a small organization of committed persons, including volunteers, but many for-profit firms are also very small. There are differences, but they are hard to pinpoint in every case.

Comparing Intergovernmental, Nonprofit, and For-Profit Contracting

The three types of contracting—intergovernmental, for-profit and nonprofit—all have different strengths and weaknesses. The public agency should be aware of these differences, both to maximize the potential strengths of each alternative and to avoid potentially ineffective arrangements.

Mere awareness of these differences, however, is not enough, for rarely does an agency have clear-cut choices among these three kinds of contracting. Competition among types of contractors will not occur without attempts to encourage competing contractors. The agency may have to diversify its contractors, perhaps by dividing contracts among different types of contractors to encourage competition. Competition among types of contractors (nonprofit versus for-profit versus government) may be as useful as competition among individual contractors (for instance, two mental health for-profit firms or two refuse collectors).

Assuming that the agency is actually able to choose among types of contractors, however, what are the strengths and weaknesses of each type? Exhibit 7 provides a general guide to each type of contract. (The exhibit is oversimplified for purposes of comparison.) For example, the exhibit suggests that governmental contracts are usually noncontroversial. Yet, relationships between different governments may be marked by controversy as, for example, when city and county have differing policies of dealing with stray dogs (one may impound aggressively and euthanize quickly, the other patrol only on complaint). In such cases, contracting by one party for the other will be very controversial. In another case, the exhibit suggests that nonprofit contractors are noted for their programmatic commitment. However, for-profit nursing homes in Sacramento County exhibit high levels of commitment to their clients (see Chapter Two).

For-profit firms possess superior strengths in internal management controls; are generally associated with lower costs, owing to the search for profit, which provides the rationale for cost-cutting behavior; tend to possess a technological edge in new equipment and techniques, again owing to an effort to cut costs; and are highly flexible and adaptable, particularly in the use of their labor forces. Essentially, the profit motive, rather than imposing an additional cost of the contractor's profit, causes a more thorough search for ways to cut costs. However, this attempt to cut costs is strongest when competition exists. Indeed, it is likely that competition itself, not the existence of a private firm, is the reason that contracting out is more cost-effective.

The weaknesses of private firms are largely related to their strengths. Small contractors are often underfunded; indeed, they may add employees and equipment only after the contract is awarded. If they are not familiar with the ramifications of the contract, these firms may develop financial problems and even go bankrupt. There are many examples of this situation, and it can be most embarrassing and inconvenient to the government unit. Private firms also require substantial monitoring because they are not as concerned with the quality of the service as are other types of contractors and may, on occasions, cut corners. Small firms are also, of course, subject to more

Exhibit 7. Intergovernmental, For-Profit, and Nonprofit Contracting.

	For Profit	*Nonprofit*	*Governmental*
Strengths:	Internal management controls	Programmatic commitment	Usually non-controversial
	Lower costs	Community support	Upgrades government professionalism
	Advanced technology	Perceived expertise	Legal status clearer
		High quality of service	Occasional benefits of fiscal, governmental equalization
	Flexibility, adaptability	Flexibility, adaptability	
Weaknesses:	Small contractors often underfunded	Small contractors often underfunded	Often high-cost solution
	Require substantial monitoring	May be difficult to control	Contractor often inflexible
	Emergency response		

severe labor trouble, since their employees tend to be lower paid and more marginal than those of other contractors. Finally, a common objection to for-profit contractors is their unwillingness to respond to emergency situations. (Chapters Three, Four, and Five deal with these issues in more detail.)

Nonprofit organizations present different opportunities and challenges for contracting out. They are widely (and usually accurately) perceived as having the program's or client's interests firmly in mind, even as much as the government agency does itself. This commitment results in generally high-quality service and a good deal of expertise, since highly skilled professional employees are attracted to these organizations. Commitment is also related to the community support that nonprofit organizations receive, both in terms of money (as in the case of United Way) and labor (as in the case of such volunteers as museum docents).

Nonprofit organizations, because they are small, are often as flexible and adaptable as for-profit organizations, largely owing to the same reasons. Nonprofit pay scales are often low, they frequently use part-time labor, and employees can often perform a wider range of tasks. While smallness has advantages in terms of flexibility, it can involve the disadvantage of under-funding (see Whitcomb, 1983). Nonprofit organizations, because of their high prestige in the community and their perceived commitment to the program, may be more difficult to control by the contracting unit. How does one criticize "committed volunteers" who also happen to be influential in the community?

Reasons for Intergovernmental Contracting

Contracting with governmental agencies, compared to nonprofit organizations, raises quite different concerns for policy-makers. Contracting with another governmental agency can be similar to contracting with a relative. Governments of all sizes and types tend to be like a family and thus are subject to the same pressures. All governments know the vagaries of elected political leaders, understand the activities of pressure groups, and are familiar with unruly recipients who behave more like citizens than customers. For this reason also, IGC often tends to be less controversial: there is less chance of a legal challenge, the stability of the contractor government agency is well known, and very few governments go bankrupt. These are immensely important advantages.

IGC often raises the professional standards of the contractee. This occurs because larger, more professional governmental units are more likely to deliver services to smaller units who may not employ as highly qualified employees.

A major advantage of IGC is the potential elimination of a number of governmental problems in the area. One example is the improvement of building inspection if the county or largest city provides the service throughout a large area. This

is true both in the quality of inspection and in the application
of uniform regulations throughout the area. The contract may
also include long-term territorial and financial agreements, such
as uniform financing of solid waste disposal plants throughout
a region under the general contractual control of the county or
state. This improves service levels and provides a larger and
more equitable basis for the service throughout the metropolitan
area.

IGC contracting has its weaknesses. It is likely to be a
high-cost solution, for the contracting agency is often larger,
more bureaucratized, and somewhat more inflexible in its use
of manpower and equipment. Salaries tend to be higher in larger
units, which means that labor costs plus overhead may be high.
Large units will sometimes subsidize smaller units in order to
"keep the market share" (keep from laying off public employees), but costs still tend to be higher.

Summary

Three primary types of organizations contract for government services. Private and nonprofit organizations, as well as
other governments, all provide services, under a range of conditions. Governments use these three choices widely, with perhaps a slight trend toward using more for-profit firms in recent
years, although the evidence is incomplete. It is increasingly
difficult to distinguish between nonprofit firms and for-profit
firms. The major distinction is often what one defines as a
proper use of profit, or possibly "surplus," in nonprofit firms. At
the local level, private contractors are most common in public
works and transportation functions, such as solid waste disposal,
and in internal support functions, such as equipment maintenance and janitorial services. Nonprofit firms are used more
often in human services, such as mental health programs (see
Chapter Two), and recreational or cultural activities, such as
museums. Intergovernmental contracting is most common in
public works and transportation functions and in human service programs such as public housing. The use of these types

of contractors varies greatly from state to state, from metropolitan area to metropolitan area, and, of course, by function.

In some locations, IGC has become a major aspect in governmental operation, contributing both to the amount of contracting out and to various types of metropolitan unification. (See Case Study 2—the Los Angeles "Lakewood plan" contract plan for municipalities—in the Resources.)

CHAPTER 8 ~~~~~~~~~~~~~~~~~~~~~~~~~~~~~

Contracting for Services to Citizens: Four Typical Contracts

Up to this point, we have explored in some detail the contracting out process and have reviewed many of the important issues, such as monitoring contracts, various contract provisions, feasibility studies, and when and when not to contract out. An actual look at some typical contracts will allow a comparison of general principles to actual agreements. Thus, Chapters Eight and Nine provide examples of actual past or present contracts or related documents. Chapter Eight considers primarily actual contracts that involve direct services to citizens.

Police Protection by Intergovernmental Contract: Hawaiian Gardens City-County

Hawaiian Gardens is a small community in Southeast Los Angeles County. It and many other cities rely on Los Angeles County for many or most of their municipal services. This is a joint agreement between Hawaiian Gardens and four other nearby cities. Each individual city had already contracted with the county sheriff for law enforcement. The cities believed that a regional arrangement for law enforcement might be less expensive. If there were police units on patrol from a central location, it might be possible to lower the number of patrol units for each individual city or increase the level of service by using the regional plan.

The costs of this regional law enforcement service are divided for the first year on a prearranged basis, probably corresponding to population or area covered, with the second-year distribution to be based on actual time or number of calls in each city.

One of the interesting parts of the contract (shown in Exhibit 8), as with all contracts under the Lakewood plan, is that the minimum service level, as well as the contract price (not shown), are set by the county. The only choice cities have is whether or not to increase the minimum level of service or whether or not to contract.

Exhibit 8. Hawaiian Gardens City-County: Regional Law Enforcement Services Agreement.

This agreement, made and entered into this 22nd day of November, 1977, by and between the County of Los Angeles, hereinafter referred to as the "County," and the Cities of Artesia, Bellflower, Hawaiian Gardens, Lakewood, and Paramount, hereinafter referred to as the "Cities."
RECITALS
A. The cities are desirous of contracting with the County for the performance of the hereinafter described law enforcement functions within their boundaries by the County of Los Angeles through the Sheriff thereof.
B. The County of Los Angeles is agreeable to rendering such services on the terms and conditions hereinafter set forth.
C. Such contracts are authorized and provided for by the Charter of the County of Los Angeles and by the Government Code of the State of California.
D. The cities have previously each contracted, on an individual basis, for the performance by the County of these law enforcement services.
E. The cities now desire, for reasons of economy, to supplement these individual agreements with one agreement for Regional Law Enforcement Services.
THEREFORE, the parties agree as follows:
1. The County agrees through the Sheriff of the County of Los Angeles, to provide, and the cities agree to accept, police protection within the corporate limits of these cities to the extent and in the manner hereinafter set forth.

Exhibit 8. Hawaiian Gardens City-County:
Regional Law Enforcement Services Agreement, Cont'd.

Except as otherwise hereinafter specifically set forth, such services shall only encompass duties and functions of the type coming within the jurisdiction of and customarily rendered by the Sheriff of the County of Los Angeles under the Charter of said County and statutes of the State of California.

2. The rendition of such service, the standards of performance, the discipline of officers, and other matters incident to the performance of such services and the control of personnel so employed, shall remain in the County. In the event of dispute between the parties as to the extent of the duties and functions to be rendered hereunder, or the minimum level or manner of performance of such service, the determination thereof made by the Sheriff of the County shall be final and conclusive as between the parties hereto.

3. Services performed hereunder may also include, if requested in writing by the cities, traffic endorsement, license inspection enforcement, the supplying of crossing guards and school safety officer, and any other services in the field of public safety, law, or traffic enforcement, or related fields within the legal power of the Sheriff to provide.

Should any one of the cities desire to receive any service from the Sheriff not specifically listed above, the City's written request must contain a statement indicating the Sheriff's willingness to provide such services.

4. There is hereby created an Administrative Committee which shall consist of the City Manager of each City and the Sheriff of the County or their designated representatives. Said Committee shall meet at the request of any one (1) member of the Committee at a time and place mutually agreeable to all members. The matters discussed at this meeting may include the review of the overall aspects of the Regional Law Enforcement Plan, the amount of service to be rendered to each City under the Plan, the allocation of the percentage of the total cost of the Plan to be paid by each City, operational standards, and any other matters relating to the administration of the Regional Law Enforcement Plan. The Sheriff of the County, or his authorized representative, shall present, upon request, statistics evaluating the effectiveness of the plan and other such information as may be useful in evaluation of the plan.

5. For the purpose of performing said functions, County shall furnish and supply all necessary labor, supervision, equipment, communication facilities, and supplies necessary to maintain the level of service to be rendered hereunder.

When if the County and any one of the cities concur as to the necessity of maintaining a Sheriff's Department Headquarters and jail facility within any one of the cities which would not normally be provided by the Sheriff, that City shall furnish at its own cost and expense all necessary office space, furniture and furnishings, office supplies, janitor service, telephone, light, water, and other utilities. It is expressly further understood that in the event such local office is maintained in that said

Exhibit 8. Hawaiian Gardens City-County:
Regional Law Enforcement Services Agreement, Cont'd.

City, such quarters may be used by the Sheriff of the County of Los Angeles in connection with the performance of his duties in territory outside of said City and adjacent thereto, provided, however, that the performance of such outside duties shall not be at additional cost to that said City.

6. All persons employed in the performance of such services and functions pursuant to this agreement for said cities shall be County employees, and no City employee as such shall be taken over by said County, and no person employed hereunder shall have any City pension, civil service, or any status or right.

For the purpose of performing services and functions, pursuant to this agreement and only for the purpose of giving official status to the performance thereof, every County officer and employee engaged in performing any such service and function shall be deemed to be an officer or employee of each City while performing service within said City, which service is within the scope of this agreement and is a municipal function.

7. Cities shall not be called upon to assume any liability for the direct payment of any salaries, wages, or other compensation to any County personnel performing services hereunder for said cities, or any liability other than that provided for in this agreement.

Except and herein otherwise specified, the cities shall not be liable for compensation or indemnity to any County employee for injury or sickness arising out of his employment.

8. County, its officers and employees, shall not be deemed to assume any liability for intentional or negligent acts of said Cities or any of them or of any officer or employee thereof.

9. Unless sooner terminated as provided for herein, this agreement shall become effective on the date on which the last signatory City signs said agreement and shall run for a period of five (5) years thereafter. For accounting purposes, the first year of this agreement shall end on June 30, 1982, except as otherwise provided herein. At the option of the City Council of each City, with the consent of the Board of Supervisors of County, this agreement shall be renewable for successive periods of not to exceed five (5) years each.

In the event said cities desire to renew this agreement for any succeeding five-year period, the City Councils, not later than December 31 next preceding the expiration date of this agreement, shall jointly notify the Board of Supervisors of said County that they wish to renew the same, whereupon said Board of Supervisors, not later than the last day of January, shall notify said City Councils in writing of its acceptance of such renewal for an additional five-year period or such other term as mutually agreed upon, otherwise such agreement shall finally terminate at the end of such five-year period.

Notwithstanding the provisions of this paragraph, any City may terminate this agreement as of the first day of July of any year upon notice

Exhibit 8. Hawaiian Gardens City-County:
Regional Law Enforcement Services Agreement, Cont'd.

---

in writing to the other parties of not less than two (2) calendar months prior thereto. In the event of such notice of termination by any City, this agreement will be deemed terminated as to all parties as of the first day of the first July following said notice.

10. Basic law enforcement service will be provided by County on the basis of a general law enforcement patrol car, or multiple or fraction thereof, and a station detective, or multiple, or fraction thereof. It is hereby agreed that the minimum level basic law enforcement service shall be determined by County as provided in Paragraph 2 herein.

11. Cities will pay for services under this contract at rates to be determined by the County Auditor-Controller in accordance with the policies and procedures established by the Board of Supervisors plus such additional amounts as determined by the Auditor-Controller that will reflect any amendments to the County Salary Ordinance related to salaries and employee benefits adopted by the Board of Supervisors for the year 1977-78.

The foregoing rates shall be readjusted by the County Auditor-Controller annually effective the first day of July of each year to reflect the cost of such service in accordance with the policies and procedures for the determination of such rate as adopted by the Board of Supervisors of County.

Cities shall be notified of the new rate established by the Auditor-Controller within the first quarter of each fiscal year.

If the cost of providing the services changes at any time following the annual first quarter adjustment, the cities shall be notified of each such change in writing, and such change, or election to modify level of service as hereinafter set forth, shall be deemed effective on the first day of the calendar month next following the giving of such notice.

The County shall prorate the foregoing rates to reflect any adjustment necessary due to a period of service of less than one fiscal year.

12. During the 1977-78 fiscal year, each City shall pay to County that percentage of the total cost of services rendered pursuant to the agreement as follows:

Artesia	7.4 %
Bellflower	29.88%
Hawaiian Gardens	7.35%
Lakewood	32.25%
Paramount	23.10%

Beginning with the second fiscal year of the Regional Law Enforcement Services Agreement, each City shall pay a percentage of the total cost of the law enforcement service level as established by Administrative Committee based on factors including time expended, numbers of cases handled and called for service experience during the preced-

Exhibit 8. Hawaiian Gardens City-County:
Regional Law Enforcement Services Agreement, Cont'd.

ing fiscal year period, or such other factors as may be recommended by the Administrative Committee.

Changes in this percentage cost, payable by each City, shall be effective only upon unanimous agreement of all member cities.

13. The County, through the Sheriff of the County of Los Angeles, shall render to said Cities within ten days after the close of each calendar month an itemized invoice which covers all services performed during said month, and said cities shall pay County therefor within thirty (30) days after date of said invoice.

14. If such payment is not delivered to the County office which is described on said invoice within thirty (30) days after the date of the invoice, the County may satisfy such indebtedness, including interest thereon, from any funds of any such City on deposit with the County without giving further notice to said City of County's intention to do so.

15. Before the start of each successive fiscal year, each City shall set aside a fund in an amount equal to the cost, or an amount 10 percent in excess of the estimated cost, of such services, which said City will receive from the County under this agreement.

The parties hereto have caused this agreement to be executed by their duly authorized officers.

A Private Contract for Engineering
Services: The Dalles, Oregon

The contract in Exhibit 9 is a one-year agreement between The Dalles, Oregon, and a private engineer whose firm is to provide the engineering services that are normally carried out by a city engineering department under the direction of the city engineer. The Dalles is a small city east of Portland on the Columbia River.

The arrangement is somewhat similar to the ill-fated experiment in South San Francisco. (See Case Study 3 in the Resources.) In The Dalles, Tenneson Engineers are to provide the staff for the engineering department, while in South San Francisco the private engineer was retained to supervise public employees and to provide advisory consultants when necessary.

A major issue in the contract is to ensure that no conflict exists between Tenneson Engineering's work for clients who operate in The Dalles and Tenneson's work for the city. Sections 9, 10, 12, 13, and 14 deal with this question, and the city may void the contract as well as collect damages for violations of these sections. Failure to perform satisfactorily, compared to conflicts of interest, requires a ninety-day notice.

Another point is that this contract is highly dependent on the city's high regard for Vernon B. Tenneson. The contract is void ninety days after he ceases to be city engineer, and, clearly, the contract is between Vernon B. Tenneson and the city, not just an engineering firm. This is usual for personal service contracts for engineering projects, but arrangements to privately supply an engineering department are much less common.

Exhibit 9. The Dalles, Oregon: Private Engineering Contract.

THIS AGREEMENT, made by and between the CITY OF THE DALLES, a municipal corporation of the State of Oregon, herein called the "City," and TENNESON ENGINEERING CORPORATION, herein called the "Engineers."
RECITALS
The City has heretofor contracted with Tenneson Engineering Corporation for the furnishing of all engineering services which would be provided the City by its own engineering department. Vernon B. Tenneson is the duly appointed, qualified, and acting City Engineer of the City of The Dalles, Oregon, at a salary of One Dollar ($1.00) per year. The City and the Engineers desire to enter into a contract whereby the Engineers will provide for the City the engineering services which would be rendered by the City by its own engineering department.
The parties agree as follows:
This agreement shall begin July 1, 1976, and end June 30, 1977.
The Engineers shall:
1. Provide the City with a complete engineering service as from time to time specified by the Council or the City Manager, so that the City shall not require any other engineering services except those for the design on reservoirs or a sewage treatment plant, dams, or other work for which the City normally retains a consulting engineer.
2. Furnish at their own expense all personnel, supplies, tools, equipment, and instruments necessary to provide a complete engineering service except certain items hereafter specified to be furnished by the City.
3. Maintain a registered professional civil engineer of the State of Oregon available for duty in the engineering office at the City Hall or on City business at all times that the main City Hall office is open to the public.

Exhibit 9. The Dalles, Oregon:
Private Engineering Contract, Cont'd.

---

4. Provide that a registered professional civil engineer of the State of Oregon is in charge of all work to be done hereunder for the City.

5. Furnish and perform all services, supplies, and duties necessary for operation and maintenance of the office of building inspector or building official, as required by the applicable ordinances of the City of The Dalles. Vernon B. Tenneson as City Engineer, or his duly authorized representative, will also act as City building inspector, or City building official, as the case may be.

6. Staff the engineering office in the City Hall so that it is open to serve the public in the same manner and at the same time as the main City Hall Office.

7. In the absence of the City Engineer, furnish a registered professional civil engineer of the State of Oregon, or a graduate engineer, to attend any City Council meeting, Council Committee meeting, or conference with City Manager or department heads as directed by the Council or the City Manager.

8. Stamp or mark the date and the name "City of The Dalles" on all original maps, original drawings, and documents prepared or used by the Engineers for the City and store or file the same at such places in the City Hall or elsewhere that the Council or City Manager may direct, and the Engineers hereby consent that all such maps, drawings, and documents shall forever remain the property of the City of The Dalles.

9. Not perform any other engineering service, public improvement work, or work of any kind for the City except as provided herein. This includes all agents, employees, and representatives of the Engineers. However, it is understood that Vernon B. Tenneson, a stockholder in Tenneson Engineering Corporation, occupies the City office of City Engineer and will perform whatever functions are required of that office under the charter and ordinances of the City of The Dalles, except as otherwise provided by this contract.

10. Not perform any surveys, drafting, or designing of buildings or other engineering services for any persons, firms, or corporation relative to property within the city limits of the City of The Dalles, Oregon. Provided, however, that the Engineers may perform work for public bodies relative to property within the city limits of the city so long as the work or product thereof does not require inspection and/or approval by the City Council, any city official or officer, employee, department, agency, or commission; and in any event no such work unless the engineers first obtain the written consent of the City Council thereto.

11. Monitor or inspect, as directed by the Council, all City construction projects, inside or outside the City, even though the same may be designed and inspected by a consulting engineering firm.

12. Not join with or have any financial or proprietary interest, direct or indirect, in any other consulting engineering firm or consulting engineer, contracting company or other firm, corporation, partnership,

Exhibit 9. The Dalles, Oregon:
Private Engineering Contract, Cont'd.

---

or association that may bid on or enter into any contract or agreement with the City of The Dalles. Provided, however, that the Engineers may perform consulting engineering services of the City, on approval of the City Council.

13. Not have any financial or proprietary interest in, direct or indirect, or mutual employees with, any firm, corporation, partnership, or association which bids on or enters into any contract or agreement to perform any type of work or furnish any type of services, labor, or material to the City of The Dalles and shall not consult with or advise any such firm, corporations, partnership, or association.

14. Not participate directly or indirectly in any business or commercial ventures or activities which involve the approval of plans or plats, or the issuance of permits by the City Engineer's Office, including, without limiting the generality thereof, subdivision of land in the City of The Dalles, to the end that there shall be no conflict of interest between the Engineers' private activities and ventures and the performance of the official duties of the City Engineer. This includes agents, representatives, and employees of the Engineers and it is understood that Vernon B. Tenneson as City Engineer is also bound by the terms of this section.

15. Except where the seal and signature, or either, of Vernon B. Tenneson, as City Engineer, is required, shall cause to be signed by a registered professional civil engineer in the State of Oregon employed by the Engineers (and seal where required) all maps, drawings, and documents prepared or used by the Engineers for the City in rendition of the engineering services, in the following manner: "_____, registered professional engineers in Oregon, representing Tenneson Engineering Corporation, Consultant to the City of The Dalles, Oregon."

16. Pay for the telephone service in the City Engineer's office.

17. "In behalf of the City Engineer" collect all monies paid for building permits, street cut permits, sewer connections, and other City services paid at the engineering office, post the same to a ledger, furnish a receipt to the payer, and keep copies of receipts and records until the annual city audit has been received by the Council, thereafter turn over such duplicate receipts and records to the City Clerk, and turn over daily to the City Treasurer all monies collected and designate on a daily summary sheet the purposes for which such money was collected, and in return receive the receipt of the City Treasurer for the amount of the turnover.

18. Provide for all of its employees State of Oregon Workmen's Compensation coverage.

19. Furnish supervision and inspection for work performed by the City Public Works Department and the Water Department, and also furnish such lines and grades as those departments may require.

The City shall:

Exhibit 9. The Dalles, Oregon:
Private Engineering Contract, Cont'd.

---

    1. Furnish for the use of the Engineers and staff the existing City Engineer's office in the City Hall.

    2. Furnish heat, light, and power for the City Engineer's office.

    3. Pay to the Engineers the sum of $6,250 per month on or before the 5th day of the month following the completion of a month's work with the first payment to be made on or before August 5, 1976.

    This agreement shall not constitute the Engineers or any of their agents, representatives, or employees as City officers or employees, but the services to be rendered to the City by the Engineers shall be subject to the supervision of the City Manager, and the Council, in coordination with the City Engineer. The City Manager may direct and coordinate the work of the Engineers in accordance with the policies of the City Council to the end that it shall be performed in a manner that will serve the best interests of the City.

    If it is discovered that the Engineers have violated any of the provisions of paragraphs 9 through 13 of the Engineers' obligations, the City shall have the right to declare null and void any such contract or agreement and the Engineers shall be responsible to the City for any damages sustained thereby.

    If the Engineers fail to, or do not properly, perform to the satisfaction of the Council, any of the obligations imposed upon them by this agreement, the Council shall have the right to terminate this agreement within ninety (90) days by written notice delivered to the Engineers at the engineering office in the City Hall. If Vernon B. Tenneson ceases to occupy the office of City Engineer of the City of The Dalles, this agreement shall terminate on the 90th day after the vacancy occurs, unless agreed by the parties. In the event of termination by either cause herein set forth, the Engineers shall make no claim against the City by reason of anything arising out of or incident to this agreement and shall completely release and discharge the City from all claims and demands arising out of or incident to this agreement. Vernon B. Tenneson as an individual also is bound by this section of the contract. In the event of termination because Vernon B. Tenneson ceases to occupy the office of City Engineer of the City of the Dalles, the reasonable salary of the person appointed by the City Manager to act as City Engineer of the City of The Dalles shall be deducted from the amount of the Engineers' compensation paid during the remaining ninety (90) days life of this contract. The total deduction shall not exceed $1,750 per month. Compensation of the Engineers shall continue during the 90-day period at the rate provided herein.

Private Fire Protection: Scottsdale, Arizona

Scottsdale, Arizona, incorporated in 1952 and chose to contract with Rural/Metro Fire Department, Inc., for private fire protection. The contract in Exhibit 10 is for the current contract from 1982 until 1993. In 1979 Rural/Metro served about 55,000 Arizona subscribers, most of them homeowners in five counties near Phoenix. Rural/Metro, from its 1948 beginning with one fire truck, is by far the best-known example of private fire-fighting companies (Poole, 1980; Armington and Ellis, 1984).

Rural/Metro has very low costs, estimated at about half the per capita fire costs in Scottsdale, which are comparable to costs in Phoenix suburbs that have their own fire departments. However, Rural/Metro's performance is comparable to these same cities on the criteria of response time, Insurance Services Offices of Arizona grading, and fire loss per capita.

Costs are kept low by at least two important techniques. First, the company has pioneered in technological innovations such as mini "attack" pumpers, remote controlled robots for entering areas too hot for humans, and lightweight plastic hose with larger diameters.

Second, Rural/Metro uses "auxiliaries"—full-time city employees also serving as on-call fire fighters. Trained as fire fighters, they receive monthly retainers plus hourly rates while fighting fires during nonduty hours. During working hours, they respond to fires as part of their normal duties. Contract Section 5.A(iii) requires Scottsdale to provide two auxiliaries for each regular fire fighter provided by Rural/Metro.

The portion of the contract included shows that the agreement is quite specific. The equipment to be provided by both parties is spelled out, as is the number of fire fighters that Rural/Metro must provide. Detailed specifications for computing modifications to fire-fighters' salaries should costs increase are also included (Contract Section 3).

Exhibit 10. City of Scottsdale: Fire Protection Agreement.

AGREEMENT made and entered into this 1st day of November 1982, by and between RURAL/METRO CORPORATION, an Arizona corporation (hereinafter referred to as "Contractor") and the CITY OF SCOTTSDALE, a municipal corporation created and existing under the laws of the State of Arizona (hereinafter referred to as "Contractee").

WHEREAS, Contractor is in the business of furnishing fire protection, security, first-aid, and rescue service in certain areas of the State of Arizona; and

WHEREAS, Contractee is a municipal corporation created and existing under the laws of the State of Arizona; and

WHEREAS, Contractee is desirous of obtaining Contractor's knowledge, equipment, and services for fire protection, first-aid, rescue, and related services and Contractor is desirous of providing such knowledge, equipment, and services to Contractee;

NOW THEREFORE, in consideration of the foregoing recitals and the mutual covenants and promises hereinafter set forth, the parties hereto have agreed and do hereby agree as follows:

1. *Term:* The term of the Agreement shall be for a period of ten years, eight months, commencing on the first day of November 1982, and ending on the 30th day of June 1993, unless said term shall be sooner terminated as hereinafter provided or as extended by mutual agreement.

2. *Consideration:* Contractee shall pay to Contractor for the period of July 1, 1982, through June 30, 1983, the sum of $193,904.00 per month, payable monthly on or before the 10th of the month for which service is provided. The consideration for the period following June 30, 1983, shall be as determined annually during the City's normal budget process. In the case of a disaster situation, the Contractor may make such additional charges as are reasonable, prudent, and verifiable to control such disasters as approved by the City Manager or his designee. Contractor agrees that Contractee may, at any reasonable time, audit Contractor's records on which the annual costs are based.

3. *Increased Compensation and Services:*
   A. The compensation hereinabove set forth shall be appropriately modified, with the approval of the City Council, in the event:
       i.   the average compensation of firemen in the five (5) largest incorporated cities of Maricopa County, Arizona, as determined on the basis of wages paid per normal on-duty hours worked, increases more than five percent (5%) in any year of this agreement.
       ii. the United States Consumer Price Index increases or decreases more than five percent (5%) in any year of this Agreement.

Exhibit 10. City of Scottsdale:
Fire Protection Agreement, Cont'd.

B.   The compensation hereinabove set forth shall be appropriately increased by the City Council in the event the level of service or the area to be served as herein described is increased. In the event Arizona State Compensation Fund rates payable by Contractor are increased for reasons beyond the Contractor's control, or if because of other legislative or regulative action, Contractor's payroll costs are increased, the City Council will consider appropriate adjustment in Contractor's compensation.

4.   *Area to Be Served:* The equipment and services to be provided by Contractor pursuant to the provisions of this Agreement shall be stationed in and assigned to the City of Scottsdale unless otherwise specified. It is specifically understood and agreed between the parties hereto that Contractor may in the event of emergency provide the equipment and services designated to its other service areas.

5.   *Equipment, Facilities, and Services:* Equipment, manpower, and services shall be provided by Contractor and Contractee as hereinafter set forth.

     A.   *Personnel:* During the term hereof, personnel shall be provided as follows:

         i.   *Fire-fighting positions full-time:* Twenty-three full-time positions through June 30, 1983. Exceptions to manning levels caused by vacations or illness shall be limited to seven (7) percent of the full-time fire-fighting positions specified by this Agreement, rounded off to the closest number when that seven (7) percent is a fraction. Contractor may utilize levels of manning called for in above schedule as 24-hour-shift personnel or day-shift personnel such as inspectors at his option, except that the funds expended in each contract period must be equal to the cost of the above manning levels as they would pertain to the 24-hour-shift personnel.

         ii.   *Support positions:* In addition to the positions outlined in Paragraph 5 Section A, Contractor shall provide a Chief and manpower adequate to provide alarm room service, routine clerical and accounting services, and such other functions as are elsewhere delineated in this Agreement.

         iii.   *Fire-fighting positions, auxiliary:* Contractee shall provide Auxiliary personnel at a proportion of two auxiliaries for each position called for in Paragraph 5, Section A of this Agreement. These personnel shall be recruited from the ranks of Contractee's employees with all wages and costs of same being borne by Contractee from funds other than those prescribed in the "Compensation" section of this Agreement. These firemen shall function in all respects as regular municipal firemen and work under the supervision and training of the designated officers of the Contractor.

Exhibit 10. City of Scottsdale:
Fire Protection Agreement, Cont'd.

B. *Fire Apparatus:*
    i.   *Pumping, aerial, and rescue equipment:* The parties shall provide the following motorized fire-fighting apparatus sufficient to equal or exceed that listed below:
        a.   Contractor: two (2) pumpers, 1,000 gallons per minute, 750 gallon reserve; three (3) pumpers, 750 gallons per minute, 750 gallon reserve; one (1) 3,500-gallon tanker with 750 gallons per minute pump.
        b.   Contractee:
           (1) 85-foot aerial ladder
           (1) Crash-structural pumper, 1,000 gallons per minute, 500-gallon reserve (airport)
           (1) Crash-rescue, dry powder (airport)
           (1) 750 gallon-per-minute pumper, 1,000 gallon reserve
           (2) 1,750 gallon-per-minute tandem pumpers
           (1) Rescue vehicle
    ii. *Limitations:* Apparatus which shall be limited to service inside the City of Scottsdale shall include: All aerial ladders, tandem pumpers, crash-rescue vehicles, and apparatus with a combined pumping capacity of no less than 1,750 gallons per minute and a tank capacity of no less than 700 gallons. Contractor may, at its discretion and from time to time, replace, alter, modify, or eliminate from service any equipment owned by Contractor, provided such action does not adversely affect any insurance rate credit to which the City is entitled because of said equipment.
    iii. *Additional apparatus:* Additional apparatus shall be added by Contractor or Contractee as indicated below during the term of this Agreement:
        a.   Contractee shall provide:
           One (1) rescue vehicle
           One (1) 750-gallon pumper with 500 gallon reserve
           One (1) aerial/scope 75-foot ladder truck
(All of the above listed equipment will be placed in service on or before June 30, 1983.)

Golf Shop Concession: County of Sacramento

Ancil Hoffman Golf Course is a very popular Sacramento County public golf course, where over 100,000 golf rounds were played in 1987. The county contracts the golf concession for golf lessons, sales of golf supplies, rentals of golf carts, and operation of the driving range and pro shop. This arrangement is normally the way that localities with golf courses operate their golf course. Golf professionals who would attract business to the golf course are independent contractors, and operation of the golf concession by public employees would probably not be successful.

Only a portion of the five-year contract is shown in Exhibit 11. The agreement provides for monthly accounting of gross receipts and monthly payments to the county, based on the rates established in the contract's Exhibit A. These rental rates range from 4 percent of equipment, merchandise, and lessons to 26 percent of the gross over $50,000 for golf-cart rentals. The minimum return to the county is $42,000 per year.

The rental and operation sections of the contract spell out how the concessionaire is to keep records (and how the county may audit them), when the golf shop is to be open, and what facilities are to be provided and how they are to be operated. The agreement even specifies when starting sheets should be delivered to the county for reconciliation with green fees and reservation receipts.

The contract's Exhibit B.1 specifies the promotion plan for the golf course. Promotion plans are by nature somewhat vague, but Exhibit B.1 provides enough specific data to allow the county to make an informed judgment on performance. Exhibit B.2, dealing with promotion of golf products, is perhaps even more specific.

**Exhibit 11. County of Sacramento:
Contract for Golf Pro Shop Concession.**

---

e. Beginning with the fifteenth (15th) day of the month following the first full month of operation and thereafter on the 15th day of each month of operations, Concessionaire shall furnish to County with a verified statement of the cumulative total gross receipts as defined herein through the close of the preceding month, for the then current year. With such monthly statement, the Concessionaire shall pay to county the rental fee for the preceding month. Note: Late payments shall bear interest from the date due until paid at maximum rate permitted by law. Payment to the County shall be made to the order of the TREASURER OF SACRAMENTO COUNTY and delivered or mailed to the office

Exhibit 11. County of Sacramento:
Contract for Golf Pro Shop Concession, Cont'd.

of the Department of Parks and Recreation, 3711 Branch Center, Sacramento, California 95827, or at such location as County may from time to time designate. Delays in mail delivery shall not cause a waiver of the late payment requirement.

f. Concessionaire shall keep true and accurate books and records with respect to each source of revenue derived from: cart rental, repairs, merchandise sales, tournament sales, driving-range activities, lessons, and special golf activities at Ancil Hoffman Golf Course, which are under the control of Concessionaire. County shall have the right, through its representative and at all reasonable times, to inspect such books and records, including State of California state tax return records; and Concessionaire hereby agrees that all such records and instruments are available to the County.

g. Concessionaire will submit to the County, no later than forty-five (45) days after the close of the business year, a profit-and-loss statement prepared by a Public Accountant licensed in the State of California. Said statement shall contain an appropriate certificate that all gross receipts during the yearly accounting period shall have been duly and properly reported to the County. In the event the monthly gross receipts have not equalled or exceeded FORTY TWO THOUSAND ($42,000) dollars for such period, Concessionaire shall simultaneously submit a sum in payment for the difference between the total amount paid which constitutes gross receipts and the sum of FORTY TWO THOUSAND ($42,000) dollars as provided in paragraph 4.b. on page 3. For purposes of this agreement, the business year shall be January 1, through and including December 31 of each year of this agreement.

h. County further reserves the right to examine all books and records at any time during the one (1) year period following termination of this agreement.

i. Concessionaire agrees that, as part of its record-keeping activity, he shall at his own cost and expense maintain such cash register equipment as may be deemed necessary by County. Such cash register equipment shall contain a continuous registering tape.

j. In the event Concessionaire is prevented from carrying on the operation contemplated herein by reason of an act of God, or other reason beyond his control, and when such is so determined by Director, then the rentals prescribed herein shall be abated for such periods of non-operation.

Operation

5.a. Concessionaire agrees to remain open every day, including Sundays and holidays, excluding Christmas, during the term of this agreement. Minimum hours of operation of the starter's office shall be as established by the Director. Hours of operation of the concession specified

Exhibit 11. County of Sacramento:
Contract for Golf Pro Shop Concession, Cont'd.

---

herein shall be subject to the written approval of the Director. Hours and days of operations to be used as of this date shall be as listed marked Attachment 2.

b. Concessionaire agrees that a competent person will be in attendance on the premises at all times and at no time will there be less than one person in charge of the concession operation.

c. Concessionaire agrees to provide Director with the name of person(s) who shall be responsible for the operation and management during Concessionaire's absence.

d. Concessionaire agrees to maintain an adequate and proper staff, not employ, and will discharge after reasonable notice, an opportunity to correct the situation any person deemed unsatisfactory in the opinion of the Director.

e. Concessionaire shall provide at his own expense all services, equipment, supplies, and personnel to assume complete control for the administration, staffing, and operation of the golf starter house and all starter functions on the Ancil Hoffman Golf Course in accordance with the prevailing rules established by the Director. If not performed to satisfaction of County, written notice will be given explaining problems and stating Concessionaire will have ten (10) days to correct situation or County will perform such services and bill Concessionaire. Concessionaire shall reimburse County for cost of such service on the 15th day of the month next succeeding the month in which the service was performed.

f. Concessionaire shall be completely responsible for the administration of the golf starter facilities and for furnishing all necessary services and supplies required in order to collect green fees and for the operation of the starting system on the golf course in accordance with the prevailing rules established by Director. Said responsibility shall include all services required in starting players on the golf course, establishing starting time, taking reservations for tee times, and providing any and all other services necessary in order to provide for the efficient operation of the starting system.

g. Concessionaire shall at his own expense provide all of the facilities, services, and operation personnel required in order to properly administer and operate the golf course starting system. Concessionaire shall not be entitled to any monies collected in the operation of the Ancil Hoffman Golf Course except for money collected in the operation of the concession specified above. Such personnel shall be employees of Concessionaire and not the County.

h. Concessionaire shall be fully responsible for the collection of all green fees, and shall account for and deliver to the County of Sacramento all monies collected with respect to such green fees. Said monies shall be deposited to the County of Sacramento account of the Bank of America as designated by the Treasurer of the County of Sacramento, and Concessionaire shall keep complete records of account with respect to such monies. Concessionaire shall make all such accounting records

Exhibit 11. County of Sacramento:
Contract for Golf Pro Shop Concession, Cont'd.

completely available for examination by the County Auditor-Controller or his authorized representative at all times.

    i. Concessionaire shall provide at his own expense all equipment and supplies required in order to administer and operate the golf course starting system, including a cash register which shall issue a receipt and keep a permanent record for each sale, said record to be delivered to Sacramento County as noted in Section 5, Paragraph j.

    j. Concessionaire shall be responsible for and shall keep neat, readable starting sheets which shall be available to County on the third (3rd) and eighteenth (18th) day of each month for the term of this agreement. All reservation receipts, green fees, and starting sheets must reconcile with each other.

Exhibit A

Rental Terms:
Minimum guarantee yearly payment to the County in the amount of
    $42,000.
Percent of gross sales of equipment and merchandise:
    4 percent of equipment and merchandise
Percent of gross for lessons:
    4 percent of all lessons sales
Percent of gross for driving range:
    13 percent of first $50,000
    22 percent of over $50,000 of all driving-range sales
Percent of gross for golf cart rentals:
    18 percent of first $50,000
    26 percent of over $50,000 of all golf cart rentals

Exhibit B

Operation Guidelines:
1. *Promotion Plan/Golf Course*
    Prepare and distribute an informational brochure and tournament calendar which will describe the golf course, facilities, services, staff, and sequence of scheduled events. Generate public awareness of Ancil Hoffman Golf Course with publicity in the print and broadcast media to:

    promote sponsored clinics utilizing PGA/LPGA professionals as
        instructors
    serve as host for national USGA qualifying events and/or a na-
        tional event upon approval of USGA annual calendar
    develop additional junior golf events
    support and/or develop fund-raising tournaments for area charities
    develop area tournaments
    promote Pro-Am tournaments for men and women

become a member of the Chamber of Commerce and listing
    member of any organization providing area tourist information
continue development of semi-annual Pro Shop–sponsored
    developments

2. *Promotion Plan/Golf Products*
    The promotion of golf products and merchandise will be directed
and coordinated by establishing and implementing a coordinated advertising program funded by a predetermined percent of the gross merchandise sales within a minimum percent of the gross merchandise sales within
a minimum of $7,500 being spent each year. Experience may dictate a
change in this amount.
    Funds will be used for:

newspaper
radio
telephone yellow pages
informational brochures
mailing list
promotional flyers to men's and women's clubs
periodic special sales and promotional clearances
flyers to various tournament chairmen with lists of selected mer-
    chandise at special rates
advertising program to plan for adequate seasonal and promo-
    tional inventory, clearance, and special tournament events
development of a promotional mailing list for discount and
    clearance merchandise and notice of coming events and
    tournaments

Summary

Chapter Eight has provided a look at the provisions of
four contracts involving direct services to citizens. The Hawaiian
Gardens agreement between cities and the County of Los Angeles
demonstrates an intergovernmental contract for police protection. The Dalles, Oregon, contract is for private management
of a city public works department. The Scottsdale agreement
is for fire protection by a private company. The Sacramento
County contract is for a golf pro shop concession on a municipal golf course. These four contracts are in the service areas
where private contracting is rapidly increasing. Chapter Nine
provides two examples of contracts for more traditional, internal
agency services.

CHAPTER 9 ⌒⌒⌒⌒⌒⌒⌒⌒⌒⌒⌒⌒⌒⌒⌒⌒⌒

Contracting for
Internal Agency Services

This chapter continues the discussion of actual contracts or related documents used in contracting out. In this chapter, two contracts or sets of specifications are discussed. Both of them deal with in-house services, such as building security and building maintenance, rather than with services provided directly to citizens.

Building Security:
California State Economic Development Department

California's Educational Development Department (EDD) contracts with Burns Security Professionals to provide building security at the EDD central building complex in Sacramento. Building security services across the nation are commonly provided privately, and about 36,000 private security guards work for government agencies, providing such services as guarding federal courtrooms or inspecting airport baggage (Stevenson, 1988). The EDD contract is a routine arrangement to secure buildings at night and to note security problems. The guards are unarmed, with a hotline to the state and city police in the event of emergencies.

The scope of work and specifications is presented in Exhibit 12. Burns Security provides evening and graveyard security during working days and twenty-four-hour service on nonworking days. The scope of work specifically delineates the areas to be patrolled, the type of security reports, and the incidents to be reported. There are specific provisions outlining the type of licenses and permits the contractor must obtain and the insurance to be provided. The contract also covers the qualifications of guards, the uniforms they are to wear, and other minor provisions.

The costs (not shown) were approximately $5,500 per month in January 1988, at the rate of about $10 per hour (less than regular EDD civil service employees). Other provisions of the contract (not shown) call for termination of the contract by either party with thirty-day notice and provisions for nonbinding arbitration over provisions of the contract.

Another clause (also not shown) provides that the contractor's performance is subject to an evaluation by EDD for "adequacy of the services performed, timeliness or response, and a general impression of the competency of the Contractor's firm and its staff." There are no performance standards, and monitoring the contract is largely by complaint.

The contract is being challenged by employee groups, because at one time security guards were state employees and civil service positions may not be contracted out.

Exhibit 12. State of California Employment Development Department: Building Security Agreement.

Scope of Work and Specifications
Scope of Work:
   Contractor shall provide unarmed, uniformed security guard service at the Employment Development Department (EDD) Central Office Complex which is composed of 800 and 722 Capitol Mall (Central Office building), 751 N Street (Solar Building), and 700 N Street (Park Complex) Sacramento, California.
Specifications:
   1.   The service to be provided shall consist of two seven-hour shifts (one shift 12 P.M. midnight to 7 A.M., the second shift from 5 P.M. to 12 P.M. midnight) on normal workdays, with 24-hour service (consisting of three eight-hour shifts on weekends and holidays).

Exhibit 12. State of California Employment Development
Department: Building Security Agreement, Cont'd.

1987
December 25, 1987 (Christmas)
1988
January 1, 1988 (New Year's Day)
January 18, 1988 (Martin Luther King Day)
(State holidays currently scheduled to be observed are listed above.)
In the event labor contract negotiations result in a change in the
scheduled dates listed herein, EDD shall give fifteen (15) days writ-
ten notice of the revised date to the contractor prior to the resched-
uled date or the date listed herein, whichever occurs first.

2. EDD shall provide a workstation at 722 Capitol Mall, Room
   W2052, for the security guards.
3. The security guards shall report to the Contract Monitor located
   in Room W3098, telephone number (916) 322-7990. The guards
   shall sign in and out daily, in Room 3098, on a log provided by
   EDD. The hours logged out shall be approved weekly by the Contract Monitor and a copy of the log shall be provided to the Contractor for billing purposes.
4. Security guards shall use a "beeper" supplied by the Building
   Agent's office to receive communications from EDD personnel
   needing to contact the guards while they are on duty. The beeper is
   used by Building Agent's staff during the working day, but will be
   made available to the security guards whose shift begins at 5 P.M.
   It will be the responsibility of Contractor's security guards to transfer possession of the beeper to the next guard on duty who will
   return to the Building Agent's staff, except for weekends and holidays when it will be transferred, in turn, to each security guard
   providing service. When the last guard goes off duty it will be
   returned to the Building Agent's staff.
5. Security Guard shall patrol the following areas and check the exterior doors for security five times each shift:
   a. The exterior of 800 and 722 Capitol Mall, 1750 N Street and
      751 N Street.
   b. The loading docks and areas behind and between 800 and 722
      Capitol Mall and 751 N Street.
   c. The park and fountain areas at 750 N Street.
   d. The State Car Pool Parking Lot at 8th and Q Streets.
6. Security guards shall monitor the following Central Office Building
   areas at the indicated times:
   a. N Street exit near 8th Street: 10:15–11:00 P.M. employees
      arrive at N Street entry near 8th Street.
   b. East loading dock: 10:30 P.M. mail truck arrives.
   c. East loading dock: 11:00 P.M. mail truck departs.
   d. 9th Street exit near N Street: 12:30 A.M. employees depart.
   e. East loading dock: 3:00 A.M. mail truck arrives.
   f. East loading dock: 3:30 A.M. mail truck departs.

Exhibit 12. State of California Employment Development Department: Building Security Agreement, Cont'd.

7.   Security guards shall prepare security reports covering, but not limited to, the following items. The security reports should be left daily in W3098 at the end of each shift.
   a.   Security reports should:
      • Identify any exterior doors not secured by State Police or Department of General Services staff.
      • Identify any exterior doors with defective hardware which might affect building security.
      • Report any incidents affecting the safety or security of the building or occupants.
      • Report any defective exterior lights.
      • Note any areas where EDD staff is working after 6:00 P.M.
   b.   Security guard shall report incidents as follows:
      • Assault, burglary, robbery, vandalism, or any suspicious activities on State property: report to State Police on Emergency Number 181.
      • Assault, burglary, robbery, vandalism, or any suspicious activities on non-State property: report to local City Police on Emergency Number 9–911.
      • A seriously injured or ill person, i.e., heart attack, stroke, seizure, etc., report by calling 9–911 and then State Police on 181.
      • Fire or smoke: Call 9–911 and then report to State Police on 181.
      • Unlocked entry door: Call the State Police on 181 and stand by until the door is secured.
      • Electrical outages, broken pipes, smashed windows, etc., notify State Police on 5–2895 and request the Building and Grounds be notified in order to effect immediate repair.
            Emergency numbers are as follows:
                        State police 181
                        City police 9–911
            Non-emergency numbers are as follows:
                        State police 5–2895
                        City police 9–449–5471
8.   Additional Instructions
   a.   Changes or additions to security guards' orders will be noted on a memo and attached to the sign-in sheet in W3098.
   b.   On occasion the security guards may be asked to monitor an area where a meeting has continued after hours or let a vendor into the building to do some work in a specific area.
   c.   All changes or additions to the security guards' instructions will come from the Contract Monitor or Monitor's designee.
9.   Licenses and Permits
            The Contractor and the Contractor's employees shall possess

Exhibit 12. State of California Employment Development Department: Building Security Agreement, Cont'd.

all licenses, registrations and permits required by the California Department of Consumer Affairs, Bureau of Collection, and Investigative Services. Such licenses and permits include the following:

- Private Patrol Operators License: Contractor shall furnish their current and valid private patrol operators number.
- Guard Registration Card: Contractor's security guards shall be registered and shall have a current and valid guard registration card in their possession while on duty.

These permits must be valid, current, and must be presented to State management upon demand. If the Contractor's license expires or is suspended or revoked, this contract will be immediately cancelled. If the Contractor's security guard is unable to present his/her guard registration card upon demand, he/she will be relieved from duty and Contractor shall provide a security guard who has an appropriate card in his/her possession.

The contract shall be immediately cancelled if Contractor is unable to provide a security guard with the proper card. Contractor shall also maintain all other business and professional licenses that may be required by Federal, State, and local codes.

10. Insurance

Prior to commencement of work under this Agreement: Contractor must have in full force and effect an insurance policy issued by an insurance company authorized to transact business in this State that provides coverage of a minimum limits of $500,000 public liability and $500,000 property damage.

Contractor shall also provide a fidelity bond in the amount of $25,000. Contractor's failure to provide a certificate of insurance will be referred to the Investigative Services for their investigation. The certificate of insurance will provide:

a. That the insurer will not cancel the insured's coverage without 30 days prior written notice to the State.

b. That the State of California, its officers, agents, employees, and servants are included as additional insureds, but only insofar as the operations under this section are concerned.

Contractor agrees that the bodily injury liability insurance herein provided for shall be in effect at all times during the term of this contract. In the event said insurance coverage expires at any time or times during the time of this contract, contractor agrees to provide, at least thirty (30) days prior to said expiration date, a new certificate of insurance evidencing insurance coverage as provided for herein for not less than the remainder of the term of the contract, or for a period of not less than one (1) year. New certificates of insurance are subject to the approval of the Department of General Services and contractor agrees that no work or services shall be performed prior to the giving of such approval. In the event

**Exhibit 12. State of California Employment Development
Department: Building Security Agreement, Cont'd.**

contractor fails to keep in effect at all times insurance coverage
as herein provided, State may, in addition to any other remedies
it may have, terminate this contract upon the occurrence of such
event.

Contractor is aware of the provisions of Section 3700 of the
Labor Code which requires employers to be insured against liability
by worker's compensation or to undertake self-insurance in accordance with the provisions of that Code, and will comply with such
provisions before commencing the performance of the work under
this contract.

11.   Qualification

Contractor's staff, including backups, must be professional
security guards and must be registered with the California State
Department of Consumer Affairs Bureau of Collection and Investigative Services. All security guards assigned to EDD must have
the physical ability and the mental alertness to effectively deal with
people and will present themselves as a visible authority, able to
maintain order, protect EDD staff and the public, and prevent theft
and damage to State property. All security guards must be qualified
and trained, plus have two years verifiable experience within the
last five years with emphasis on crowd control.

12.   Uniform

Guards shall be dressed in a uniform which is appropriate
and is approved by the local law enforcement agency authorized
to regulate uniforms worn by private security guards.

13.   EDD Requirements

EDD requirements are that each security guard will circulate
and be visible to employees and/or the public at all times. It is accepted that the security guard may adjourn for authorized lunch and
breaks; however, he/she shall remain on the premises and be available at all times. Should a disturbance or any other problem arise,
it is expected that the security guard shall take command of the
situation and shall take appropriate action to restore order within
reason and within the parameters of the law. In case of major distur-
bances, it is expected that the security guard will call the California
State Police and/or the local authorities for assistance.

14.   Direction and Responsibility of the Security Guards

EDD management shall be responsible for the general direction of the security guards in that EDD may request the security
guard to patrol the parking lot, the lobby, or any other area needing
attention. The contractor shall be responsible for the supervision
which includes security guard's work habits, appearance, and overall performance. To meet this end, Contractor shall provide EDD
management with a local "hot line" which will be a phone number
where poor work performance and or unsatisfactory work habits
may be reported. Contractor's supervisors shall schedule, at each

Exhibit 12. State of California Employment Development
Department: Building Security Agreement, Cont'd.

---

location, a minimum of two unannounced visits per week to observe·
the performance and the work habits of the security guard.
15. Contractor must provide full coverage for each shift.
16. Contractor shall provide security guards who hold current credentials
and will perform First Aid and Cardio-Pulmonary Resuscitation
when necessary.

Janitorial Services: Maintenance of the
California Franchise Tax Board Office

The Franchise Tax Board is California's income tax collection agency. Most of its offices are housed in a very large
building in suburban Sacramento, and the janitorial services
are contracted to a private firm. The building has a working
population that fluctuates between 2,000 and 4,000 individuals,
and during tax return peaks it is used twenty-four hours a day.
The building itself has 446,000 square feet of cleaning area,
including the 600 exterior windows and 160 toilet fixtures—a
major cleaning project. A minimum of 152 person-hours between
6 A.M. and midnight, Monday through Friday, are required
in the specifications to provide routine cleaning. Portions of the
thirty-six-page set of specifications for the contract are presented
in Exhibit 13.

The solicitation to bid is significant because of the requirement that potential bidders walk through the bidding site. Section E deals with the state's role in contract administration. It
details the inspection of janitorial services and some of the remedies that the state has as well as clarifying the use of a complaint
system. Section F, performance and terms, gives the state the
right to extend the contract unilaterally (to prevent lowballing).

Section J includes detailed minimum of cleaning quality
requirements. For example, the number of floor finish coats is
specified as well as the nearness to the baseboard. Section K,
schedule of cleaning requirements, delineates the frequency of
cleaning. For example, toilet rooms must be wet mopped or
scrubbed with a disinfectant each day and on weekends and in
areas having a swing shift.

Exhibit 13. State of California Franchise Tax Board:
Janitorial Service and Window Cleaning Contract.

Section E. The Role of State Personnel and Responsibility for Contract Administration

The State Office Building Manager has the overall responsibility for the administration of this contract.

Custodial Inspectors have responsibility as follows: Determining the adequacy of performance by the Contractor in accordance with the terms and conditions of this contract; acting as the State's representative in charge of work at the site; ensuring compliance with contract requirements insofar as the work is concerned; and advising the Building Manager of any factors which may cause delay in performance of the work.

Custodial Inspectors are staff of the Building Manager and are responsible for the day-to-day inspection and monitoring of the Contractor's work. The responsibilities of the custodial inspector include, but are not limited to: inspecting the work to ensure compliance with the contract requirements; documenting through written inspection reports the results of all inspections conducted; following through to ensure that all defects or omissions are corrected; conferring with representatives of the Contractor regarding any problems encountered in the performance of the work; and generally assisting the Building Manager or his representative in carrying out his responsibilities.

1. Inspection of Services

All services, which include services performed, material furnished or utilized in the performance of services, and workmanship in the performance of services, shall be subject to inspection and test by the State to the extent practicable, at all times and places during the terms of the contract. All inspections by the State shall be made in such a manner as not to unduly delay the work.

If any services are not in conformity with the requirements of the contract, the state shall have the right to (a) require the Contractor to immediately take necessary steps to ensure future performance of the services in conformity with the requirements of the contract; and (b) make monetary deductions to reflect the reduced value of the services performed.

In the event the Contractor fails to take necessary steps to ensure future conformity with the requirements of the contract, the State shall have the right to either (a) procure or furnish, upon such terms and in such manner as deemed appropriate, services required by the contract and charge to the Contractor any cost to the State that is directly related to the performance of such services; or (b) terminate this contract for default in accordance with the "Default" clause provisions, contained in these specifications.

2. Default Clause

If the contractor fails to adhere or perform to the provision of this specification, the State has the option to terminate the contract. If the contract is terminated by the State for "default," the contractor will be removed from the job immediately.

**Exhibit 13. State of California Franchise Tax Board:
Janitorial Service and Window Cleaning Contract, Cont'd.**

---

3. Occupant Complaint Program
The State will institute a customer complaint program as a means of assisting in documenting certain kinds of service problems. This occupant complaint program will be considered in evaluating the Contractor's performance and in making deductions.

Section F. Performance and Terms

1. Option to Extend the Term of the Contract
The State shall have the unilateral option of extending or renewing this contract for two (2) consecutive additional periods of twelve months each upon the same terms and conditions as are contained in this contract at the time said option(s) are exercised.

Said options shall be upon formal written notification (mailed or otherwise furnished) to the Contractor at least thirty (30) calendar days prior to the expiration of the contract. The Building Manager shall have given preliminary notice of the State's intention to renew at least sixty (60) calendar days before this contract is to expire. (Such a preliminary notice will not be deemed to commit the State to exercise the option.) A document will be executed by both parties to extend the life of the contract.

If the State exercises the option or the first additional twelve (12) month period, the contract as renewed shall be deemed to include the option provision for the second additional twelve (12) month period. However, the total duration of this contract, including the exercise of any option(s) under this contract, shall not exceed three (3) years.

Bidders are cautioned that the exercise of the options is a State right, not a contractual right on the part of the Contractor. If the State exercises the option(s) within the time frame prescribed herein, the Contractor shall be contractually bound to perform the services for the option period(s). . . .

Section J. Cleaning Quality Requirements

General
Services performed under this contract shall be subject to inspection and approval by the Building Manager. This section outlines the minimum acceptable standards.
Floor Maintenance
A. General
For all operations where furniture and equipment must be moved, no chairs, wastepaper baskets, or other similar items shall be stacked on desks, tables, or windowsills. Upon completion of work, all furniture and equipment must be returned to its original position. Baseboards, walls, stair risers, furniture, and equipment shall in no way be splashed, disfigured, or damaged during these operations. Proper precautions shall

Exhibit 13. State of California Franchise Tax Board:
Janitorial Service and Window Cleaning Contract, Cont'd.

---

be taken to advise building occupants of wet and/or slippery floor conditions; this applies during inclement weather as well as during cleaning operations. All tools and equipment shall be maintained in clean condition at all times and neatly stored each night in the assigned storage areas. All waxed surfaces must be maintained to provide safe anti-slip walking conditions.

B. Sweeping and Damp Mopping

After sweeping and damp-mopping operations, all floors shall be clean and free of dirt streaks; no dirt shall be left in corners, under furniture, behind doors, or on stair landings and treads. Likewise, sidewalks, entrances, garages, and other assigned areas shall be swept clean of all dirt and trash. No dirt shall be left where sweepings were picked up. There shall be no dirt or trash under desks, tables, or chairs.

C. Wet Mopping and Scrubbing

The floors shall be properly prepared: thoroughly swept to remove visible dirt and debris; removal of gum, tar, and similar substances from the floor surface is required. On completion of the mopping and scrubbing, the floors shall be clean and free of dirt, water streaks, mop marks, string, etc., and properly rinsed and dry mopped to present an overall appearance of cleanliness. All surfaces shall be dry and corners and cracks clean after the wet mopping or scrubbing. When scrubbing is designated, it shall be performed by machine or by hand with a brush.

D. Floor Finishing

The job of floor finishing includes the cleaning and applying of finish to asphalt, rubber, vinyl, and linoleum floor surfaces.

1. Sweeping: Sweep floors thoroughly. Remove all gum and adhesive materials.

2. Stripping: Remove all old finish or wax from floors, using a concentrated solution or a liquid cleaner. Cleaner is to be applied with a mop and scrubbed with an electrical polishing machine with scrub brush or a medium-grade scrubbing pad. Extremely stubborn spots, gum, rust, etc., shall be removed by hand with a scouring pad dipped in the cleaning solution. Corners and other areas that the polishing machine cannot reach shall be scrubbed and thoroughly cleaned by hand. Care shall be exercised so that baseboards, walls, and furniture shall not be splashed or marred. Cleaning solution shall be taken up with a mop or a water pickup and the floor rinsed twice with clean water to remove all traces of cleaning solution. Do not flood floor with water; use only enough water as required for good rinsing. Floor shall be allowed to dry thoroughly for good rinsing.

3. Finishing: Apply a minimum of four coats of floor finish, allowing sufficient drying time between each coat. The last coat only should be applied up to but not touching the baseboard. All other coats should be applied to within four inches of the baseboard. (Note: Should there be more than eight hours delay before applying finish after the floor has been cleaned or between coats, the areas must again be cleaned to remove surface dirt and scuff marks before applying finish.)

Exhibit 13. State of California Franchise Tax Board:
Janitorial Service and Window Cleaning Contract, Cont'd.

---

4. Periodic Spray Buffing: Sweep floor thoroughly. Damp mop to remove any spillages. Spray buff floor, using floor-polishing machine, synthetic fiber pad, and spray equipment containing 50 percent water and 50 percent floor finish of the same type as on the floor. Spray only worn areas and buff immediately to blend in.

Schedule of Cleaning Requirements

1. General

The contractor shall furnish all labor, supplies (including restroom supplies and wastebaskets and liners), materials, equipment, and supervision and perform satisfactorily the services at the frequencies and during the times specified herein. The services shall include all functions normally considered a part of workmanlike, satisfactory janitorial work.

Full performance of all daily services specified in this contract will be required on the first official working day of the contract period. The Contractor shall service all toilet rooms to maximum capacity during the afternoon of the contract day. Dispenser stock of paper supplies and hand soap remaining at the termination of the last official work day shall not be removed.

These schedules are included to describe the level of the services which this contract is intended to include. The performance will be based upon results, not upon the frequency or method of performance.

2. Daily Services (for day-shift occupants)

A. Toilet Rooms (inclues child-care center and private toilet rooms)

    1. Sweep and wet mop or scrub floor with disinfectant detergent.

    2. Clean all fixtures—water closets, urinals, washbasins, mirrors, waste receptacles, and dispensers—with a disinfectant detergent. Polish all restroom fixtures. . . .

    5. During the day, empty waste receptacles, police rooms, replenish supplies, and clean washbasins as traffic demands, and upon request of the Building Manager. . . .

    7. Paragraphs 1., 2., and 5. shall again be performed in areas with a swing shift and on Saturdays and Sundays.

Summary

Chapter Nine has covered two State of California contracts for routine housekeeping functions—janitorial services in a large office building and building security for another large building. Now that several contracts have been reviewed (Chapters Eight and Nine) and many contractual provisions have been discussed in earlier chapters, attention should be directed toward ways managers can improve their prospects for successful contracting out.

PART IV

Ensuring Success in Contracting Out

Although ensuring success is the topic of this part, only Chapter Twelve specifically addresses this area, summarizing the book as a whole. However, Chapters Ten, Eleven, and much of the Resources section deal with the politics of contracting out and cover enough of the difficulties of contracting out to largely ensure success if certain dangers are avoided.

Chapter Ten concerns the politics of contracting out. Managerial politics involves the relationship of the manager to department heads, legislators, and citizens. The politics of lubrication is reflected in the many examples of the way contractors are forced (or choose) to obtain contracts by campaign or personal contributions to public officials. The politics of risk avoidance involves the use of contracting to direct all or a portion of the risk for new programs from government officials to contractors. Rule politics means dealing with the expected and unexpected impact of rules that affect contracting out (such as New York's Wickes law, which requires that contracts be divided up among different contractors). Finally, the politics of direct election is shown in three examples of how direct elections over a contract or about politicians directly associated with a contract affect contracting out.

Chapter Eleven specifically concerns unions and employees and the political difficulties created by their opposition to contracting out. Generally, public employee fringe benefits and often wages are higher than in private firms. This is generally accepted, although management efforts to document this difference are often controversial. Dealing humanely and effectively with employees displaced by contracting out is another issue, which can sometimes be solved by giving these workers employment rights with the contractor. This solution, of course, angers public unions, since it means fewer jobs, usually at a lower wage scale, and weaker public sector unions. The chapter gives ten brief summaries of contracting out against strong employee opposition.

Chapter Twelve summarizes the book with eight do's and don'ts for managers considering contracting out. These may seem a bit obvious, for they almost constitute what one might call common sense. Common sense, however, is not always used. Do's for contracting out include being open and direct; mastering all details; remembering that the agency, not the contractor, is ultimately responsible for the contract; and, finally, contracting only for legitimate reasons. Don'ts for contracting out include not undertaking controversial contracts; not getting too deeply committed to a contractor, process, or even contracting out itself; not contracting out when even the faintest suggestion of corruption exists; and keeping citizen views of the service foremost in mind.

The Resources include nine case study examples, both long and short, that show successes as well as failures in contracting out. A selective review of contracting out on an international basis is also included.

CHAPTER 10 ∽∽∽∽∽∽∽∽∽∽∽

Handling the Politics of the Process

This and the following chapter deal with the politics of contracting out: who gets what and when and why they get it. Contracting out deals with the intersection of money, power, jobs, profits, and political influence. It is naive to believe that all contracting issues can be settled on the basis of merit, even if there were agreement on what merit is.

This chapter deals with politics and contracting in general, focusing on political events and circumstances that arise from the particular nature of contracting out. Chapter Eleven focuses on personnel issues, particularly the impact contracting out has on jobs and the attempts that unions and employees make to defeat contracting out. This chapter covers several aspects of contracting out politics, in the following order: (1) managerial politics, or how contracting out plans are initiated by managers; (2) the politics of lubrication, or how money, in the form of campaign contributions or actual bribes, "lubricates" the process of selecting contractors or the decision to contract out; (3) the politics of risk avoidance, or how contracting can reduce political risks involved in beginning new programs; (4) the politics of rules, or how legal provisions (or the lack thereof) are adopted (or not adopted) for political reasons; and (5) the politics of direct elections, when contracting decisions are made by the voting public (other than where the electoral issue primarily involves employee issues, as covered in Chapter Eleven).

Managerial Politics

Managers have to work in a political environment and, at the minimum, avoid or circumvent political forces that would defeat administrative initiatives. For example, a proposal to contract out a city program innocently put on the council agenda in the expectation that the council, without any advance notice, will discuss the matter on its merits is doomed to failure. The time has to be right, actors (such as department heads) have to be "lined up," the community (or at least influential segments of it) should agree to contracting, and the legislative body must be sympathetic. Such events do not occur by accident; managerial politics is the way to ensure that they do occur.

There are three basic groups of influentials that have to be sympathetic (or at least neutral) for a contracting out proposal to receive serious consideration (Marlin, 1984). The community and community leaders have to be at least neutral, the affected departments have to be at least neutral (or be neutralized by the manager), and the governing body usually has to be positively inclined.

Citizen Groups and the Community. At the state or federal level, most interest groups (other than organized labor, which usually resists contracting) show little concern about contracting out or are favorably disposed because they believe it will save money. Contracting out rarely conflicts with community tradition at this level, for there is rarely an identifiable community. At the local level, however, community traditions are crucial. The city council normally reflects these traditions clearly, but the role of community groups in expressing support for any potentially controversial topic can be decisive.

Influential citizen groups usually include those interested in government activities (such as the League of Women Voters) and neighborhood groups (such as the Arden Oaks Association or Taxpayers of Daphne Grove). These groups are usually favorably disposed toward contracting out and should be contacted early. Another group of organizations are trade and business or professional groups. These groups also are inclined to favor contracting out because it promises to make government more "businesslike." Members of this latter group tend to be quite influential in the community, and their support for or opposition to contracting out is very important.

A study of cities that contracted out their refuse collection service showed that only one citizen group in the cities surveyed had opposed contracting out, for the reason that city workers would lose their jobs ("Customers Rate . . . ," 1981). After a change to private contracting, however, local groups will object if there is a decline in level of service (such as no backyard collection or no overfilled cans picked up) and if a complaint system does not work well.

The media are another segment of the citizenry that can make or break contracting out proposals. Most newspapers or television stations are not much concerned with what may seem to be a minor issue. However, the media are intensely concerned with any matter that may seem controversial or of public concern, such as city employees being laid off or the possibility of a strike. These actual or potential controversies sell newspapers and television advertising space.

On occasion, individuals or individual businesses become influential in decisions to contract out. Their support must be courted and their views taken into account. Sometimes the leaders of businesses involved in contracting will have opinions— usually, of course, favoring contracting out.

The media, individual influentials, and community groups must, in most cases, be satisfied that contracting out is desirable, will not cause too much controversy, and will not damage historical community traditions. The job of convincing these groups often falls on the manager, although in theory such sales work is the job of elected officials. Community advocacy is difficult to balance, for too much administrative advocacy may be obviously political, while too little may not develop enough support for the plan. In most cases, managers obtain approval of the council for such actions and, if they can, try to get council members to publicly advocate contracting out. If managers advocate the plan, it is usually in a low-key informational talk or private conversation, for no manager wants to get "too far in front" of the council and thus become politically vulnerable.

Occasionally, community groups, under contract from the city or other granting unit, actually provide the service. They then no longer are interested onlookers or "veto groups" but actual contractors. Like any contractor, their bids must be reviewed and their programs monitored and evaluated. Unlike other contractors, however, they have substantial political clout. The 1982 International City Management survey reported that as many as 8 percent of all city and county cultural and arts programs, 6 percent of all day-care programs, and 5 percent of crime prevention patrols are provided by contracts with neighborhood groups (Valente and Manchester, 1984).

These groups can become a separate political force. They are not at all reluctant to place considerable pressure on the city or on federal granting agencies to renew the contract, regardless of actual performance. Richmond (Virginia) experienced this situation in administering Community Development Block Funds. The city contracted with neighborhood groups for downtown economic development, housing rehabilitation, and job training. Richmond used formal contracts to ensure performance and ensure that these groups met federal requirements. However, monitoring proved difficult. Special city monitoring agencies were created rather than using city departments. This created new relationships between the federal granting agency, the neighborhood groups, and the monitoring agencies. The community groups placed heavy pressure on the federal government to maintain a grant program that would permit the city to contract with them. One U.S. labor official commented that "city politics dictated that we had to keep these people happy" (Kettle, 1981, p. 367).

Managerial politics involve dealing with community groups, and this task is even more complex when these groups, which have substantial political influence, actually become the contractor for city projects.

Department Heads and Middle Managers. Department heads are the individuals who are most directly affected by contracting out. Objections from and complaints by department heads are taken seriously by council members and often by community influentials, because department heads may long have had ties to the community and thus many supporters there. Department heads cannot veto contracting out proposals in the sense that many community groups can, but their reservations or objections can predispose community groups or council members to oppose contracting out proposals. Furthermore, if department heads are not at least neutral about contracting out services, they are likely to give lukewarm support, making it more difficult for the contract to succeed.

There are two categories of department heads. Some are directly involved in the service being contracted out. Others, while not directly affected, may be concerned about whether services in their department will be the next ones contracted out. Department heads whose services are being considered for contracting may resist because they are fearful of change, because they fear losing control of the service to a contractor, because they feel that their duties and responsibilities are being diminished, or because they actually believe that the contract will not save money or maintain service. In any case, these department heads are likely to believe that they will have less responsibility and potentially lower salaries in the future. No matter what their professional assessment of the program to be contracted out, the situation is likely to be viewed as a personal setback.

It may be possible to counteract these reservations by providing complete information to the department head so that she understands the need to contract out. It may help to explain that her supervision of the contract and development of a monitoring program will enhance her position as a valued member of management. Department heads cannot always be won over, however, and sometimes changes in personnel have to be made. (If the manager's contracting out proposal works out badly, the changes in personnel may involve the manager, not the department head.)

Lower-level managers are often neglected during the transition to contracting. This is unfortunate because they often become the contract monitors. As monitors, they have an enormous impact on how the contract will be evaluated and how the contractor will be treated. These managers, program directors, and division heads have to be convinced that contracting out is necessary or at least is a fait accompli. Then they can be convinced, if they do not already know it, that a successfully managed and monitored contract will also work to their advantage.

Department heads who are not directly affected by contracting out may nevertheless be greatly concerned. Fearing future contracting out proposals, they may raise all sorts of objections to the proposal, hoping to eliminate any contracting. Their departments may be plagued by loss of morale or fear of layoffs if the department is involved in contracting or indirectly affected through the "bumping" of more senior employees from other departments.

Again, providing full and honest information does more than any other tactic to reassure doubting or recalcitrant department heads and lower-level employees. Providing such information is possible only if the legislative body has first been alerted to the possibility of contracting out and at least given its blessing to exploring the idea. Department heads, or citizen groups for that matter, cannot (or should not) be contacted without first contacting the legislative body. Management-initiated plans to contract out without legislative approval are usually doomed to failure and are sure to elicit objections from department heads.

The Governing Body. Legislators hold a wide range of views on contracting out. These views are generally similar to widely held community values, or legislators' assessment of these values. Frequently, however, their views are idiosyncratic, based on personal opinion, affiliations with groups opposed to or in favor of contracting, or other reasons. In most cases, legislators are committed to least-cost solutions to service delivery issues, and most can be convinced of the value of contracting if a proper feasibility study has been done and if the process of contracting out does not threaten community values or become too controversial. Effective managers keep the legislative body fully informed at all stages of the contracting out process, from the beginning of any feasibility study to the final selection of a contractor. No legislator likes to be surprised or uninformed on such a potentially controversial topic.

Marlin (1984) lists six major concerns that legislators frequently raise about proposals to contract out:

1. Can the contractor be held responsible to the public? (If so, this will require a properly drawn contract.)
2. Will the contract threaten the jobs of current employees? (Answers to this question vary with the contract. Proposals that do not somehow protect employee rights and employment—for example, by requiring the contractor to employ them—often become quite controversial.)
3. Will local contractors be selected? (An open search for the best contractor, regardless of location, conflicts with the natural desire to reward residents, who are voters, contributors, and possibly friends or neighbors. This is a ticklish area, which is handled somewhat differently in each city and sometimes in each case.)
4. Will cost savings be only temporary? (This question is related to the fear of lowballing, and the techniques discussed in Chapter Five to keep control of the contract deal with this issue.)
5. What happens if the contractor defaults? (Again, techniques for keeping control of the contract, such as partial contracting or requiring performance bonds, will generally answer this question.)
6. How will citizen complaints be handled? (The complaint system can be controlled by the city, by the contractor, or shared, as outlined in Chapter Five. If this question becomes a major issue, a wise manager will suggest that the city control the process.)

Deceptiveness. Managerial politics includes more than orchestrating political forces, anticipating the objections of interest groups, and making contracting out proposals appear highly palatable. Sometimes it involves practices that may involve some deception. At the federal level, this may mean using misleading estimates to get a project or contract approved by legislators or top managers (or disapproved, as the case may be). As one official commented, "We know that if we tell the Department of Defense across the river how much something is going to cost, they may scrub it. And they know that if they tell the Congress how much it's really going to cost, the Congress may scrub it. . . . So you start with both sides knowing that it is going to cost more" (Cooper, 1980, p. 461). Deliberate miscalculations such as this do occur, possibly more often than commonly admitted. Such actions can be explained by the argument that every party to the contract knows what is going on, but this hardly justifies the practice. While deceptive activity is unfortunately sometimes part of the manager's political arsenal, most managerial political activity is straightforward and open.

Managerial politics involves a host of sensitive activities that, taken individually, are administrative rather than political. The entire set of activities, however, involves a complex balance of precise timing, attention to detail, a blend of openness and caution, and awareness of community and legislative sensitivities. Successfully maneuvering through this mine field is a true political (and administrative) triumph.

Lubrication Politics

The politics of lubrication is what most people think of when they consider contracting out politics. Money lubricates the political system, in many cases having a direct effect on who gets a contract or what the conditions for fulfilling the contract will be. Contracting out involves a great deal of money—well into the billions of dollars at all government levels. To maximize their access to these sums, contractors and consultants invest money—through campaign contributions or even bribes—in politicians who will be sympathetic to contracting out. To the consultants and contractors, this is simply the cost of doing business. To politicians, it is also the cost of doing business, for reelection campaigns are expensive. (For a few, bribes or gratuities are part of the unreported fringe benefits of the job.)

Contractors and consultants who want business and politicians who receive contributions continue to exert pressure to contract out more projects, often to specific contributors.

A cynic once noted, "all unprofitable functions ultimately will be governmental functions. Conversely, profit-making operations will be moved from government to privately owned organizations" (Ayres, 1975, p. 459). Since 1975, contracting out and other forms of privatization have increased. The increased volume of potential business has no doubt increased the role money plays.

In New York City, twenty-three consulting firms gave over $100,000 in loans and campaign contributions to local political candidates. In return, they received over $60 million in fees from the city and the Transit Authority. The Transit Authority once did most of its work in-house but now contracts out over half of the design work (AFSCME, 1983).

In Massachusetts, the consulting firm of Daniel, Mann, Johnson and Mendenhall (DMJM) pled guilty in 1981 to fraud charges in connection with political campaign contributions made in return for DMJM obtaining a $2 million design contract. DMJM paid a $1,000 fine plus another $105,000 to the state after the State Ethics Commission concluded that there was "probable cause" that the contributions were illegal. A special Massachusetts corruption commission reported in 1981 that in state and county design contracts in the 1960s and 1970s, "corruption was a way of life" and that "political influence, not professional skill" was the primary criterion for consulting work. A nonpartisan climate of corruption was primarily created by a "quid pro quo system in which campaign contributions were exchanged for state contracts" (AFSCME, 1983, p. 76). Between 1962 and 1974, three state administrations routinely awarded design contracts for millions of dollars in return for political contributions (AFSCME, 1983).

Garbage and rubbish collection contracts seem particularly vulnerable to corruption. SCA Services of Ohio, a garbage collection firm, has been involved for years in questionable contracts and has been charged with ties to organized crime. In January of 1980, SCA Services of Ohio pled no contest to a charge that it paid $20,000 to bribe two Ohio township trustees to keep a $425,000 trash collection contract and to have trustees raise local taxes to pay for increased collection fees (AFSCME, 1983).

Campaign contributions or bribes, at least for trash collection activities, seem to be international in scope. Waste Management, another trash hauling firm, was charged by the Securities and Exchange Commission with making illegal payments to foreign political parties and also with maintaining a secret slush fund for unlawful payments. The payments were to the Progressive Conservative Party of Canada to help ensure that its subsidiary could open a large landfill north of Toronto with provincial government approval (AFSCME, 1983).

A Los Angeles suburban area newspaper reported, "refusemen have spent and are spending thousands of dollars a month for lobbying and legal fees in their fight over [city] rubbish hauling contracts. The stakes are high—an estimated $10 million in eventual gross receipts. . . . Several candidates for the . . . City Council received contributions from refuse interests. . . . Two incumbents listed such contributions" (Ayres, 1975, p. 460).

Campaign contributions are not limited to small-time contractors. ARA, a large national company, is the nation's largest operator of food services and school buses and is a large operator of nursing homes, health care services, and trucking lines. In the late 1970s, ARA was accused of mob ties, although the company denied it and no charges were ever filed. However, in 1977 ARA voluntarily admitted that it made questionable and possibly illegal payments totaling $393,000 and, over six years, received $504,000 in illegal rebates. These payments included $23,400 in state and local campaign contributions that were admittedly "illegal" and another $11,550 that was legal but improperly recorded. ARA was not charged with a crime. In 1981 a member of the Boston School Board pled guilty to extorting $50,000 from ARA for a $40 million school busing contract for about 27,000 students (AFSCME, 1983).

In 1980 the *Chicago Tribune* reported that newly elected mayor Jane Byrne's administration awarded lucrative noncompetitive city contracts to firms and individuals who contributed over $1,000 to her campaign, despite Byrne's 1979 campaign promise not to give any contracts to contributors of over $1,000. During the 1979 campaign, Byrne charged incumbent Mayor Bilandic with "sweetheart deals" with C. F. Murphy and Associates, an architectural firm, noting there was a relationship between campaign contributions and contracts awarded. However, after Byrne defeated Bilandic in the primary, Murphy gave $30,000 to her campaign, and after her election, a Murphy affiliate received nonbid consulting contracts of over $150,000 (AFSCME, 1983).

The list of infractions could go on and on—and AFSCME's *Passing the Bucks* (1983) does go on for 100 pages, citing example after example of where contracting out has been involved, or appears to be involved, in influence peddling, corruption, shoddy services, and cost-ineffective contracts. AFSCME's point is clear: In all too many cases, firms that desire consulting and contracting contracts make heavy contributions to public officials. These contributions seem to be the ante for entrance to the contracting poker game. There is simply too much contractor money available and too many politicians who need that money for their campaigns to assume that firms will not try to use money to influence the selection of contractors.

This is particularly true in consulting contracts, where traditionally the importance of obtaining the best, or highest-quality, firm, without bidding or reference to the price, is commonplace. All too often, the right firm is the one that has made campaign contributions. And among two or more reputable firms, who can tell which is the best? Is not the firm that cares deeply about the political process, often by contributing to all candidates, the better choice? Many people, and perhaps most legislators who have to run for office, take this position.

The problem is not simply the greed of private companies. Often politicians are equally hungry for campaign funds or are simply interested in enriching themselves. They initiate the demand for funds, as in the Boston School Board case.

Formal bidding and selection processes, as discussed in Chapters Four and Five, can eliminate some of the more obvious abuses of the contracting out process—that is, of course, if the governing body wants to eliminate them. By far the majority of legislative bodies want to eliminate such abuses; however, this may not eliminate the appearance of politics. Where large contracts are available, contractors who wish to stay in the good graces of elected officials will continue to make contributions or will continue to be pressured to make such contributions.

Wesemann (1981) notes that while corruption is the major problem of contracting out, it is no worse than other municipal activities, such as building inspection or zoning. If this is true, the real danger in contracting out is not corruption per se (although far too much exists) but that the appearance of corruption may cause legislators and public executives to shun contracting out even when contracting would improve public services.

Corruption, if limited in definition to illegal activity, usually plays a relatively minor role in major contracts such as defense procurement. There are, of course, scattered and sometimes serious cases of fraud and illegal activity in contractors' delivery of weapons systems or in billing for them. Pork-barrel politics, however, is the major source of improper behavior. Pork-barrel politics involves which region, state, or congressional district gets contracting activity. Members of Congress are extraordinarily sensitive to the effect of contracts and military installations or procurement in their districts. A major government installation, such as a military base, or construction of a major military project, such as the Supercollider, are major prizes, often going only to key Congress members in key committee positions.

Construction, while important, arouses less concern than the threat of termination. Lambright (1976), writing about large-scale technology programs in terms that apply equally well to any large federal contract, notes:

> A cancellation decision does not just stop a program; it ends it. Moreover, it drastically disrupts careers of those associated with it, including government administrators, private contractors, and scientists and engineers. The termination of large-

> scale technologies hurts regional economies. What
> causes pain locally triggers congressional rescue ac-
> tivity. The constituency of a large-scale technology
> program is never more in evidence than at the time
> of termination [p. 48].

Congressmen are thus driven to resist the end of contracts because they affect the lives and jobs of their constituents. Eliminating, terminating, or canceling contracts is thus subject to
the bitterest kind of politics, for loss of a base or military contract is hazardous to a congressman's health (that is, reelection).

Federal agencies are not above coopting legislators by the
judicious use of contracts. Spreading bases, projects, and contracts among a number of districts in order to commit a large
number of congressmen to the project is by now an art form.
Congressmen are only too glad to authorize these locations,
and it is difficult at times to tell who is coopting whom. As
Lambright (1976) comments:

> Contracting out provides enormous flexibility
> for a technoscience agency in selecting companies in
> the districts of key legislative constituents. Loca-
> tional politics can be used by the agency to enlarge
> the program's geographical, legislative clientele.
> Contracts and subcontracts combine the interests
> of regional economics, unions, industry and legis-
> lators with those of the program. . . . Government
> by contract is cooptation by another name. It pur-
> chases legislative loyalty without necessarily increas-
> ing congressional scrutiny into executive decision
> making [p. 132].

As long as money, geographical choices, and votes are
at stake, political decisions will continue to be made about who
gets contracts, for how long a period, and in which location.
When the contract or project is large enough, pork-barrel politics
will rule, to the detriment of program efficiency and effectiveness.
On the other hand, if large contracts were made only on the basis

of economy and efficiency, managers who determine economy and efficiency would make all decisions, and major contracts would be decided on the basis of managerial politics. Given these alternatives, most people would probably opt to let their elected representatives make these decisions. In any case, some kind of political decision making will determine large contracts as long as the government contracts out.

Risk Avoidance

On occasion, contracting out can be used to reduce or avoid the political risk of starting new or untried programs. This is generally the case when a new or substantially expanded program is initiated. Sometimes these expanded programs are contracted out because in-house employees do not have the technical expertise or tools such as an expanded and more complex data-processing system. Sometimes an expansion or a new program involves new equipment that the agency does not have or cannot afford. However, sometimes these official reasons mask unofficial, more political reasons.

Political leaders often respond to popular demands for new programs. In doing so, they are primarily interested in initiating the program rather than being sure that it is operated properly over a long period of time. Politicians receive public attention for starting programs, not for managing them well. They exert considerable energy in making the political arrangements and compromises involved in initiating any new program. Thus, they are impatient to get the new program started. If an existing department cannot expand services quickly enough, the use of contracting out often meets the immediate need.

Contracting is often a lower-risk option. If the new program is popular and is operated well, the service can continue to be contracted out. If the new program is popular but not well operated, the service can be continued by agency staff. If the program is unpopular, no matter how well or poorly operated, the contract need not be renewed.

If the service is unpopular, no permanent agency staff have been committed. Few resources other than time and money have been expended: the private contractor shouldered all of the risks. In this way, risky programs can be created with a reduced political risk of creating an ineffective or unpopular program, since problems can be blamed on the contractor (Sharkansky, 1980).

Sometimes expansion of a program is popular and might well be done by regular staff or with the addition of new staff. However, on occasion, the service can be contracted out for a variety of political reasons, all related to reducing political risk. During 1986 and 1987, California, under Governor Deukmejian, had a policy of contracting out highway surveying, allegedly at a higher cost than hiring more Department of Transportation surveyors. Opponents claim that the purpose of using private contractors was to defuse any political criticism that the number of state employees had risen during Deukmejian's administration ("State Sued . . . ," 1986). Actions can be taken to guard against charges of "payroll padding," even though the contract may be more costly than in-house services. Total budget figures are subject to dispute, but changes in the total number of employees can be measured more exactly.

A variant of the technique of avoiding political risks by keeping employee levels down is to place the newly expanded program off budget by financing it by fees or charges, using these fees or charges to finance the costs of the contract (Sharkansky, 1980). Refuse collection may be paid by property taxes or by direct charges to homeowners. The difference is that the city budget is lower when homeowners pay direct charges. In this case, an economic virtue (direct charges for specific benefits) becomes a political virtue (reduction of the city budget).

Avoiding, or at least sharing, the risk involved in the construction of private prisons provides another example of political risk avoidance. Prison contracting is controversial (see Chapter Two), but overcrowding is also a risk, since courts sometimes intervene to demand lower inmate populations in specific prisons or jails. State agencies can thus justify contracting out as a new alternative to prison overcrowding, particularly since private contractors can build new prisons faster than can public agencies. Prison contracting has the further advantage of sharing with the private sector the responsibility for the corrections problems ("Pros and Cons . . . ," 1987).

Rule Politics

Rules and regulations involving public services and the way they are authorized, provided, and evaluated often have a considerable impact on contracting out. Some rules are designed to protect the public, such as rules prohibiting certain building materials, but these rules have inadvertent effects, as when such laws prevent new technological developments. Some rules are designed to shelter individuals and groups from competition, such as laws that require payment of the prevailing wage (which is the union wage in many metropolitan areas). Some rules tip the balance for or against public decisions to contract out, such as provisions for referenda that may overturn legislative decisions. Finally, some rules are not meant to be followed but merely exist as formal admonitions that few follow, such as requirements for competition in defense weapons procurement.

Inadvertent Rules. This first category of rule politics is only political in the sense that its results have political implications. A building ordinance may specify a certain thickness of doors for fire prevention, only to find later that some building materials maintain fire protection but do not meet the letter of the law. Perhaps the new material is a quarter-inch thinner than prescribed by the building code. Attempts to change the law delay the use of new materials. Also, these attempts meet political opposition from builders who claim the old materials are safer but who really prefer the economic advantages of the old law. As in so many cases, a law or rule may have been relatively noncontroversial when adopted but later changes in technology can have political implications.

Day care is a good example of the effect of outmoded rules. Day care, not typically a local function, is usually provided privately and regulated by government, although government occasionally arranges day-care services. Between 1970 and 1980, the number of women in the work force with children age six or under grew from one-third to one-half (Woodson, 1984).

Responding to this demand, in 1980 approximately one-quarter of the 1,780 cities and counties surveyed by the International City Management Association operated day-care facilities. Of these 436 agencies, 37 percent contracted with nonprofit agencies, 35 percent with profit organizations, and 6 percent with neighborhood groups (Valente and Manchester, 1984). In the three-quarters of the cities and counties not arranging for day-care services, government heavily regulates providers, primarily because of political and social sensitivity of the issue. Some of this regulation is understandable, because the service is new and governments are still uncertain how to deal with it.

Woodson (1984) is quite critical of the day-care regulatory activities of local governments. He comments on the difficulty of local governments in adjusting to day-care problems and their attempts to apply outmoded rules to day-care centers:

> A District of Columbia woman who has run her day-care center out of her home in a residential section of the city since 1978 faces jail unless she closes her doors. . . . City officials cited her for zoning violations. . . . Many of the parents of the children in her care do not feel they can find the same quality care at affordable rates elsewhere in the city.
>
> In Augusta, Maine, one enterprising woman opened a day-care program in a seniors' nursing home. . . . She must respond to ongoing—and seemingly unnecessary—flak from state and city licensing authorities relative to the "potential" risks of mixing children and elderly citizens in a single environment.
>
> The sanity lapse of many day-care regulations in Washington, D.C., was highlighted by one day-care operator who testified before a zoning board: "You're telling us that we cannot operate a day-care center in a residentially zoned middle-class neighborhood with a large number of working mothers, but we can operate a center in a commercial zone between two topless bars" [pp. 151, 159].

Woodson goes on to note that zoning regulations, staff requirements, and building codes designed for elementary schools are applied to day-care centers, making them expensive to start up. Churches, which provide many day-care centers, are also plagued by expensive regulations, such as requiring staff members to have master's degrees in early childhood education. Woodson argues that "public policy must address the issue of whether the legal protections and quality controls are effective, logical and have reasonable costs" (p. 159), particularly since they increase the quality of service far beyond what most children have in their own homes.

Day-care center rules will eventually be changed to meet the needs of working mothers, for what Woodson rails about is primarily the lag time involved in modernizing outdated regulations. Fortunately, because of the recent growth in the number of day-care centers, only a few operators have vested interests in these old rules.

In other areas, change will be more controversial than that involving day-care centers, for those with economic investments in older technologies or rules will resist changes, whether or not the public is better served by a change. For example, requirements have apparent face validity when they require that key staff in certain programs have certain specific minimum educational requirements but are less valid for new programs. Even so, professional groups made up of those who have the educational credentials can be expected to oppose any changes in rules.

Intended Rules. In other cases, rules are specifically designed to benefit or protect certain groups, such as workers in specific industries. The Federal Department of Transportation temporarily stalled Sacramento's new light rail system in 1986 because the cars were determined to have been assembled with parts not made in America. Local officials deny this, charging that the rules were changed after the contract was signed. In any case, the requirement for American-made parts was a rule presumably created to benefit the steel workers.

In New York there is an even clearer case. In 1980 the city closed Wollman skating rink in Central Park for an estimated two-year repair job estimated at $4.9 million. Six years later the city was $12.9 million poorer and the rink was still incomplete. The city announced that it had to spend another $3 million and two years on the repair. To avoid this further delay, the city accepted a challenge from Donald Trump, the flamboyant contractor, who promised to do the job for $2.8 million in less than a year. If he went over budget or took longer, he would do the job free. He completed it for $2.3 million in five and a half months. (To add insult to injury, a $200,000 report commissioned by the city to find out the cause of city delays was itself five months late.)

Officials blamed the city's delay on its decision to use state-of-the-art technology (Trump used traditional ice-making methods), on design errors, and on delays in letting contracts (which let leaks develop in exposed refrigeration coils). They also attributed Trump's success to being able to pick top contractors who would produce quickly or risk losing future business with the billionaire developer.

The major reason for the city's cost overruns and delays, however, was the delay in signing contracts with four separate contractors. Under New York's Wickes law, which does not apply to private contractors, state and local agencies must hire separate contractors for plumbing, construction, electrical, and heating and ventilation, using the lowest bidder. City officials and Governor Mario Cuomo have tried to have the Wickes law repealed, claiming it costs taypayers $100 million per year, but contractors and labor unions have resisted repeal successfully, intensively lobbying the state legislature. The city avoided having Trump subject to the Wickes law (it was a city contract) only by declaring that rebuilding the rink was an emergency measure ("Private Effort . . . ," 1987).

Rules are rarely neutral, for they benefit some and damage others. Sometimes rules have inadvertent results and can usually be changed, although those benefited will usually resist the changes, even if they are obviously necessary. In other cases, the rules are not designed to be neutral, and any change will involve a major political battle.

Direct Elections

Sometimes the contracting out process involves direct political action through elections of various types. Sometimes the contract itself is on the ballot through a referendum. More commonly, proposals to privatize services become an election issue through the identification of candidates with the proposal. Less frequently, poor service may be the reason for popular opposition to specific candidates. Whether contracting out involves direct elections depends on a number of issues. Is there a provision for referenda on disputed contracts? Can legislators associated with an unpopular contract be recalled? Are elections for legislators held about the time that an unpopular contract is under consideration? Are employee groups or unions active in the electoral process (see Chapter Eleven)? Are important groups in the community opposed to or supportive of contracting out? Are citizens informed about and interested in public services? Three elections are discussed here to illustrate the range of issues and situations that can arise.

Hall County, Georgia. Located northwest of Atlanta, Hall County was threatened with losing fire and ambulance services when federal aid ran out and a local ambulance provider withdrew. County commissioners, aware of a neighboring county's contract for fire service, tried contracting out. Since deadlines forced their hand, the commissioners hastily hired a private firm for both ambulance services and fire protection. There was some public outcry before the contract was signed, and a citizens' group recalled the commissioners. However, the new commissioners chose to continue the contracts under a more formalized process. The new contracting out process included legal advertisements, bid specifications, prebid information, a prebid conference, and formal final bid submissions. These formal procedures appeared to meet the objections of the citizens.

The present contract is a three-year, fixed-fee contract for all but two cities in the county and provides that the contractor will operate all aspects of the fire and ambulance program, including hiring and firing employees, meeting state requirements, and providing a full range of fire and ambulance services. The contract sets specific personnel standards and minimum staffing levels. Hall County leases all fire and ambulance equipment to the contractor, pays utility and fuel bills, and monitors performance. The county projects annual savings of $100,000 to $200,000 per year, while keeping quality consistent. Hall County commissioners make the following suggestions about contracting out fire services: (1) Proceed slowly, (2) consult all elected officials as well as the fire chief, (3) issue a prepared statement explaining the reasons for contracting out, (4) establish a special committee to review the bids, and (5) be prepared for criticism from fire department employees as well as citizens ("Case Studies . . . ," 1986).

Kalamazoo, Michigan. The City of Kalamazoo credits its privatization efforts for gaining enough voter support to pass a special mass transit levy. The proposal failed by only twenty-nine votes initially, but won easily by a two-to-one margin the second time. The special levy replaces the current general fund support for mass transit with support from other sources so that general funds can be used for other purposes. The new levy continues the present level of services.

Voters changed their minds for two reasons. First, a group of candidates ran on a "privatization platform," promising to bring better transit service through contracting out. This campaign ploy publicized privatization opportunities. Second, the city implemented transit privatization measures before the second vote. These measures included contracting out three bus routes, contracting out the repair of passenger shelters, and contracting out radio maintenance. This apparently improved services and caught the voter's eye ("Privatization Helps . . . ," 1987).

Southern California. In suburban Los Angeles, a controversial rubbish collection contract was voted down by a three-to-one margin after the mayor and two councilmen, who pushed the exclusive contract through the council, became the subjects of a district attorney investigation.

A rubbish hauling contract, which has brought
a district attorney investigation into circumstances
behind its award, was cancelled Tuesday by voters.

The contract was defeated 6,356 to 2,191. Proposition A was put on the ballot by referendum when the award to Refuse Company . . . [no names were in the original account] without competitive bidding was opposed by two councilmen. Mayor _____ and councilmen _____ [the two later pled no contest in court] voted for the exclusive contract [Ayres, 1975, p. 460].

Analysis. Hall County ran into electoral difficulty because it acted too hastily in fire service and ambulance contracting, particularly when fire service was to be newly contracted out. Kalamazoo found that adopting contracting out measures for the transit system helped convince voters to ratify a tax levy for that transit service. Voters in a suburban Los Angeles city rejected a rubbish contract because of suspected collusion between councilmen and the contractor.

In each of these cases, good contracting out principles were politically advantageous and bad contracting out practices were damaging. Hall County supervisors initally acted hastily, ignoring good practices that later supervisors instituted. Kalamazoo found that voters apparently liked contracting out, once the city tried it. The Los Angeles suburb found that corruption is bad politics as well as bad contracting out practice.

Summary

There are five general categories of contracting out politics. Managerial politics involves managers in the political aspects of initiating contracts. Lubrication politics concerns the use of money, particularly campaign contributions, to advance certain contractors over others. Risk-avoidance politics involves the reduction of political risk in initiating new contracts. Rule politics involves the application of both inadvertent and deliberate government rules and their consequences. Direct elections intervene whenever voters must approve a specific contract or vote for politicians associated directly with a controversial contract. Normally politics is seen as a negative force, or at least something that must be managed or even guarded against. However, good contracting practice can also be good politics, whether it is electoral, managerial, rule, or risk-avoidance politics. Bad contracting practices, well intentioned or not, often cause political troubles. Contracting out, like many other government practices from personnel to budgeting, is a process where strict adherence to both legal details and good management practice pays political dividends.

CHAPTER 11 ᴧᴧᴧᴧᴧᴧᴧᴧᴧᴧᴧᴧᴧᴧᴧᴧ

Dealing with Employee and Union Opposition

Contracting out and the fate of public employees whose jobs have been contracted out has two sides. The best-publicized side involves highly politicized issues surrounding the intense efforts of employee groups to save their jobs through internal opposition, civil service rights, appeals to conscience, and direct electoral activity. In all of these attempts, the role of a strong and vocal union is important and often provides the basis for a successful challenge. This opposition to contracting out occurs, as might be expected, regardless of the economic "merits" of the case. Jobs, economic security, and careers are at stake. In such cases, the abstract merits of contracting are of little concern to employees and unions. The issue is, or quickly becomes, highly politicized. This part of the employee's relationship to contracting out is a major issue in most contracting decisions, particularly in the more highly publicized ones.

The other side is the human aspect: how to deal humanely and effectively with displaced employees. In some cases, the decision to contract out was not a reflection on employee performance but simply a recognition of wage costs, technological advances, or the cost of new equipment. It may be cheaper or more effective to contract out, but this fails to take into account the human costs. Fortunately, there are ways to reduce these human costs (which are covered in the section on employee displacement). Using these ways of reducing the human and economic costs of employee displacement adds up to good politics and is a crucial tool for the politically wise manager.

The Cost of Public Employees

Very few public functions would be contracted out if it were demonstrably clear that private contractors were more expensive. Contracting out is usually done to save money. True, there are some psychological, managerial, and philosophical reasons for contracting out that are not directly economic in nature (see Chapters One, Two, and Three). However, whenever the public is convinced that private operation is less expensive, most routine and some sensitive government functions are usually contracted out. Since labor consumes up to 70 to 80 percent of many municipal budgets and a large, although lesser, proportion for other government levels, employee costs are the major cost item eliminated by contracting out.

One major employee cost, in addition to direct wages, is fringe benefits. In many cases, the private contractor's wages are as high as or higher than those of the city, county, state, or federal government. Rarely, however, are the fringe benefits as high. Sick and vacation time allowances are lower, and thus there are more total days worked. Frequently, the contractor provides no retirement plan. In the Ecodata study of southern California cities (Stevens, 1984), there were retirement packages, but in Camden, New Jersey (discussed later in this chapter), there were none.

Private contractors also reduce labor costs in other ways. Private employees often work longer hours and accomplish more in a given time than their public counterparts. (This is usually attributed to stronger management that has more responsibility for hiring and firing. It may also be because contractors also have a somewhat younger work force.) Private employers use more part-time help, thus reducing the cost of fringe benefits, and they use less skilled help, which reduces costs. (Increased flexibility of more highly skilled employees, as when a maintenance employee can change fuses or unclog toilets, is an expensive luxury that apparently improves service very little.)

The Ecodata study of reduced costs through contracting out is verified by several other reports. In the late 1970s and early 1980s, many Sunbelt cities reduced spending and increased efficiency through contracting out (Pierce and Susskind, 1986). (High employee costs were not cited as the reason.) Cities aggressively pursued these efficiency strategies because of the loss of federal dollars. Contracting was eased by lack of union opposition, since the Sunbelt has fewer unions than other parts of the nation. In addition to contracting, several cities are now combining fire and police departments, sometimes by having employees serve as police officers who respond to fires. Where unions exist, they resist this "double duty" fiercely, because jobs are at stake.

In the 1970s the State of Michigan contracted Title XX (social services) and Comprehensive Education and Training Act (CETA) work to private nonprofit social service agencies. The state chose neither to assign the work to the Department of Developmentally Disabled Services (DDS) caseworkers nor to hire additional social workers with expertise. The DDS caseworkers lacked expertise. Hiring additional employees would have reduced flexibility in the work force in the case of cutbacks, while contracting with private firms spread support for social services throughout communities within the state. In this case, lower employee costs were less important than flexibility and political support. However, additional flexibility is an intangible benefit to employers that is widely recognized by managers and is often as important as lower costs (DeHoog, 1984).

Management studies on labor costs are not always carefully done and, in fact, frequently involve some bias toward contracting, often understating monitoring and contract administration costs or overstating the costs of public employees. In 1976 and 1977, the official cost of federal employee pensions changed three times in fifteen months, giving the appearance of political manipulation. In August 1976, President Ford's Office of Management and Budget (OMB) set the cost of retirement plans so that government costs could be compared with those of private contractors. The rate went from 7.0 to 24.7 percent, thus ensuring that government costs, compared to private costs, would be nearly 18 percent higher than previously. The OMB called this "new guidance." Employee groups complained, and the OMB, under newly elected President Jimmy Carter, reset the rate at 14.1 percent in June 1977. However, perhaps as some sort of compromise for the range of hazily defined groups on both sides of the issue, the rate was reset at 20.4 percent in November 1977. OMB legitimized the latest figure as follows: "This factor was produced by the Civil Service Commission's actuarial method, as modified and validated by the General Accounting Office, using economic assumptions supplied by the Council of Economic Advisers" (Sharkansky, 1979, pp. 138–139). However, three changes in fifteen months probably destroyed any belief in the figure's reliability, regardless of how carefully it might have been calculated.

As long as either management or labor makes cost studies in highly charged areas such as contracting out, these estimates are unlikely to be received well or believed at all. The situation becomes even worse when questionable methodologies are used or flip-flops in position (as in the case of the OMB) occur.

Dealing with Displaced Employees

Whether or not there is opposition to contracting out, management must face an unpleasant task: What is to be done with those employees who will be displaced by the contracted service? When unions are involved, the task will be more complex and difficult. Even when there is no union pressure, the ability to deal effectively and fairly with employees is crucial if contracting out is to be effective.

Displaced employees garner a good deal of sympathy from both citizens and legislators and their placement can become a volatile political issue. Managers should be certain that plans for displacing employees will actually be carried through. One city projected contracting out savings based on a 70 percent reduction in the refuse disposal crew, with the remaining employees to be transferred to other city jobs. However, the council was unwilling to lay off employees and finally voted to redistribute them to other public works functions. The net result was an expanded municipal work force and no savings under the private contract (Wesemann, 1981).

This situation illustrates one way of handling displaced employees: redistributing them to existing positions in the agency. The agency can transfer all employees, some employees who do not go to work for the contractor, or all employees who desire to stay with the agency, or it can employ some other alternative. One way to handle redistribution is to limit it to employees with substantial seniority. If personnel rules permit, redistribution can be limited to employees with skills usable elsewhere. Often employees are asked to choose between the contractor, a layoff (sometimes with severance pay), or moving to another job or department. Employees in this or a similar position should be required to make a one-time choice, rather than, for instance, trying employment with the contractor and then electing to return to the public employer. Such changes can be disruptive to the contractor, the agency, and the employee.

Occasionally, a contractor is required to hire displaced workers, or at least consider them for employment. This is feasible when jobs require no special training or special skills (such as rubbish collection), when the contractor's work force is not already committed, and when the contractor is willing to accept such a provision in the contract. This was done in the Prince George's County data-processing project (see Case Study 1 in the Resources), where employees were given an opportunity to work for the contractor (Shulman, 1982). In most cases, such a provision may cause contractors to increase their estimate. It is not clear how long most displaced employees remain with the contractor in this case, or even how frequently such a provision is included in contracts. However, this provision makes employee reductions more palatable to politicians.

Attrition and layoff are two common ways to reduce the work force. In most cases, the reason for cutbacks is not contracting out but program staffing decreases or reduced revenues to the agency. In any case, the question is how the work force should be cut back.

Attrition relies on employee turnover to reach lower staffing levels. With rapid turnover, lower levels will be quickly reached. Slower turnover levels take correspondingly longer. With slow turnover, some sort of additional action, such as employee transfers, will be required to reach desired staffing levels.

If a planned attrition program is developed, positions will be held vacant until enough employees have left the organization to meet desired levels. This is usually referred to as a "hiring freeze."

Layoffs are simply the termination of employees, usually by seniority, and are done without prejudice. Employees can and often do return to the agency at a later date in a similar, or even the same, position. However, layoffs can occur at specific dates, such as when the contractor replaces the public program. If some employees, such as supervisors and senior staffers, are to be retained to monitor the contract, the remaining employees can be laid off. The public agency then has no responsibility for their salary, which makes possible the savings envisioned by the contracting proposals. Thus layoffs, as compared with attrition, in theory immediately produce cost savings.

In practice, it is not this simple (see Greenhalgh and McKersie, 1980; Feldt and Anderson, 1982). Attrition has but one agency cost—"holding" unnecessary employees until they quit or can be absorbed elsewhere in the agency. (With low turnover, this can amount to a high cost.) In contrast, a layoff policy has a large number of smaller costs, most of which are difficult to quantify. Layoffs involve official reduction-in-force (RIF) policies that cost a certain amount to administer. Layoff costs mount rapidly and frequently match or surpass attrition costs.

There are three large losses due to layoffs. One is chargebacks by unemployment insurance, usually in the form of future rate increases. Another loss results from voluntary "quits" due to job insecurity. These voluntary quits are usually the most mobile and valuable work-force members. Because they are valuable, they have to be replaced and their replacements trained. Third, there is productivity loss due to job insecurity. Workers concerned about layoffs do not work as hard, or they spend time looking for other jobs.

Finally, there are minor costs—for example, the cost of the preferred rehire system for laid-off employees, the loss due to some increases in alcohol abuse (studies have established this loss), and a final small loss to the government unit of income and sales tax receipts by unemployed workers. (This is a loss to the government as a whole, not to the specific department making the layoffs.) One New York State empirical report indicates that if all intangible costs are included, it is usually cheaper to rely on attrition than to lay off employees (Greenhalgh and McKersie, 1980).

With adequate planning, attrition can be used, although most changes from public to private provision are not carefully planned. The remaining employees are usually reassigned, if there are not too many, and if possible the contractor is asked (or required by the contract) to hire them or at least give prior consideration to them. Layoffs usually occur as a last result, and many employees, through preferential hiring or seniority, usually end up back on the agency payroll in one position or another.

Citizens and taxpayer groups often applaud anticipated savings from employee layoffs, but in many jurisdictions it is politically dangerous to propose layoffs. Thus, when long-term layoff costs are added to the potential political repercussions employee layoffs often cause, layoffs are usually not a cost-effective or politically effective solution (National Commission for Employment Policy, 1988). Another solution—such as planned attrition, employee redistribution within the agency, or contractor employment—is usually a more practical answer.

Labor's View: Cost Figures Are Highly Debatable

Not surprisingly, organized labor believes that the costs of contracting out are usually severely understated. First, labor regards actual cost savings attributed to contracting as highly illusionary, rarely actually occurring. Second, even if there are cost savings, labor claims that they are outweighed by other drawbacks of contracting out, such as the loss of public control, the likelihood of corruption, and the decline in the quality of public services.

Gerald McEntee (1986), president of the American Federation of State, County, and Municipal Employees (AFSCME), attacks contracting out vigorously:

- *Higher costs.* . . . When making cost comparisons, governments often omit the costs for contract preparation, administration, service monitoring and renegotiation. Often the cost of using in-house facilities or equipment is omitted as well. . . .
- *Poorer quality of services.* The profit motive provides an incentive to cut corners on service quality—to hire inexperienced transient personnel at low wages, skimp on contract requirements, or provide inadequate supervision. . . .
- *Reduced accountability of public officials to citizens.* The motivation of public officials in contracting is often to just wash their hands of administrative hassles. But providing public service is *their* responsibility. . . .
- *Loss of flexibility.* Public managers directing a public work force have a large degree of flexibility in responding to unforeseen circumstances; on the other hand, a contractor has the clear right to refuse to do even the smallest task that isn't in the contract. . . .
- *Corruption.* Using consultants and contractors to perform public services frequently produces widespread corruption—bribery, kickbacks, collusive bidding, conflicts of interest, charges for work never performed. . . .

With more competent public management, there would be no need for contracting. Good public sector managers should be able to achieve the same economies and efficiencies that private managers achieve—and without the added problems brought by contracting out. . . . As more public services are shifted to the private sector, we move from an open and accountable society to a closed, secretive society easily subject to manipulation [p. 10].

Opponents of contracting out are on shaky ground when attacking contracting on the basis of cost. Most studies have shown that contracting costs less than public provision of services. The issue is whether the lower costs of private operation are negated by intangible benefits that the public sector gives up when it contracts out. In some areas, the union argument is on solid ground: Corruption is a fact of life in some situations. Wesemann (1981), an advocate of contracting out, admits that "the only persuasive argument unions can develop against contracting for municipal services is corruption" (p. 87).

In some cases, contracting provides poorer quality of service, just as McEntee charges. However, public provision of services can also be characterized by low productivity and/or low quality. Both cases exist, and definitive examples are highly subjective. There are no convincing studies that point in either direction. The hard-to-measure nature of many public services, such as police and fire protection, further confuses the issue. In addition, slight variations in many services are hardly noticeable under either public or private provision, as when street trees are trimmed two times every three years rather than annually.

One could continue to debate each specific AFSCME charge against contracting out without coming to a conclusion. What is crucial to recognize is that the unions can have a good deal of influence over contracting out. Much of the public sector is unionized, and unions almost inevitably oppose contracting out. From their point of view, either jobs will be lost if private contractors hire fewer employees, or well-paid jobs will be replaced by poorer-paying jobs in the private sector. (Since fringe benefits, if not salaries, are usually lower, this view is technically correct.) Another reason, not usually stated but important to AFSCME, is that union jobs are often replaced by nonunion jobs. This weakens public sector unions. It should be no surprise that where unions have influence, they oppose contracting out.

Public sector unions, such as AFSCME, have attracted relatively more members than their private sector counterparts in recent years. While the influence of public sector unions has declined in the past fifteen years, they are still extremely powerful in large urban areas, particularly in midwestern and eastern states. Public sector unions were able to win wage gains of 5.7 percent in 1986, compared to 3.2 percent for private sector unions. One U.S. Chamber of Commerce labor law specialist complains that government managers do not resist unionization because they have little incentive to control labor costs. He claims that increasing privatization of public services is the only way to avoid the "problems created by the increasing unionization of government workers" ("Problematic Labor . . . ," 1987, p. 5).

Unions have at times resorted to strikes, the ultimate sanction against contracting out. Philadelphia garbage collectors struck in July 1986, partly to fight the city's intention to contract out, which cost several thousand union jobs in recent years. Before a court ordered the union back to work, 45,000 tons of garbage had piled up. The union did not win restrictions on the city's ability to contract out in the settlement, but it had served notice that it was willing to strike to enforce its wage and nonwage demands ("Philadelphia Costs," 1986).

At the other extreme, a small issue arose in the California State University system when, at several campuses, management proposed to contract out custodial work. Custodians at the Northridge (near Los Angeles) campus marched into the manager's office. When he would not hold a meeting to discuss contracting out ten positions, the custodians filed a grievance ("Custodians Fight . . . ," 1987).

It appears that in both Philadelphia and Northridge, the unions were unsuccessful in blocking contracting out, but they made it clear that it would be unpleasant for management to contract out. Unions will make themselves felt in terms of inconvenience and disruption if management is intent on contracting out.

Results of Union and Employee
Opposition to Contracting Out

Employee and union opposition to contracting out takes a toll. Managers report that employee and union opposition is the second most frequent reason for dropping plans to contract out. (The first is legal prohibitions against contracting.) The International City Management Association (ICMA) recommends that employee and union involvement in plans to contract out can prevent small problems from later becoming more serious problems (Shulman, 1982). This, of course, will work when actual layoffs are not contemplated, as, for example, when additional work is involved and contracting out merely prevents employment of additional public employees.

Some employers have reached extensive agreements with their employees over contracting out agreements. The State of Massachusetts has a formal agreement with its union members. Massachusetts has agreed that no work will be contracted out unless it can be proved that no state staff are available or able to perform the service (Report on the National Association, 1986).

At the other extreme, some agencies create competitive conditions in which public employees work and bid against private contractors. Phoenix and Minneapolis, among others, follow this policy for refuse collection. In Phoenix, city employees have bid against private contractors for refuse collection and park landscaping. Even so, Phoenix city manager Marvin Andrews does not want to contract out over 50 percent of city services, because the city would face prohibitive capital expenses if city employees won back the service from private contractors. In addition, if all services were contracted out, it might cause "labor unrest" ("Andrews: Policies . . . ," 1986).

Whether specific agreements are reached with unions or whether employees actually compete with private contractors, the possibility of union and employee unrest weighs heavily on the minds of most managers, as Valente and Manchester (1984) note: "Although contracting is a way to circumvent outmoded rules and restrictive practices of the civil service and unions, these institutions may impose such a high cost for switching that it will not be attractive economically" (p. 17).

These high costs are psychological and political, but they also take an economic toll in managerial time and effort. Union contracts may require that contracting out be bargained with the union. In such a case, the union will not be easy to deal with. If by some chance an agreement over contracting is reached, the contract will be full of such provisions as severance pay, vacation pay, and sick pay, which quickly counteract any contracting out savings.

Local ordinances, state law, or judicial interpretations of law may prohibit or restrict layoffs or contracts that give agency work to non–civil service workers. If layoffs occur, civil servants may have elaborate "bumping rights" that disrupt work in many departments. Affirmative action laws or agreements may, in effect, prevent contracting. Pensions present additional problems. Unfunded pension plans normally will involve a substantial payout to each employee if the employees withdraw from the plan.

Managers and executives who have been burned by employee opposition to contracts are often convinced that strong employee opposition, particularly with union support, will almost always destroy plans to contract out. However, this is an exaggeration, because, as the following cases show, there have been occasions where employee opposition did not foil plans to contract out (and a substantial minority of cases where it did).

Cases of Contracting Out Where Union or Employee Opposition Exists

To illustrate the range of union and employee opposition to contracting out and to examine the form such opposition takes, ten short cases of contracting out involving employee opposition follow. While these are not a representative sample, they do portray a wide variety of situations from which some conclusions about employee opposition can be drawn.

Camden, New Jersey. Camden contracted out its refuse collection service in 1974. Camden was a declining central city. Dominated by the mayor, the city's refuse collection service was heavily populated with patronage appointees and was providing generally poor service. It was a high-cost system plagued with severe overstaffing. To reduce costs, the mayor proposed contracting. After the initial decision to contract out, sanitation employees walked out but came back at the mayor's request. They engaged in a work slowdown when the actual contract was signed, which was followed by an unsuccessful lawsuit against the contract. However, the contract switch was made, with about twenty-five employees eventually joining the private contractor and thirty-five being reassigned to other departments at reduced wages. Those who worked for the contractor received higher wages but lower fringe benefits, including no pensions (Berenyi, 1979).

Milwaukee, Wisconsin. Milwaukee decided to contract out solid waste disposal in the early 1970s. The city terminated its employees, sold its collection equipment, and arranged with a contractor for collection of solid waste. At a later date, lawsuits against the contract were filed, and eventually a court ruled that the contract was unlawful. Ruefully, the city had to cancel the contract, rehire employees to collect refuse, and acquire equipment. Restarting the city operation from the beginning came at a great cost in time, money, and embarrassment (Fisk, Kiesling, and Miller, 1978).

San Francisco, California. San Francisco was anxious to reduce costs by privatizing. The city voters passed a measure, in November 1976, changing the city charter to allow contracting with private parties. After it passed, management services at General Hospital were contracted to American Management Services. The contractor aggressively cut costs, reducing the number of porters 30 percent, from 139 to 100. Employees complained that the contractor also cut service, citing dirty specimens and laboratories, employee harassment by management, selective cleaning of rooms and areas for high-ranking individuals, and dirty restrooms. Porters staged a sickout to protest these conditions and the reductions in employee levels (Platt, Barnes, and Bishop, 1983).

Akron, Ohio. Mayor Roy Ray of Akron proposed contracting out trash-hauling services in 1981. The proposed contractor was already serving some residences in the city and proposed to extend the contract. The proposed cost was lower than for residences already being served by the contractor. The union called the proposal lowballing, pointing out the exclusion of certain costs, such as dead animal pickup. Furthermore, the union compiled figures indicating the city was already operating at a $100,000 profit, compared with the estimated $500,000 contracting out profit. Substantial public debate ensued, but within eight days of the contracting proposal, the union and the city agreed to revised collection routes and stops per route. City officials said that the revamped city agreement would save more money than contracting out (AFSCME, 1983).

West Chester, Pennsylvania. The Borough of West Chester proposed to contract out trash collection in December 1981. The unionized eight-man sanitation unit was to be replaced by private service. An overflow crowd of citizens turned out to support the sanitation workers, who averaged twenty years of borough service. The crowd, representing a large cross section of the community, vociferously opposed the proposed contract, claiming that quality would suffer and costs would increase. Some citizens said they would be willing to pay higher taxes to keep the service in-house. As a result of the meeting, borough officials elected not to contract out the service (AFSCME, 1983). Although the account does not mention the role of the union in protecting its members, the union no doubt worked very hard to maximize citizen opposition at the meeting.

Fort Walton Beach, Florida. Fort Walton Beach had a negative experience when it proposed privatizing fire services. The newly elected mayor was looking for savings and approached a private fire-fighting service. However, the fire-fighting union interpreted discussions with the private firm as evidence of bad faith, since the city was simultaneously negotiating a union contract. (The newly elected mayor termed this a "coincidence.") The union successfully petitioned to place a referendum on the ballot that, if adopted, would have prohibited contracting out police and fire services in the future. After a fierce election campaign (expenses totaled the highest in city history), the voters turned down the referendum 3,634 to 2,537. However, the city, now free to contract out, chose to consider simply renewing the fire-fighting contract. One observer said the conflict "burned out" the mayor and council and that they would probably not soon reconsider privatization ("Privatization Fire . . . ," 1986).

Fairfield, California. Fairfield successfully (at least to date) contracted out fire protection service for peak hours between

3 and 11 P.M. This contract service supplemented city fire fighters' regular twenty-four-hour shift. The eleven contract employees perform other tasks than fire fighting, and this flexibility is the reason that the city favors the program. The existing fire-fighting union was approached about the eight-hour shift, but the union rebuffed the idea. Fire fighters preferred the existing twenty-four-hour shifts. After the city contracted out the peak hour shift, the union filed two lawsuits, contending that contracting out was illegal. One suit was dismissed, the other is pending ("Trying a New Way . . . ," 1986).

New Orleans, Louisiana. New Orleans was required by the federal Environmental Protection Agency to close its incinerators and landfill site. The city decided to contract for several reasons. First, the successful contractor (rather than the city) could be required to dispose of wastes collected under the contract. Second, the city regarded city collection as expensive. Finally, the new mayor was anxious to contract out the sanitation division because he could not control patronage. The contractor, already serving part of the city, helped by preparing bid specifications to ensure continuity of the present level of service. A power struggle between the sanitation division head and the mayor delayed implementation of the contract. This allowed attrition of some potentially displaced workers to occur, and, finally, 10 percent of the city's waste services was contracted out. Implementation went smoothly because the union already represented the contractor's employees and negotiated a contract with the contractor in advance of the change to private collection (Armington and Ellis, 1984).

Pekin, Illinois. Pekin had its landfill site closed by the State of Illinois in 1976, forcing a refuse collection change. The firm operating a private landfill contracted with Pekin to also provide refuse collection. The firm marketed its services aggressively, conducting a cost study of the city refuse disposal system, demonstrating the firm's capacity, and arguing its case publicly. Pekin viewed the contract alternative as a way of avoiding the wage demands of city workers. After contracting out was approved, the twenty-three employees of the Sanitation Department were laid off. The union opposition to the change received little public support (Armington and Ellis, 1984). (Unions had no statewide status at that time, and the city was not required to bargain collectively.)

Covington, Kentucky. Covington experienced rather strong union opposition to its plan to contract out refuse disposal in 1975. Covington wanted private operation in order to reduce costs. The union enjoyed some public support and sued the city to prevent contracting out. However, the judge upheld the city, and the city then signed the contract. The sanitation workers were redistributed to other jobs by the city. The contract proved to be about 14 percent cheaper in the first year of operation, mostly due to lower fringe benefits paid to contract workers (Armington and Ellis, 1984).

Summary of the Cases

What do these ten cases reveal? First, generalizations should be limited, since seven of the cases involved refuse disposal. Refuse disposal is a commonly contracted service, with a number of private operators available in every metropolitan area. Since it is highly labor intensive and often filled with patronage employees, it is vulnerable to more efficient private operations that use advanced equipment and have a more productive work force.

However, the cases contain some valuable information and some insights into employee or union opposition. The opposition to contracting took the following forms:

Court challenges	4
Work disruptions	2
Referenda	1
Public debates	2
No serious opposition	2

One surprising item that stands out is the use of lawsuits to resist contracting out attempts. Lawsuits were used in four of the ten cases. This lends credence to the view of the ICMA that legal objections, followed by union and employee resistance, are the most common reasons contracting out proposals fail (Shulman, 1982).

In addition to lawsuits, a variety of means to resist contracting out were used, including slowdowns, public debates, and a referendum. Employee resistance may have occurred in other ways—for example, how the effect of contracting affected the morale of employees is not known.

Union opposition prevented contracting out in three cases: Akron, West Chester, and Milwaukee. In Fort Walton Beach, the union lost the referendum battle but appears to have won the contracting out war. In 40 percent of the cases, then, union opposition prevented contracting out.

Perhaps the four cases where effective opposition developed were ill-considered attempts to contract that should not have occurred, union or no union. This is impossible to say, however, just as it is impossible to say that the six successful contracting attempts were well thought out. The lesson of these ten cases is that union and employee opposition to contracting out can be expected, often in the form of lawsuits, and that such opposition is often successful.

Summary

Contracting out is almost always justified by cost reductions. Private contractors can reduce their costs for services primarily because they have lower labor costs, particularly in employee fringe benefits. Employees and unions, not surprisingly, are not impressed with the economic merits of this argument, which to them are highly questionable. Thus, unions and employee organizations ferociously resist contracting out, for it means the loss of jobs, salary, and union membership. Unions and employee groups comprise the most formidable block to contracting out, other than any legal constraints. This is a fact of life facing anyone planning to contract out.

One way to limit employee opposition is to treat employees humanely and responsibly, relying on attrition, reassignment, or placement with the contractor for displaced employees. Equitable treatment of employees is not only the responsible thing to do but is also politically wise, since employees and their unions are quite able, in many cases, to defeat contracting out proposals. The ten short cases in this chapter make this quite clear.

CHAPTER 12 ∿∿∿∿∿∿∿∿∿∿∿∿∿

Strategies for Success in Contracting Out

By now most of the major issues—as well as the facts and details—of contracting out have been reviewed. However, managers and political leaders need more than facts and technical details. They have to know when to use the facts they have, when to ask for more information, and when facts (or yet more facts) are not particularly useful. This is when judgment is called for, and this chapter is about the use of judgment. Since judgment is applied individually and to specific situations, the views in this final chapter certainly are not to be applied universally— but they still are good advice in general.

This final chapter is really a summary of the preceding eleven. Are the technical details important? How, when, and why do you use the information in these first eleven chapters? When all is said and done, what does all the material about contracting out discussed in these chapters really mean?

The preceding chapters are summarized in eight very general do's and don'ts. These do's and don'ts are advice— wisdom, if you will—distilled from the preceding chapters. Certainly not universal wisdom for managers, they are logical conclusions of the facts, information, and insights of the foregoing discussion.

217

Four Do's

Be Open and Direct. Contracting out is a policy issue that should be dealt with openly and honestly. Closeting plans to contract out generally results in fiercer opposition once plans are revealed. It is tempting to operate behind closed doors, particularly when opposition can be expected the moment contracting plans are revealed, but there is little evidence that plans hatched in private result in better contracts than openly agreed-on covenants.

It is one thing to review the law, the history, and the pitfalls of contracting out in private. It is quite another to complete extensive feasibility studies, comparative analyses, and even to prepare contract documents without prior authority of the legislative body. Very preliminary studies are a necessity before the manager can recommend a more comprehensive study. However, elaborate plans made privately do not command much credibility when opponents finally become aware of them. A formal request to the legislative body or chief executive to initiate a contracting out study is a much better way to begin.

Operating openly and directly has its advantages. Better information can be obtained. Employee groups and unions will not be enthralled by the prospects of contracting out, but their comments about the impact on employees and their views on what provisions are needed to protect employees are useful and cannot be obtained elsewhere. Publicity about a study alerts many contractors and providers to the prospects of business, provides more information about suppliers, and ultimately increases competition. Community groups, when an actual geographical community such as a city is involved, can debate the issues. Department heads' and middle managers' intimate knowledge about the service being considered for contracting can be tapped. Their questions about service quality and their new role as monitors and contract managers can be dealt with directly and promptly.

The credibility of the feasibility study and of the manager are also at stake. Managers have to be analytical and clearheaded when evaluating the likely impact and feasibility of contracting out, but they also have to be "honest brokers" in getting agreement from competing interests over facts, issues, and values involved in the contracting process. In addition, managers have to be salespersons when getting a contracting out program approved. None of these three roles—analyst, broker, and salesperson—is enhanced if the process is not regarded as open and the managers not seen as honest.

Master All Details. Contracting out covers many specific items—all of which are important—and the top manager should master these crucial details. However, contracting out is really no different from other potentially controversial programs. In every case, including contracting, the manager is expected to master most details if she wants to effectively advocate or even discuss dispassionately the issue at hand.

The manager must be in control of the legal issues. Does state law permit contracting and, if so, under what conditions? What are the legal implications of employee layoffs, contractor selection, bid requirements, or revoking the contract for nonperformance? These are questions for legal counsel, but the manager's ability to answer them, at least generally, will do much to defuse initial opposition and increase confidence in a contracting out recommendation. It is not reasonable to expect managers to act as lawyers, but it is wise for managers to appear knowledgeable in the early discussion of contracting out. Legislators or chief executives can ask the attorney for specific details if they want detailed information.

The same argument applies to many other areas involved in contracting out. The manager should have a grasp of the major purchasing details, such as bid specifications, negotiated and formally bid contracts, and availability of contractors. He should likewise have answers to questions about the financial implications of a contract, such as the cost of layoffs, the probable cost of contract service, the agency's cost of monitoring and bidding, and specific estimates of the amount of money to be saved by contracting out. Many of these figures, of course, can only be estimates based on comparable situations in other jurisdictions. Even so, the manager's credibility, as well as the fate of the contracting out proposal, depends on mastery of the financial details.

Any manager seriously arguing a contracting out proposal should also be conversant with program details. If the contract is street sweeping, the manager should be able to explain how a contract might affect sweeping schedules, if any new parking regulations will be necessary, if there are likely to be changes in sweeping times, and so on.

Questions about program monitoring and the contractor's responsibility for performance will arise. The manager should be able to deal knowledgeably with all aspects of monitoring and performance questions and should also have some knowledge of contract provisions to compel performance (see Chapter Six).

The need for the manager or chief executive to have complete mastery of details varies with the issue. Sometimes contracting out involves a high-level policy or political issue, and there is a correspondingly diminished interest in the details. Such is the case when a governor is interested in contracting for specific areas to keep employee levels low. In this case, the specific costs and most of the details are less important, and the case may be settled on purely political grounds, with little reference to technical facts. However, even in these cases, there eventually will be reviews of the performance of the contract, and political figures may then wish that they or their staff had paid more attention to these technical "details."

Often the proposed contract does not break new ground. The contract may simply be the extension of an existing contract or a contract for services of a kind already routinely accepted by the agency (such as a financial audit or professional engineering study). In such cases, there is less expectation that the chief executive will be intimately conversant with all details, and the manager will be more likely to be able to rely on the staff for information. However, someone in the agency should be intimately familiar with every contract.

Remember That the Agency Is Ultimately Responsible for the Contract. In the final analysis, service delivery is up to the agency. When things go wrong, the agency bears most of the pressure and discomfort of complaints about the service or criticism of the contractor. No amount of sophistry about contractor responsibility will satisfy any users or citizens. The agency must take some action to improve the service, whether or not the contractor is at fault.

This is far from self-evident. Even as managers and political leaders proclaim, "Of course, we are ultimately responsible," they sometimes behave in ways that imply, "It's the contractor's fault." This is evident when a city contracts with the largest intergovernmental contractor, usually the county, and then blames the county for service problems without seriously considering other alternatives. This is also apparent when managers overlook less than effective service by a private contractor, giving as a reason the lack of competitive alternatives, instead of aggressively searching for alternatives.

Accepting full responsibility means intensive, proactive monitoring rather than simply processing complaints. Matters such as performance specifications, performance standards, inspections, observations, and written contractor reports should be part of every contract (see Chapter Six). Training employees in contract monitoring methods and assigning competent employees to the monitoring process are also the manager's responsibility.

In assuming full responsibility for the contract, the manager should insist on agency protection clauses in the contract and be willing to use them. There are times when the contractor does not perform and should be penalized for such failures, with the ultimate sanction of voiding the contract being a real possibility. Insisting on the sanctions in the contract will do much to keep out contractors who will not or cannot provide top service.

Insisting on sanctions includes the willingness to actually change contractors when necessary. This is no small matter, partly because changing contractors is sometimes controversial and always unpleasant, but even more because it is a time-consuming job. It usually involves rebidding the contract, reawarding a bid, arranging new monitoring systems, and many other technical matters that take time and effort. Managers who are not deeply committed to the public service are usually reluctant to spend this much time. If the contractor is not failing abjectly, it is often easier to avoid the use of sanctions.

Another example of putting the agency first is the willingness to use city forces to develop benchmark costs or to provide a competitive alternative to complete reliance on an outside contractor. Although some cities (such as Phoenix and Minneapolis) have the city's solid waste collection service compete with private contractors, this technique is rarely used. This is probably because it takes more effort than simply relying on either public employees or outside contractors. Contracting with several private agencies is another way of demonstrating that the agency cares about services and is willing to experiment and innovate to obtain the best mix of public and private services.

Contract Only for Legitimate Reasons. There are a number of very good reasons for contracting out. In many, if not most, cases, contracting out is less expensive than in-house service. When the true cost of contracting out for the same level of service is less than all costs of providing the service, contracting out should be used. When contracting out is the only way to obtain scarce, temporary, or highly technical services, contracting out should be used. (This assumes that no amount of good management in the form of recruiting and adequately paying public employees can overcome these problems.)

There are several other good reasons for contracting out. Sometimes it is useful to contract out in order to establish benchmark costs that can serve as a measure for future provision of that service, whether public or private. (Often, partial contracting through dividing the work among several contractors and the agency itself, as is occasionally done in the case in refuse disposal, is used for this purpose.) Occasionally, as in many small cities, contracting out is a policy adopted to maintain limited commitment to a range of municipal services.

A final effective use of contracting out involves the need to acquire private financing for major capital items, such as a new prison or wastewater plant. If agency financial problems face increasing public demand, the agency may simply have to rely on private financing. One difficulty with private financing is that it may often involve private operation of the new facility as the quid pro quo for financing. Under these circumstances, it is hard to separate construction and financing costs from operating costs. However, the use of contracting out to obtain financing is now well established.

There are some arrangements that confuse and complicate the contracting out process. Some contracts are designed to reduce service levels, thereby diverting attention from the unpopular (although sometimes necessary) act of cutting service levels by pointing to reduced costs. It is far better to openly cut staff and reduce services than to contract out to achieve the same result. These kinds of contracts add bidding and contract administration costs to the agency, which could have been avoided simply by facing the need to cut back services.

Another undesirable use of the contracting out process is to transfer difficult or seemingly intractable problems to the contractor, as when the agency or city wishes to get rid of unpopular unions or employees. It is tempting to wash one's hands of employee relations problems by contracting out the service, but such a step rarely solves the real problem. Not only does the agency run the risk of having the union or employees drag their feet and raise a political issue, but the problem—usually lack of good management—will remain. If the root problem is not solved, future problems will arise in other situations.

A good rule to follow is the "sunshine rule": Any reason for contracting out that cannot survive in sunshine (that is, in complete openness) is not a good enough reason. For example, if the reason for contracting out cannot withstand a hostile press conference, it may not be a good enough reason. Thomas Jefferson said the same thing over 200 years ago when writing to a friend: "Whenever you are to do a thing, though it can never be known but to yourself, ask yourself how you would act were all the world looking at you, and act accordingly" (Jefferson, [1775] 1974, p. 126).

Four Don'ts

Don't Contract Out When the Policy Is Controversial. Contracting out is ill advised if the proposal is controversial, has strong opposition, or will divide the community. Controversy normally develops from unions and employees who face the loss of jobs or, at least, the prospect of lower-paid jobs with the private contractor. Opposition can also develop simply because opponents oppose contracting in principle, the likely contractor, or losing agency control over the function. There are many reasons, good or bad, for opposing contracting out. In general, where there is strong opposition, contracting out is, more often than not, a bad idea.

Since there are many cases where contracting out has worked in the face of strong opposition, such as in Berwyn, Illinois (see Case Study 4), it may seem odd, even cowardly, to suggest that one not contract out in the face of political opposition. The problem with contracting out given such opposition is that attention to the real advantages of contracting out will be lost in recrimination about side issues, such as the loss of some public sector jobs. The real issues—such as increased quality of service and obtaining better financing or better equipment—are likely to be lost in arguments over the possible loss of jobs.

Contracting out can become controversial and divisive rather than being viewed as a neutral management tool for improving services. If approved over substantial opposition, there are greater risks of contractor reluctance to bid because of dislike of controversy, and even existing contracts may be endangered by fallout from the specific controversy. And, as happened in South San Francisco (see Case Study 3), controversial contracts may flip-flop back from contractors to public provision, with all the difficulties that ensue.

If contracting out, for any reason, is controversial, it is probably not wise to force the issue against opposition. A better strategy is to attempt to convince opponents over time that contracting out is an effective solution to the problem facing the agency. If it is a serious service delivery problem, for example, the situations that lead to consideration of contracting will later point to contracting. If they do not arise again, perhaps it was best not to contract in the first place.

Don't Burn Bridges Behind You. Another rule about contracting out is largely common sense. Wise managers and politicians avoid actions that commit them to a single course of action: they do not make permanent, absolute changes. In other words, they never "burn their bridges behind them." Prepare for the possibility that things may go wrong with the contract—it may receive no bidders, the contract may be declared invalid by a court, the contractor may perform poorly, political leaders may change their minds on the desirability of contracting, or any of a hundred unexpected events may occur.

Not burning bridges means always being able to make necessary changes to correct contracting out problems. These corrections can be for very serious problems, such as having a contractor declare bankruptcy, or relatively minor matters, such as small contract infractions. The principle is that every likely occurrence should have a remedy that still permits contracting out or, in extreme cases, allows an orderly return to in-house service provision.

A host of things can go wrong with the best-planned contract. Some of these problems are primarily technical. In these cases, not burning bridges means being able to make adjustments without endangering the contract or contracting process. Is there only one bid, and that too high? The bidding process should provide for the ability to reject all bids. Have citizen complaints increased? The agency should have monitored the contract well enough to determine whether the contractor has really failed to perform, and the contract should have provisions for the deduction of money in the event of lack of performance. It should not be necessary to review the whole contract in such cases. Have legal problems surfaced in awarding the contract that, although minor, require some time to correct? Be sure that the rules for the award allow the agency time to correct these problems and that the contract provisions bind the successful contractor or all bidders so that they must maintain their offers for a reasonable period of time. Is there reason to believe that a contractor will receive no competition for a forthcoming contract renewal bid and that she intends to present a much higher bid for a renewal? Be sure that the contract contains a provision that contracts may be extended for a certain amount of time at the current rate, while you seek an alternative supplier. (Lowballing works only when an agency has not endeavored to develop competition for the contractor.)

There are a number of techniques, most widely used, to prevent agencies determined to contract out from burning their bridges. Unless you are positive that you have found a contractor who will (1) bid low on the contract, (2) meet with ease all performance specifications, (3) be immune to labor or financial difficulties, and (4) return time after time to the bidding table with a rock-bottom bid, you should consider the need for the techniques that follow.

The contractor may have little competition, so you should consider (1) partial contracting, with city forces doing some of the work (see Chapter Six); (2) creating competition by working with other agencies, such as another government agency; or (3) dividing the work among several private companies. Mechanisms such as performance or contract interruption bonds (see Chapter Six) also help in such cases, although large bond requirements themselves may depress competition.

The worst bridge fires are those caused by emotional commitments to contracting out. This is just as unwise as absolute commitment to in-house services. Emotional or psychological commitments to contracting out prevent considering the reduction in costs or improvements in service that can be gained by switching to in-house performance or even to alternative private contractors. This kind of blindness can be seen in contract cities' managers and political leaders, who often pay dearly for the security of a permanent, convenient contractor such as the county (Chapter Seven).

Contracting out is an administrative tool for improving public services. Commitment to contracting as a "way of life" or to contracting as "the answer" to problems ranging from labor relations to paring expenses is neither good management nor good politics.

In a complex, fast-changing world, agencies need to preserve the ability to provide public services in a variety of ways and forms. Psychological commitment to a specific way of providing services jeopardizes needed flexibility.

Don't Contract Out When There Is the Least Hint of Corruption. Scandals have often tarnished the reputation of contracting out. Opponents of contracting make their most convincing point when they point to actual or alleged corruption in the contracting process. Supporters of contracting out admit that corruption may be the bête noire of the contracting process. The seriousness of corruption or scandals cannot be overemphasized, although all the money lost by dishonesty in contracting is probably only a fraction of that lost by managing honest contracts poorly or entering into unwise but honest contracts.

Likewise, contracts that present even the appearance of potential impropriety should be avoided. Public trust is crucial to the contracting process. Good contracts can be marred by their association with improper contracts. Contracting out, like Caesar's wife, should be above suspicion. Many people are eager to think the worst of contracting, and the scent of scandal, let alone its actual appearance, may damage the process.

The items that spark suspicions or fears of improprieties can be (1) negotiated bids, (2) sole-source contracts, (3) secret meetings about contracts or with contractors, (4) incomplete public information about the contract, and (5) failure to disclose any government official's ties to contractors.

Avoiding potential scandals does not mean refusing to contract. Even if there is some intention, or merely willingness, by various parties to engage in illegal activity, such activities can often be avoided by contract provisions calling for full disclosure or competitive bidding, with the bids opened and awarded in public. Likewise, contract specifications can be carefully drawn and rigorously enforced.

Illegalities occur most often when the opportunity arises, and opportunities arise most often when checks against dishonesty are weakest. Criminal activities in contracting destroy public support for the entire contracting process.

Don't Forget Why You Are (or Should Be) Contracting Out. The basic reason for contracting is to preserve the quality of the service being rendered. Thus, the ultimate test is whether citizens are satisfied with public services. If they are satisfied, changing to a contract is probably not a good idea. If they are not satisfied, making some change is necessary. Of course, contracting out is often done specifically to cut costs (or to obtain financing, scarce skills, or advanced equipment). But it is important to keep in mind the basic issue: Contracting out should occur to provide more effective public services or at least to maintain current services at lower cost. Any other reason trivializes public services and leads inevitably to weak programs, whether public or private, that are badly managed.

The argument for contracting out to save money is that the public will not or cannot pay for services. However, citizens are more than willing to pay for those public services they appreciate. They rarely demand lower service levels because they are paying too much; they usually want to pay less for some preferred level of services. The issue is providing the level and quality of service desired; if contracting out does this at less expense, it should be done. The first question should be, however, to discover an acceptable level of service. Only then should the mode of service delivery—contract or public—be considered.

Police patrol units provide an example. For many years, cities used two-person patrol cars in high-crime areas—and paid a high cost—because they were concerned with officer safety. (Some cities still use them.) This high-cost way of delivering police services was justified by citizen desires for such a level of police protection. It became clear later that improved police-headquarters communication and changed patrol techniques made one-person units effective. This change also spread a limited number of officers over a wider area, with only the added cost of additional patrol cars. At that time, the public came to accept (to the extent that most citizens were aware of the change) a different level of service. The police budget was no lower, but there were more patrol units in the field. At this time, other agencies using one-person units became possibilities for contracting, since their service delivery systems were now similar. Contracting out was a possibility. The issue was primarily the level of service and only secondarily financial.

Lower costs are only one advantage that contracting out has over in-house provision of services. It may be easier to obtain financing from private sources; scarce managerial and technical skills may be more readily acquired by contracting out the service; technologically advanced equipment may become available upon contracting; and contracting may free managerial time for other issues. These should be secondary issues, however. The crucial question is whether the service is being effectively delivered. If the service is wholly satisfactory as currently provided, the agency should not change.

If the public believes that certain services should be delivered in a certain way (police by a city, refuse disposal by a contractor), this is probably the way they should continue to be delivered. Ultimately, citizens demand public services of a certain level and type, regardless of whether they are being provided by public or private employees. The agency's job is to provide those services efficiently and in a way acceptable to the recipients. If the service is contracted, it should be only because quality of services can be maintained most effectively.

Summary

This book has covered the background and extent of contracting out, as well as suggestions for when and when not to contract out (Part One), and most of the technical issues in contracting (Part Two). It has discussed the major kinds of contractors along with six sample contracts (Part Three) and the political aspects of contracting out (Part Four).

This final chapter accomplishes several purposes. It summarizes the political aspects of contracting by summarizing eight do's and don'ts for managers, politicians, or civic leaders considering contracting out. These do's and don'ts are more than mere political advice, however. They encompass, in a commonsense way, the issues raised in the first eleven chapters of this book. The four do's are to be open and direct in all dealings about contracting out; master all details of any contracting out proposal; remember that the agency, rather than the contractor, is ultimately responsible for the contract; and contract only for legitimate (not merely legal) purposes. The don'ts are to avoid controversial contracts, avoid permanent commitments to a contractor or contract that cannot be terminated or resolved without embarrassment, zealously avoid even the faintest aroma of corruption, and keep citizens' preferences and attitudes firmly in mind.

These do's and don'ts will not prepare the contract, select the lowest bidder, or monitor the contract. They will ensure, however, that effective contracting becomes more likely, that poor contracts become less likely, and that contracting out will be considered on its merits.

Resource A

Contracting Out Case Studies

This Resource contains the case studies and background material that exemplify in some detail the richness and complexity of contracting out. The basic issues of contracting appear in each chapter; the specific examples appear here.

Case Study 1, contractor operations management of Prince George's data-procession operation, indicates that outside technical competence can help resolve internal problems. Despite lack of good performance standards and some controversy over employee displacement, the contract saved at least $350,000 the first year, with no serious decline in quality.

The Lakewood plan (Case Study 2) is a rather extensive and highly institutionalized system in which the County of Los Angeles provides a wide range of services to municipalities. These services range from the routine, such as engineering staff services, to the sensitive, such as law enforcement. The county sets service standards and prices. The agreements are a classic case of intergovernmental contracting.

The South San Francisco case (Case Study 3) shows how injecting a revolutionary organizational change into a social system not prepared politically and socially for it led to rejection of the change. In this case, a traditional, blue-collar city rejected a change to a privately managed public works program, despite evidence that the change actually saved money. Contracting out may not be for every unit, and failure to prepare the agency for contracting out will further dim the prospects for change.

Berwyn, an ethnic community west of Chicago, at first glance, resembles South San Francisco (Case Study 4). Here, however, strong-arm partisan politics pushed the change through, and garbage collection is still contracted out ten years later. Corruption, as well as bureaucratic and political intransigence, doomed in-house services.

Contracting out has more than its share of successes, but there are also some monumental failures. Five of these failures are reported here. They involve pervasive corruption exaggerated by political intervention in the federal General Services Administration (Case Study 5); incompetence of the federal Department of Energy in contracting out far too many consulting services with far too little gained in return (Case Study 6); criminal neglect in Beverly nursing home services that resulted in substandard nursing care and the deaths of patients (Case Study 7); private incompetence by Datacom Systems in collecting fines for unpaid traffic tickets, which led to national media coverage that embarrassed Yonkers, New York, and New York City (Case Study 8); and, finally, private mismanagement on a grand scale of the Convention Center in Baltimore, which, although finally corrected by the city, left a trail of unpaid bills (Case Study 9).

The final part of the Resources deals with a phenomenon of increasing importance: international privatization, including contracting out. Privatization, including contracting out, is widely seen as an alternative to government ownership or operation. In addition to general reports of privatization in countries as diverse as the Philippines and Jordan, three examples are given. Canada contracts out programs such as snow removal and part services. Great Britain has sold off many of its holdings in private corporations as well as requiring local authorities and the National Health Service to contract out many services hitherto provided publicly. Falck, an eighty-year-old corporation, provides ambulance and fire protection to a majority of Danish municipalities and has grown in a country with a large public sector, even though all employees are, by law, unionized.

Case Study 1: Data Processing in Prince George's County

Description. This project concerned the Prince George's County (PGC) (Maryland) Office of Central Services and involved a management contract with Planning Research Corporation to manage and operate the county's central data-processing functions. (See Prince George's County, n.d., for a complete account of this case.) PRC's responsibilities included effective operation of the central computer in the county Administration Building; related scheduling of standard products; defining elements of data entry; maintaining and modifying existing systems; and, with county approval, developing new systems at the rate of six man-years per year. The contract with PRC was for a minimum of five years. Performance incentives were built in for exceeding contractual obligations. The county maintained a five-person contract administration unit.

Costs and Benefits. Estimated first-year savings in FY 82 were $350,000. A fixed price, four-year contract for 1983–86 was designed to continue this annual savings. Benefits included cost savings and other productivity assets, such as the ability of PRC to attract and maintain a well-balanced technical staff, to make staff changes compatible with changing technical requirements, and to apply a broader base of professional know-how to the operation and enhancement of the existing system. The county experienced problems in all of these areas prior to the contract.

Implementation Issues. Initial results since the PRC takeover in July 1981, indicated conformance with contractual commitments and achievement of initial goals and plans under the facilities management concept. Considerable staff time, in addition to the utilization of outside consultants, was anticipated in order to properly prepare a request for proposal and a comprehensive contract document to ensure that the county was adequately protected.

The explanation of the Prince George's County data-processing contract was from county sources and does not indicate the range of issues that the county faced. For some time, the county had not been completely satisfied with the data-processing operation, for a number of reasons. Doubtful of the likelihood of improving in-house operation, management entered into the present facilities management contract, which has some interesting provisions as well as some employee problems.

The contract has a 14 percent incentive fee, which ranges from 7 percent below bid price if performance is unsatisfactory to 7 percent above bid price for top-rated service. Performance is rated by a team of county employees using a formal rating system, but evaluation of quality is hampered by lack of straightforward performance measures.

Uneasiness over the proposed contract led to declines in employee morale and productivity of the data-processing operation. Arranging the transfer of employees to the contractor also proved to be difficult, although about 60 percent were eventually transferred to the contractor with guarantees of ninety-day employment.

Most county users were relatively satisfied with the services, which appear similar to those under county operations. Prince George's County representatives made a number of recommendations for similar facility management contracts, most of which involved the political, human, and behavioral aspects of a major change, rather than involving technical issues (Valente and Manchester, 1984).

Case Study 2: The Lakewood Plan

Background. The Lakewood plan is the classic IGC arrangement, at least as far as cities are concerned (Sonenblum, Ries, and Kirlin, 1977). The Lakewood plan is named for the city in Los Angeles County (California) that inaugurated in 1954 the extensive system of county contracts to cities. A city can purchase all or part of every municipal service, from police protection to county personnel services. The rates are preset, as is the minimum level of services, but the city can generally ar-

range for levels of service above the minimum. This system of
services has developed over the years from an experiment to
a stable system of services that thirty or more cities use. All of
these cities incorporated since 1954, at least partially because
they had the option of contracting with the county.

The Lakewood plan demonstrates the range of issues surrounding IGC, illustrating some of its best and worst aspects.
It is a proven plan in which all contracts have been tested over
time and in a wide range of conditions. The contracts involve
county employees who provide a uniform minimum level of
areawide services, so the plan contributes to political and administrative unification in the area. The contracts have a preset
price and minimum level of service, neither of which can vary,
so the contracting parties are relieved of negotiations. The potential city recipient can see how the plan operates elsewhere before
entering into a contract. The plan, supported by state legislation, is largely invulnerable to legal challenge. In the 1950s the
state also helped by giving cities shares of the sales tax. This
was sufficient to allow incorporation of communities based on
using the sales tax to pay for county services. These sales-tax
receipts alleviated incorporation opposition owing to fear of
higher property taxes.

From the narrow perspective of the recipient city and from
a broader perspective of metropolitan unification, the Lakewood
plan has been a resounding success. From some perspectives,
however, the system has a darker side, as a later section will
show. First, it is necessary to examine the system in some historical and operational detail.

History. Contracting with municipalities began early in
the century, with 1907 contracts for tax assessment and collection. During the 1930s and 1940s, the county entered, on a
limited basis, into contracts with cities for building permits and
inspections, animal control, street maintenance, personnel services, and planning and zoning. These initial contracts set the
stage for the more complete array of services to be later offered.
A direct cause was the continual criticism of the County of Los
Angeles by the City of Los Angeles for allegedly subsidizing
unincorporated areas. The city pressed for either incorporation

or special tax districts for communities desiring urban levels of services. The county, loath to change, feared that incorporations would decrease its influence. Eventually realizing that incorporations were inevitable, the county began to devise ways to retain its dominant position in the urban area.

In 1954 the City of Lakewood became the second city in the county since 1930 to incorporate. Justification for incorporation was largely that no increases in local taxes were necessary, because the city would contract with the county for all services and pay for them with revenues available to incorporated cities. This position was easier for future cities to maintain, since in 1958 state law increased all city revenues. One cent of the sales tax went to the community from which it originated, if the community was incorporated. This further fueled incorporation activity. Between 1956 and 1965, thirty-one cities incorporated, all but three heavily dependent on the county for municipal services.

Of these thirty-one cities, eleven incorporated to gain property tax advantages; ten incorporated for home rule purposes or for land-use control; six incorporated to avoid annexations to adjoining cities; and four were dissatisfied with county services (Sonenblum, Ries, and Kirlin, 1977). Whatever the reason, the availability of county services under contracts was a major reason for incorporation, and many fewer cities would have incorporated if they faced the job of creating their own services. (This prospect may have convinced many to contract with the county after incorporation, even if they had not originally intended to do so.)

The availability of relatively inexpensive county services and a source of revenue from sales taxes have kept property taxes down, since by 1970 twenty-one of the new cities had no property tax (Sonenblum, Ries, and Kirlin, 1977).

The key issue favoring incorporation was apparently not the full range of municipal services available, since few cities used all services. Rather, it was the availability of police services provided by the sheriff. Indeed, those few new cities that chose to create their own police departments did not contract for many other services.

The reason that police services proved so crucial was twofold. First, the service was somewhat subsidized, because state laws compelled sheriffs to offer minimal police services to unincorporated areas. The cost of contract services thus included a subsidy presumably equal to the cost of this minimal service, which the sheriff had to provide anyway. Second, the sheriff, a potent political figure, made many options available to cities, including one-man patrol cars and variations in levels of service. These were all designed to suit individual municipal tastes for service (Kirlin, 1973).

By 1973 the wave of incorporations had declined because contract service costs, particularly for law enforcement, were increasing. The sheriff's activities that were rendered at less than true cost have been limited, and the cost has gone up accordingly. Consequently, demand for county contract services has stabilized.

The Extent and Type of Lakewood Plan Intergovernmental Contracts. Most city contracts involve six county departments: Sheriff, Roads, Health, Engineering, Hospitals, and the Registar/Recorder. The Sheriff, Roads, and Engineering Departments accounted for the largest share of the $19.3 million in 1973 contract revenues. The Registrar/Recorder had a contract for elections with seventy-seven of the seventy-eight cities in the county, while the other five departments provided from two services (Hospitals) to twelve (Sheriff).

Table 14 describes similar contracts twelve years later in 1985. The most popular contracts by then were general services agreements, presumably covering elections, with eighty-three of the eighty-four cities. Other popular contracts were with the Health Department for general services (eighty-one cities); with the district attorney for local prosecutions (sixty-seven cities); with the Public Works Department for subdivision parcel checking (fifty-eight), traffic signal maintenance (fifty-six), and sewer maintenance (thirty-nine); and with the sheriff for general law enforcement (thirty-six), traffic law enforcement (thirty-five), and detective services (thirty-five).

The figures in Table 14 provide some detail and indicate the range of the county's services. The existence of little-used

Table 14. Municipal Contracts Selected by Los Angeles County (1985).

Department	City Contracts
County clerk	
Microfilm storage	12
Health	
General services	81
Massage parlor/technician examination	6
District attorney	
City ordinance prosecution	67
Animal care	
Animal control	30
Animal shelter	5
General services	
General agreement	81
Public works	
Street maintenance	12
Traffic signal maintenance	56
Construction inspection	5
Building inspection	30
Sewer maintenance	39
Parcel map check	58
Master house map service	21
Engineering staff service	27
Sheriff	
Helicopter patrol	5
General law enforcement	36
Business law investigation	10
Crossing guard	3
School safety	2
Community relations	18
Traffic law enforcement	35
Detective services	35
Bicycle safety/pedestrian office	1
Disaster law enforcement	0

Source: Los Angeles County, 1985.

services, such as crossing guards, shows that the county is ready to offer almost any service that may be desired.

County provision of services is well accepted by all cities, not just contract cities. Since only thirty-seven cities were contract cities (members of the Contract City Association and not associated with the Independent Cities Association), independent cities also use the county for specific contracts. The only differences between contract and noncontract cities are (1) contract cities use more county contracts; (2) contract cities contract more often for police services (thirty-three of thirty-seven contract for general law enforcement); and (3) contract cities are younger (over thirty contract cities have incorporated since the Lakewood plan became available in 1957).

Setting Contract Prices and Service Levels. When dealing with private or nonprofit contractors, price is a crucial issue. Whether the price is negotiated or comes in a sealed bid, it can rarely be predicted precisely in advance. Although the level of service can be negotiated with contractors, contracting is not officially justified as a means of cutting or raising levels of service.

This process is reversed in the Lakewood plan. The contract rate and minimum service levels are already established. Additional levels, although available in most cases, are rarely purchased by cities. For each county contract service, the county auditor publishes an annual price list. The contract price is stated as an hourly charge per type of employee to be assigned under the contract. The law enforcement and traffic contract, for example, is an annual rate for all traffic and patrol cars (Sonenblum, Ries, and Kirlin, 1977). This price cannot be negotiated, for it is based on items set by state law. The intrusion of state law occurred because the legislature, at the urging of contract cities, established the principle of a specific subsidy, recognizing the responsibility of the county to provide a minimum level of service to incorporated areas. County departments, since they cannot set or negotiate prices, now claim that they do not seek contracts but only respond to requests.

The county requires minimum levels of service, which are established by the departments offering the service. Street maintenance contracts read: "Ordinary maintenance and repair of streets within the City . . . shall be maintained and repaired in the same manner, to the same extent, and kept in a similar condition of suitability as similarly situated County highways." Law enforcement contracts read: "It is hereby agreed that the minimum level of basic law enforcement shall be determined by the County" (Sonenblum, Ries, and Kirlin, 1977).

For all contracts other than law enforcement, the county performs the work as requested under the contract provisions and then bills the city on an hourly basis. Under a contract for traffic signs and markings, for example, the county will repaint lane lines as often as it deems necessary to maintain a minimum level equivalent to county streets. The county will then bill the city for hourly costs specified in the contract. The city may ask for additional work at the specified rate, but may not reduce the level of service. In effect, the city trades loss of control over the service in return for certainty of price, a highly professional service, and flexibility of operations. (The city has no employees hired and only a year-to-year contract.) However, the cost is substantial. By the mid 1970s, the Roads Department was losing contracts to private contractors, particularly street sweeping and signal maintenance (Sonenblum, Ries, and Kirlin, 1977).

The Lakewood Plan in Perspective. Every IG contract is unique, and the Lakewood plan is worthy of attention only because of its scope. Because it is such a comprehensive and well-used system, it has substantial impact on the metropolitan region as well as having a specific impact on the cities it serves.

Two major policy issues arise from the Lakewood plan. The first is that cities will not consider alternatives to providing their own services unless alternatives, such as the Lakewood plan, are available. The second is that once a contract is reached, cities rarely abandon county contracts for cost, but only because the service is perceived to infringe on local control (Sonenblum, Ries, and Kirlin, 1977).

Contract cities are generally poorer than independent (noncontract) cities and spend less money than noncontract cities. Contract cities "give up a measure of local control in the hope of gaining economy and reduced financial burden. In this they succeed, but they also purchase less service" (Sonenblum, Ries, and Kirlin, 1977, p. xix).

The levels of service in Lakewood plan cities were often quite low, since the cities were spending less than independent cities but buying a service that was relatively more expensive. Providing relatively low levels of service was the only way to do this. County services were highly professional but, due to their costs, were only used at a low level, particularly in law enforcement. Low levels of service and less local control were acceptable only because the cities were newly incorporated and had not become (and did not want to become) accustomed to higher levels of service.

From a broader perspective, the Lakewood plan has been a mixed blessing. The plan is a model of efficiency and has unified governmental management throughout much of the county. On the other hand, the availability of the plan has also fragmented the area, since cities incorporated because the plan was available.

Miller (1981) alleges that (1) incorporations made possible by the Lakewood plan encouraged the suburbanization of businesses and residences, weakening the tax bases of older cities such as Compton, a mostly black city; and that (2) the Lakewood plan represents a successful attempt to reduce property tax burdens and limit the expansion of government operations (rather than simply being a neutral administrative tool for efficiency).

The first criticism, that the Lakewood plan further fragmented the governmental area at the expense of older cities, claims too much for governmental cooperative arrangements. The suburbanization trend was much too powerful a movement for the Lakewood plan to halt. In America, suburbanization and its consequences wait for no one—government or otherwise. The second criticism, that the Lakewood plan aimed to reduce tax burdens and limit governmental growth, is hardly news to any close observer. In fact, these are two of the primary reasons for contracting out by cities and other governmental units.

Miller (1981) also observes that the efficiency or inefficiency of county operations was never considered in the decision to incorporate. Since incorporation almost always included the decision to contract with the county, this supports Sonenblum, Ries, and Kirlin's (1977) view that decisions to contract were not economic decisions.

The Lakewood plan points out some of the issues inherent in IGC. IG contracts, as contrasted to private contracts, place emphasis on cooperation, informality, and contractors who understand government operations. These contracts clearly do not turn on the issue of costs, at least not in Los Angeles County, and are less politically and administratively dangerous than private contracts. The Lakewood plan tends to support the general observations about IG contracts made in Chapter Seven.

Case Study 3:
Private Contracting in South San Francisco

Background. On May 31, 1972, the City of South San Francisco (California) initiated a major reorganization that provided for private management of the city's Ecological Department. (See Levinson, 1976, for a full account of this case.) The move was both controversial and short lived, as the following account reveals. South San Francisco lies directly south of San Francisco, immediately adjacent to San Francisco International Airport. An industrial suburb, its 47,000 people were primarily blue-collar workers, mostly from Northern European ethnic groups. There was considerable conflict between old-timers, who were very traditional, and newcomers, who often supported change. Labor organizations were influential in local politics. City employees, who usually lived in the city, were politically influential and often obtained their jobs based on whom they knew rather than what they knew.

In the early 1970s, South San Francisco faced a slight economic downturn, which resulted in the city using past years' reserves to finance current operations. The council, split as usual, did not seem to be exercising financial leadership.

A new city manager, Gale Dreisbach, had been hired in 1971 and took immediate action to cut expenses for the coming year. He froze department budgets and new employee hires, contracted out payroll preparation to a bank, and created a new finance department. Dreisbach was also concerned about the effectiveness of the Engineering Department. He conferred with VTN, a large private civil engineering firm, about contracting out the city's public works functions. (VTN had previously worked for South San Francisco on engineering projects.)

At Dreisbach's request, VTN reviewed several cities similar to South San Francisco, concluding that South San Francisco operated most functions at higher costs than other cities. These costs were attributed to inefficiencies, lack of coordination among the nine different departments doing public work functions, and lack of control resulting in cost overruns. VTN proposed a major reorganization of engineering-related functions, with VTN organizing and directing the city engineering department.

The reorganization was to create a Department of Ecological Development. It was to be headed by a VTN vice-president, Fred Hull, who also would be director of Public Works, city engineer, and director of Parks and Recreation. At the same time, the VTN vice-president would hold his private position, working full time for the city for six months and half time the other six months. VTN would provide a group of consultants to help the city handle all engineering aspects. These consultants were to operate as needed, to save the costs of full-time city employees. The new Department of Ecological Development was to include the departments involved with planning, engineering, building, streets, the marina, sanitation, landscape, and the garage. The plan was projected to save some $430,000 the first year.

VTN received a one-year contract at a closed-door council session that lasted over four hours. The contract had not been discussed with department heads or city employees and had not been mentioned in the press. This radical reversal of administrative policy was made possible by a change in the city council at the last election, which gave the "new city" faction a three-to-two majority on the council, although the vote on the reorganization and contract was unanimous.

The unexpected change, which included the dismissal of five city engineers, caused considerable controversy among employees. The employees, traditionally politically active, objected strenuously through their union. Union opposition in South San Francisco, a strong-union, blue-collar, industrial city, was a force to be reckoned with. A threatened strike within a month of the contract was averted at the last minute.

The VTN Experiment. From the start, VTN's operations were plagued by opposition from unions, employees, and a vocal council minority. (After voting for the contract, the minority "old city" faction soon began to routinely oppose most VTN projects.) Objections to VTN were mainly based on the secrecy and lack of debate over the change, the terminations of the city engineers, and an increased turnover rate of city employees. Underlying the conflict were two issues: employee opposition and a council division between old and new city employees.

Because of bitter opposition, small issues loomed large. The council minority criticized VTN manager Hull and city manager Dreisbach over management of a rat-proofing ordinance for new buildings, renewal of a city–school district joint powers agreement, and even testimonials for retiring employees. Anything VTN proposed became controversial, and the bills for VTN were always approved by a split three-to-two vote. A capital improvement budget was challenged by a dissident councilman. Hull's position of ecological director, in the view of many, involved a conflict of interest, as he was a vice-president of VTN at the same time. VTN's semiannual report to the council, showing savings over municipal operation, did not appease opponents of the contract.

The VTN controversy reached an impasse when city councilman Gordon Boblitt died when a truck he was repairing slipped off its blocks, crushing him. His election a year earlier had given the "new city" faction a three-to-two council majority, the margin by which VTN's work was being approved. Boblitt's death left the council split two to two, and votes for VTN work projects began to lose.

Before the election to replace Bobblitt could be held, VTN chose to ask the council to release them from the contract three months prior to the end of their contract year. VTN president Vin Westfall asked the council to terminate the agreement because they could not do a professional job with the present division on the council. He noted that an administrative pay plan, a master drainage plan, a joint city and school board plan to construct a baseball field, a revised sewer rate structure, and even a request to apply for a marina feasibility study had all been turned down or received opposition.

Even the request to withdraw was subject to council wrangling before it was finally approved. VTN agreed to complete existing projects for the city to ensure some transition to a new system, but two-to-two votes on the council continued until the election a month later. The VTN contract, although it was now void, and the restructured city government became the central issue in the campaign. An anti-VTN member of the "old city" group was elected, with a plurality of the votes cast, and gave the anti-VTN faction a three-to-two majority.

The new council also reasserted its power by restricting the city manager's power to hire and fire department heads. Realizing he had fallen out of favor, Dreisbach resigned shortly thereafter.

The VTN experiment had relatively little impact on South San Francisco, even though VTN remained as the consulting engineer for the balance of the year. The next budget for the city largely restored the pre-VTN organizational structure. Direct contracts between department heads and council, previously restricted by Dreisbach, increased. The number of city employees began to rise as departments expanded their organizations. The number of employees increased from 285 during the VTN contract to 350 two years after the contract was terminated. The operating budget soared 35 percent in the year following the VTN contract.

Despite the figures, observers are divided over the amount the VTN contract saved, with one newspaper describing savings as "nickles and dimes," compared to the official estimate of VTN and Dreisbach that the contract would eventually save $400,000 annually. Most of the savings were from hiring fewer employees; public works personnel services were $10,000 lower in the VTN contract year than the previous year.

Ironically, a year after the VTN contract termination, a regular council election resulted in the defeat of the original two anti-VTN council members. This was no pro-VTN vote, since all candidates agreed that the VTN issue was dead and buried.

Two years later, one of those original members won election again on an anti–city manager ticket, and shortly thereafter the council dismissed Dreisbach's replacement, only two years after he had been appointed. South San Francisco had returned to the pre-Dreisbach and VTN pattern of administrative instability.

Analysis. The South San Francisco contracting experiment failed for several reasons. The major reason was that the city's political situation was too unstable for such an innovation to work. The council was split, differences between old and new residents were great, and the history of the city involved a politically influential set of municipal employees. Contracts similar to VTN work best in "contract" cities (see Chapter Seven) where there is no preexisting municipal staff or no long history of city services. In addition to these reasons, the VTN plan was conceived and adopted in secret, engendering additional controversy; the position of the VTN consultant as a city and private official posed a potential conflict of interest, was a source of irritation, and confused lines of communication.

Case Study 4:
Refuse Collection in Berwyn, Illinois

Background. In 1975 Berwyn (Illinois) switched from municipal to private refuse collection. The decision was a highly charged, partisan decision in which management and cost considerations played a minor role. (See Berenyi, 1977, for a complete account of this case.)

Berwyn, a city of 50,000, lies twelve miles directly west of downtown Chicago. Known as the "Republican suburb of Chicago," it is a middle- and lower-middle-class community whose residents are primarily of Slavic and Bohemian descent. Berwyn grew rapidly in the 1920s as a haven for immigrants who wanted to escape from Chicago. It is a tightly knit community in which many citizens have lived all their lives. Over 25 percent of the population is over sixty-five years of age. The city is also known for political partisanship, personalistic politics, and substantial use of patronage. Local politics appears to represent individual goals rather than ideological convictions, since politicians have been known to switch parties. Individual goals seem to fuel partisanship, and intense partisan divisions played a crucial part in the decision to contract out refuse disposal.

Contracting Out and Union Opposition. Berwyn was plagued by labor strife in the 1970s, particularly by refuse collectors and police. Pay was usually the issue, resulting in strikes in 1972 and 1974. The 1974 strike was marked by confusion resulting from the city's inability to establish a management negotiation team. A committee composed of the mayor, three aldermen, and the public works director eventually met without the formal consent of the council. At that time, one Democratic councilman first broached the possibility of saving money by contracting out refuse collection.

In the council elections of 1975, Republicans, campaigning on the issue of repealing the utility tax, swept all but one Democratic councilman out of office. The Public Works Department was another Republican target, since it was considered ineffective and expensive. With exquisite timing, the garbage collectors struck the city on election day.

This strike, like the 1974 strike, was marked by union demands for wage increases and additional fringe benefits. It lasted three weeks, during which time residents were asked to store refuse, Water Department employees refused to report to work, and police threatened to strike. The mayor, a Democrat, and the councilmen, all Republicans but one, blamed each other for the strike. As in the past, the city could not form a united negotiating committee, and the mayor had to empower the city council, acting as a committee of the whole, to negotiate. The union won a 41-cent-an-hour wage increase plus additional fringe benefits. The council then had to find cost savings to pay for the wage increase and to make up for losses due to repeal of the utility tax.

The council, angered and frustrated, voted for the resignation of the public works director. This precipitated a bitter confrontation between the administration and the council, resulting in the council backing down in the face of mayor-generated public support for the director. Relations between the council and the department remained icy, however.

Later that year, the union indicated that it wanted further wage increases and fringe benefits, effective January 1976. After some unproductive bargaining sessions with the union, the council called a special meeting to consider contracting out refuse collection. There it heard private scavenger firms make presentations and instructed that bid specifications and advertisements for bids be drawn up. The council also submitted a counterproposal to the union, largely rejecting the union proposal.

At the next meeting, the council, in a surprise move, invited firms to bid on a proposed contract during a council recess. Their bids were opened that same night, and the council accepted the lowest bid. The city garbage collectors were terminated, and they were invited to apply for jobs to the low bidder, Clearing Disposal Company.

As a result of the council action, the union promptly began picketing the city. Since all union members honored the picket lines, Clearing Disposal could not take possession of the city trucks and could not collect refuse. The mayor resisted vigorously the council plan, since it involved partisanship aimed at him, a loss of patronage, and a loss of mayoral authority. He vetoed council actions but was promptly overridden by the council.

To bolster its public image in the face of apparent public support for city operation, the council introduced a cost-benefit analysis to compare the private contract to city refuse collection; this analysis showed substantial savings under private collection. The council also ordered striking employees back to work. In response, the mayor, with the union and an aggrieved contractor, filed suit against the contract. The council countered with its own lawsuit, charging the union with an illegal strike.

The strike, and thus the new contract, depended on a favorable court ruling. The court refused to take sides, merely ordering employees to return to work and cease picketing, postponing until later all other questions. This settled the situation, and the council promptly put policies concerning the private contract into effect. Trucks were turned over to Clearing Disposal (to be returned if the court later ruled against the council on the merits of the case), employee salary rates were set, and Clearing Disposal's supervisory position over employees was clarified.

The court later ruled in favor of the city council, which then confirmed the contract, dismissing twenty-six of thirty-three public works employees, with the understanding that they could be reemployed by Clearing Disposal. This action completed the formal transition to private collection.

Results. The contract resulted in some significant changes in Berwyn collection. Clearing Disposal originally hired all fifteen city employees who requested employment, but only three remained nine months later. Apparently, they worked harder for Clearing Disposal than for the city, although the pay was higher. There was also less absenteeism. Refuse pickup practices changed to a specific route for each day rather than the city practice of a specific area each week. Finally, Clearing Disposal also reduced the number of collection trucks and the size of crews, from two to three persons.

The actual savings were in doubt. Under five different assumptions, the change resulted in a loss of 6.3 percent (−$43,411) or a gain of 1.0 percent, 7.4 percent, 11.0 percent or 17.1 percent ($125,895). However, the debatable nature of the savings did not deter the council from feeling that it had won the battle. This battle was most significant, because garbage collection has been contracted out ever since.

The victory only partly (if at all) improved collection services or reduced costs. The battle, ostensibly over poor and inefficient collection practices, was really over political power and, to a lesser degree, over some control over a previously dominant union. The Berwyn case illustrates that contracting out is by no means always an administrative or efficiency question—it is often simply part of the political struggle, in this case between a mayor, a council, and a union.

Case Study 5:
Federal General Services Administration

In the late 1970s and early 1980s, the General Services Administration (GSA) was the subject of a nationwide investigation that produced indictments of 200 federal employees and contractors on charges of false claims and kickbacks on GSA contracts (see Hanrahan, 1983). One former GSA employee received a six-year prison sentence for receiving kickbacks of over $600,000. Contractors overbilled the government for work or never did the work in the first place, confident that GSA officials would not report them because of the kickbacks they had made. One Hyattsville (Maryland) painting contractor reported that he paid off GSA officials with trips, money, prostitutes, and free painting jobs on their houses. Many GSA contractors were routinely paid for work done by government employees, or for applying one coat of paint and being paid for two, or for painting the same wall over and over again. Some dummy companies were paid for work not done.

In the Baltimore area, abuses were rampant. In the Customs House, one contractor installed an engine-room heating system improperly. Moisture condensed, ruining the ceiling. A second contractor was called in to repair the damage at extra government expense. In another Customs House room, a plumbing contractor, fixing a floor drain, broke a wall, which had to be repaired by GSA employees. The contractor was not charged for the extra expense.

In the Baltimore Appraisers Store, a contractor installed fire sprinkler heads on the seventh floor, while GSA employees did exactly the same work on the eighth floor and could easily have done the floor below. At the Federal Middle River Depot, a contractor installed a new computer room, but GSA employees had to replaced ceiling tiles that were installed improperly. Their time was charged to building maintenance.

There was plenty of dishonesty on the part of both GSA and contractors, but much of the problem rests with the politicization of the GSA and with legislative and executive branch pressures to award contracts to certain contractors. Arthur Sampson, GSA administrator in 1974, commented, "A Congressman or a Senator has the right to make a recommendation for his constituents. . . . If I've got three firms and they're all equal and the Vice-President has made a recommendation, I'd go with the Vice-President or with Senator Montoya or Senator Scott" (Hanrahan, 1983, p. 64). Montoya and Scott had positions influencing GSA budgets and patronage, respectively. Congress has never been much concerned in GSA performance as long as states and districts get their share of government offices, leases, and purchasing contracts.

Case Study 6:
Federal Department of Energy Consulting Service

A review of consulting practices in six agencies by the General Accounting Office found numerous shortcomings in the way these agencies used consulting contracts (see Comptroller General, 1979). The Department of Energy (DOE) was selected as representative of these agencies and because GAO has been critical of DOE on other occasions.

One $29,000 contract for technical analysis and support for assessing the technology base included tasks such as meeting support, maintaining various reports, and maintaining project planning documentation. A DOE official said that most of the work was typing support necessitated by personnel ceilings.

Another $453,000 contract was for assessing industry research and development activities. Of the contract, $300,000 was for a subcontractor who did the work, while the prime contractor "performed in a supervisory role and opened doors to obtain the data required under the contract." The sole-source contract stated that the contractor could do the work.

A DOE sole-source contract was for outside advice to DOE about the Trans-Alaska Pipeline System. The contract had been modified three times, increasing the price from $55,000 to $198,000 and the period of performance from one year to twenty-seven months. A fourth modification, for twelve more months and an additional $115,000, was pending. The hourly rate had increased from $22 per hour to $40 per hour after the contract was signed.

DOE awarded a $343,000 contract for analysis of resource development on Indian reservations to "help the agency in policy development." DOE officials could not explain or document any use of the results.

DOE also awarded a contract for $27,000 to prepare testimony about a regulatory issue. It was a sole-source contract because of time pressures. However, DOE never used the testimony, because the agency felt that the contractor was defining government policy, which is the agency's responsibility.

Of the twenty DOE consulting contracts GAO examined, fourteen involved sole-source contracting, where the contract is awarded without bidding. Twelve involved extensions of the contractual period for performance. Twelve more involved contractual modifications, most of which increased the total contract substantially and extended the time to complete the work. Eleven were signed during the last quarter of the fiscal year, when uncommitted funds are commonly spent for marginal purposes to avoid having to turn the money back. In seven cases, DOE could or should have used in-house capacity to complete the contracted project. In six cases, DOE made little or no use of the results. In four cases, the contract was for an unsolicited proposal, suggesting that DOE had to be told what needed to be done; in four other cases, the primary contractor largely or entirely subcontracted the contract. Finally, in three cases, DOE contracted with former employees, presumably when the work should have been completed before the employee resigned.

Case Study 7: Beverly Nursing Home Care

Beverly Enterprises is the nation's largest for-profit nursing home chain (see AFSCME, 1983). Between 1977 and 1982 in its home state of California, Beverly was cited for 173 major patient care violations. Twenty-six of these involved an imminent threat of death or injury. Beverly's Florida facilities were fined $15,115 for continuous staffing deficiencies. Beverly's District of Columbia facility was found to have unlawful understaffing and nonworking medical equipment.

In the early 1980s, Beverly paid $188,500 for five wrongful death lawsuits in Michigan, Georgia, and Florida. In 1983 two additional suits for wrongful death were pending. In Texas during 1978, a state attorney general's report found that many Beverly homes provided abusive and substandard nursing care. In 1983 the United States charged Beverly's Georgia facility with refusing to provide care to indigent patients, a requirement for any nursing home that receives federal aid for construction of facilities.

Case Study 8: Scofflaws, Computers, and the Datacom System Corporation

Datacom Systems Corporation of New York City took over the Yonkers (New York) Traffic Court program to send notices and collect fines from traffic scofflaws—those people who had three unanswered summons or unpaid parking tickets within eighteen months (see AFSCME, 1983). Newspaper reports termed the Datacom operation a disaster. Initially, nearly 200 people were notified that they were scofflaws. These motorists claimed that they had already paid their fines, some up to six years earlier. When they called Datacom to complain, they found no working phone number. They then called the Traffic Court to register their complaints and to try to straighten out the records. This was just the situation that the contract had been designed to correct.

Datacom had a similar program in New York City. ABC's "Eyewitness News" reported that many people had their cars towed and auctioned off for nonpayment of traffic fines they had already paid. Other motorists protested that they were not given a chance to make final restitution, although this was required before any impounding. Datacom had subcontracted with the towing companies, and these companies were purchasing the impounded cars at auction, in violation of city law. Allegedly, some arrangements for purchase of cars were made before impoundment.

Yonkers also almost contracted with Datacom for city computer services. Datacom had hired a previous city computer system director, reputed to be politically influential, as its marketing director. The proposed contract had a number of deficiencies. First, it was to be awarded without competitive bidding. Second, Datacom could subcontract the computer contract and with only the city manager's, not the council's, approval. Since Datacom had done the contracting feasibility study, it may have gained inside information and could benefit from its own feasibility recommendation. Finally, the city planned to abolish its own computer information department once Datacom took over, so there would be no capacity to replace Datacom. After public objections, partially based on Datacom's Traffic Court work for New York and Yonkers, the proposed contract was turned down by the city council.

Case Study 9: Convention
Center Management in Baltimore

In March 1982, a year before the contract was to have expired, Baltimore terminated the arrangement with Facilities Management, Inc., to manage the city's Convention Center, Convention Bureau, and Civic Center (see AFSCME, 1983). City officials alleged that the contractor ran up deficits as large as $800,000 in its management of the three facilities, that financial records were in "shambles," that Facilities Management tried to hide these serious financial problems from the city, and that creditors were being paid late or not at all.

The Convention Center suffered the most severe problems. The officials appointed to replace Facilities Management reported that the contractor had left financial records in chaos. There were boxes of unpaid bills, with unsigned checks attached, some dating back almost a year. In addition, $211,000 in checks had been written to cover some bills for the Convention Center and the Civic Center, but these checks had never been sent. One bill for $11,000, dated November 1980, was stuffed among papers in an office desk.

Facilities Management had underestimated the year's utilities bills by $400,000, which may have been why other creditors were being paid late. However, Facilities Management was quickly investing the city's payments of $250,000 to them in short-term, six-day bank notes and was not using these fees to pay creditors.

The city filed suit against Facilities Management, claiming mismanagement and breach of contract. The suit was settled out of court, with Facilities Management turning back $800,000 of city operating fund advances and with the city paying $100,000 to the firm in disputed management fees.

Analysis of Cases 5 Through 9

The DOE and GSA federal cases were based on reports to Congress by its watchdog, the GAO. The GAO has a highly nonpartisan reputation. The remaining three cases were based on reports in *Passing the Bucks* (AFSCME, 1983). AFSCME is fiercely opposed to contracting out because it claims that contracting out is not really cost-effective and that it subordinates public services to the search for profit by private firms. However, most of AFSCME's reports are from newspaper accounts and published reports. It is clear that the five accounts do represent contracting at its worst.

The GSA case shows corruption at work in the whole contracting process within an environment of political influence. The DOE case shows that poor performance can be expected when an agency lacks interest in managing contracts. The Baltimore Facilities Management case simply involved an instance of extraordinarily bad performance by the contractor. The Datacom case also represented very bad performance, although Yonkers might have been expected to check the performance of Datacom in New York City (presuming Datacom's performance had been known at that time). Certainly Datacom's ticket-tracking performance in Yonkers should have ruled out further contracts for computer service programs prior to a full-scale controversy.

Perhaps the most interesting case is that of Beverly Enterprises. Beverly performed poorly and endangered (or even lost) lives. Why then was Beverly rehired or retained in several states over several years? It was probably done to cut costs in publicly operated nursing homes, and this may have succeeded, at a terrible cost, because Beverly understaffed facilities. One wonders if publicly owned facilities would have fewer injuries and a better record than Beverly, given that fiscal pressures would have tempted legislators to lower public staffing levels.

It hardly excuses Beverly's sad record to recognize that private or nonprofit groups are often held to higher standards than public agencies. One analyst notes, with respect to the case for privatizing prisons: "The government can, in fact, require much better conditions at private prisons than exist in many public institutions'' (''Supporters . . . ,'' 1987). This argument may apply as well to nursing homes and other social programs. Financially strapped governments are tempted to grant lower-cost contracts to private firms. They know (or suspect) that this may result in lower staffing totals (hence lower-quality service). However, they are unwilling or unable to operate the institutions with as few public employees as private operators will probably use. (If the contractor met minimum staffing standards, there would probably be no profit.) Thus, the responsibility for understaffing is shifted to a private party, who is repaid for this responsibility by getting the contract. The problem lies not with contracting out as much as it resides in an unwillingness or inability to recognize the full cost of nursing homes and perhaps of all other social services.

The next most interesting case is that of DOE, which (along with several other federal agencies) seemed to routinely mishandle consultant contracts by not demanding competitiveness, not demanding performance after the award, and not utilizing the results of the contracts after the work was done. The DOE case is useful because it shows that while contractors may not have performed well, the major problem in consultant usage is often weak agency management. Such use of consultants may be one reason that consultants, grant recipients, and contractors refer privately to the federal government as ''Uncle Sugar.'' Federal agencies usually defend themselves against these and similar charges by pointing to restrictive staffing limits that necessitate outside contracts to accomplish an unreduced work load.

If we could eliminate corruption and political influence, monitor performance from the onset of the contract, and observe basic management principles in planning, awarding, and utilizing contracts, contracting out would not be particularly controversial. This is a lot to ask—and probably amounts to wishful thinking. However, the right environment—where corruption is minimal and planning optimal—continues to be key for success in contracting out.

RESOURCE B ∾∾∾∾∾∾∾∾∾∾∾∾∾∾

International Interest in Contracting Out

The privatization movement is not limited to the United States, but is international in scope. And as part of the privatization movement, contracting out government services to private parties is receiving more attention.

In many countries, such as the Philippines and Jordan, the emphasis is on denationalization of state-owned enterprises. In Jordan this involves airlines, bus systems, and the telecommunications industry. In the Philippines it involves resort hotels, bulk cargo ships, cement plants, and a shoe factory ("Privatization Abroad . . . ," 1987).

Great Britain

England's public sector, under the Conservative administration since 1979, has been privatized substantially, taking three major directions. First is the sale of parts of nationalized industries—such as British Telecom, British Petroleum, British National Oil, and shares in other firms such as Jaguar. Second is relacing the control by state monopolies (for example, allowing private firms to compete with the Post Office). Third is more extensive use of contracting out (S. Young, 1986).

Local authorities now contract out school meals, cleaning, park maintenance, catering, gardening, laundry, and refuse collection. The use of private contractors varies widely, however. By 1984, only eighteen of 117 local elections had approved private refuse collection. All road construction and maintenance above a certain value must be contracted out, and certain freeway lanes are maintained by private contractors. All new construction and most building maintenance are done privately (S. Young, 1986). The armed forces contract heavily. The Marine Branch of the Royal Air Force, involving launches and support craft, is now contracted out. The servicing of navy ships and air force aircraft, veterinary services, legal services, and education corps are now under private contract (P. Young, 1986). London Regional Transit (LRT) began to contract out in 1984, emphasizing small suburban routes initially and using three-year contracts. The original bidding awarded sixty-five routes, and about 10 percent of LRT's total bus miles per year ("Privatization Jolts . . . ," 1987).

In these British cases, contracting out did not always go smoothly as some might have hoped, since there were not always bidders for contracts. In addition, because of Conservative views of the value of privatization, work was sometimes contracted even though this cost more than doing it in-house. Some observers believe, however, that the privatization trend is irreversible (S. Young, 1986).

Canada

Since the 1950s, the six municipalities of Metropolitan Toronto have contracted out snow removal, awarding seven contracts (one for every maintenance district) every three years. Metro employees monitor the snow-removal efforts, which are divided among contractors and its own employees. Metro employees melt and remove snow after it is plowed by private contractors. Private contractors plow the annual snowfall of fifty-five inches and salt the streets. The salters, plows, and other equipment are contracted for. This division of labor has been worked out over thirty years, and both parties are apparently satisfied ("Privatization in Metropolitan Toronto . . . ," 1986).

The Ontario provincial park system is expanding the contracting out system for its parks. Eighteen of the 138 parks will be privately operated under the plan. The minister of natural resources notes that contract operation has worked well in the past for small recreational parks used by the public for overnight camping ("Contracting Out . . . ," 1986).

Denmark

In Denmark, privatization means Falck, although many Danes do not know that the Falck Corporation is privately owned. Actually, the popular red-and-white trucks, while owned privately, offer a range of both public and private services.

Sophus Falck began in 1906 with a rescue station in Copenhagen that was designed to help local fire fighters. By 1918 Falck organized an ambulance branch station and within a decade set up private fire brigades and private repair road service, by subscription. Presently Falck ambulance service covers 98 percent of Denmark, and 62 percent of all municipalities are served by fire services.

Falck's 6,300 employees (including 1,300 paid reservists) served in 134 rescue stations in 1980, turning a profit of $1.3 million on $117 million gross revenues. About half of this income came from public contracts for municipal fire, ambulance, and patient contracts, and almost as much came from private subscriptions for such services as road repair.

Falck employees receive up to twenty months of training in a range of services during their first few years in the company. In addition, Falck uses special information services—such as television, radio, and newspaper reports on road conditions and traffic—operating almost like a government.

Falck has no particular wage advantages over other employers. All its employees are members of SID, the largest trade union in Denmark. SID has proven to be an aggressive bargainer, and Falck in recent years has experienced work stoppages (Stewart, 1982).

The World

Privatization is expanding worldwide, and it appears to have little to do with ideology. "Seventeen of the world's most populous nations are initiating measures to privatize state-owned industry, relax price controls, or otherwise increase competitions," reports observer William Chandler. He further comments:

> Market-based economies regularly outperform those that are centrally planned, particularly in land, labor, and energy productivity. . . . Between 1970 and 1980, total agricultural productivity declined by one-third in the Soviet Union, Romania, and Poland. By contrast, it increased steadily in the United States and Japan.
>
> The world today is posed at a turning point in economic management. Many African nations, plagued with agricultural decline, have begun to extend market incentives for agriculture. Latin American nations, plagued with debt, have moved to sell off state-owned companies. . . . Many nations are increasingly leaving the internal workings of economics to market mechanisms. Those that have—notably China, Hungary, and Zimbabwe—are reaping the rewards. Those that have not—Mexico, Nigeria, and Egypt—are faced with falling living standards ["The Hunger Project," 1986, p. 1].

Contracting out is not likely to become a major issue in underdeveloped countries, for it is generally limited to countries with developed public and private sectors. Even so, the above words reflect that populous countries are privatizing, and contracting out is certainly one way to privatize, as the examples of England and Canada show. As demonstrated by Falck's success in Denmark, however, contracting out may have to be uniquely suited to the institutions and values of each country.

REFERENCES

Advisory Commission on Intergovernmental Relations. *Significant Features of Fiscal Federalism, 1981–82*. Washington, D.C.: Advisory Commission on Intergovernmental Relations, 1983.

Advisory Commission on Intergovernmental Relations. "1984— Not A Good Fiscal Year for Big Brother." *Intergovernmental Perspective*, 1985, *11* (1), 4–7.

American Federation of State, County and Municipal Employees. *Private Profit, Public Risk*. Washington, D.C.: American Federation of State, County and Municipal Employees, n.d.

American Federation of State, County and Municipal Employees. *Passing the Bucks*. Washington, D.C.: American Federation of State, County and Municipal Employees, 1983.

"Andrews: Policies without Politics." *City and State Magazine*, 1986, pp. 22–30.

Armington, R. Q., and Ellis, W. *This Way Up*. Lake Bluff, Ill.: Regnery Gateway, 1984.

Auditor General. *The State Needs to Improve Its Control of Consultant and Service Contracts*. Sacramento: Auditor General of California, 1986.

Ayres, D. "Municipal Interfaces in the Third Sector: A Negative View." *Public Administration Review*, 1975, *35* (5), 459–466.

261

Berenyi, E. "Berwyn, Illinois: A Case Study of a Change in Organizational Arrangements for Residential Refuse Collection." Unpublished paper, Center for Governmental Studies, Graduate School of Business, Columbia University, 1977.

Berenyi, E. *Camden, New Jersey: A Case Study of a Change from Public to Contract Refuse Disposal.* New York: Center for Government Studies, Graduate School of Business, Columbia University, 1979.

California Tax Foundation. *Contracting Out Local Governmental Services in California.* Sacramento: California Tax Foundation, 1981.

"Case Studies Show Private Fire Protection That Works." *Privatization,* Sept. 21, 1986, pp. 4–5.

Center for Governmental Studies. *Service Evaluations and Policy Priorities: A Survey of DeKalb Citizens.* DeKalb: Center for Governmental Studies, Northern Illinois University, 1985.

Chi, K. *The Private Sector in State Correctional Industries: The Control Data Program in Minnesota.* Lexington, Ky.: Council of State Governments, 1985.

Chi, K. "Private-Public Alliances Grow." *State Government News,* 1986, pp. 10–12.

City of Charlotte, South Carolina. *City Budget.* City of Charlotte: Charlotte, S.C., 1980.

Coleman, W. *A Quiet Revolution in Local Government Finance: Policy and Administrative Challenges in Expanding the Use of User Charges in Financing State and Local Government.* Washington, D.C.: National Academy of Public Administration, 1980.

Collett, M. "The Federal Contracting Process." *The Bureaucrat,* 1981, *10* (2), 18–19.

Community Communication Company v. *City of Boulder, Colorado,* 70 L. Ed. 2d 810 (1982).

Comptroller General. *The Department of Energy's Practices for Awarding and Administering Contracts Need to Be Improved.* Washington, D.C.: U.S. General Accounting Office, 1979.

Comptroller General. *Controls over Consulting Service Contract at Federal Agencies Need Tightening.* Washington, D.C.: U.S. General Accounting Office, 1980.

Comptroller General. *Civil Servants and Contract Employees: Who Should Do What for the Federal Government?* Washington, D.C.: U.S. General Accounting Office, 1981.

Comptroller General. *Information from Previous Reports on Various Aspects of Contracting Out Under OMB Circular A-76.* Washington, D.C.: U.S. General Accounting Office, 1985a.

Comptroller General. *NASA Not Complying with OMB Circular A-76.* Washington, D.C.: U.S. General Accounting Office, 1985b.

Comptroller General. *Analysis of DLA's Dealing with the Pines Corporation During 1985.* Washington, D.C.: U.S. General Accounting Office, 1986a.

Comptroller General. *Contracts with Employee Organizations Should Be Terminated.* Washington, D.C.: U.S. General Accounting Office, 1986b.

Comptroller General. *DOD Initiatives to Improve the Acquisition of Spare Parts.* Washington, D.C.: U.S. General Accounting Office, 1986c.

Comptroller General. *Procurement of Piston Rings for the F-16 Aircraft.* Washington, D.C.: U.S. General Accounting Office, 1986d.

Comptroller General. *Project 12,000 at the San Antonio Logistics Center.* Washington, D.C.: U.S. General Accounting Office, 1986e.

Congressional Budget Office. *Contracting Out: Potential for Reducing Federal Costs.* Washington, D.C.: Congressional Budget Office, 1987.

"Contracting Out for Nickels, Dimes and Dollars." *Privatization,* July 2, 1986, pp. 1–2.

"Contracting Out Jobs Challenged." *Sacramento Bee,* Aug. 16, 1982, Sec. A, p. 4.

"Contracting Out Recreation Parks, Too." *Privatization,* Dec. 12, 1986, p. 7.

"Contractor Provides Correction Services to State and Federal Agencies." *Privatization,* July 7, 1987, pp. 2–3.

Cooper, P. "Government Contracts in Public Administration: The Role and Environment of the Contracting Officer." *Public Administration Review,* 1980, *40* (5), 459–468.

Crutcher, J. "Privatizing the U.S. Postal Service." *Government Union Review*, 1984, *21*, 1–11.

"Custodians Fight Back—Contracting Out Strikes Again." *University Employee*, 1987, pp. 1–8.

"Customers Rate Refuse Service." *Waste Age*, 1981, *10* (11), 84–88.

DeHoog, R. *Contracting Out for Human Services*. Albany: State University of New York, 1984.

Doherty, D. "Private Contracting in Municipal Operations: Rochester, New York." *Urban Resources*, 1985, *6*, 29–36.

Feldt, J., and Anderson, D. "Attribution Versus Layoff: How to Estimate the Costs of Holding Employees on Payroll When Savings Are Needed." *Public Administration Review*, 1982, *42* (3), 178–182.

"First 'Sludge Privatization' Agreement Reached." *Privatization*, Nov. 7, 1987, pp. 1–2.

Fisk, D., Kiesling, H., and Muller, T. *Private Provision of Public Services*. Washington, D.C.: Brookings Institution, 1978.

Florestano, P., and Gordon, D. "Public Versus Private: Small Government Contracting with the Private Sector." *Public Administration Review*, 1980, *40* (1), 29–34.

"France Looks to Private Prisons." *Sacramento Bee*, Nov. 20, 1986, Sec. A, p. 5.

Greenhalgh, L., and McKersie, R. "Cost Effectiveness of Alternate Strategies for Cutback Management." *Public Administration Review*, 1980, *40* (6), 575–584.

"Handling Children and Youth Services Through Contracting." *Privatization*, Oct. 7, 1987, pp. 6–7.

Hanrahan, J. *Government by Contract*. New York: Norton, 1983.

Hatry, H., Fisk, D., and Winnie, R. *How Effective Are Your Community Services: Procedures for Monitoring the Effectiveness of Municipal Services*. Washington, D.C.: Urban Institute, 1977.

Hayes, T. *Service Contracting*. San Diego: Metro Associates, 1984.

Henderson, L. "Intergovernmental Service Arrangements and the Transfer of Functions." In ICMA's *1985 Municipal Year Book*. Washington, D.C.: International City Management Association, 1986.

"The Hunger Project." *World Development Forum*, 1986, *1* (4), 1.

"Infrastructure Privatization After Tax Reform." *Fiscal Watchdog,* Oct. 1986, pp. 5–8.

International City Management Association (ICMA). *1985 Municipal Year Book.* Washington, D.C.: International City Management Association, 1986.

"Is FAA Privatization Program Meant to Fly?" *Privatization,* Dec. 7, 1986, pp. 1–8.

"Jails, Corporate Style." *Privatization,* Sept. 7, 1987, pp. 7–8.

Jefferson, T. "Letter to Peter Carr, August 19, 1775." In F. Mosher and others (eds.), *Watergate: Implications for Responsible Government.* New York: Basic Books, 1974. (Originally published 1775.)

Johnson, G., and Heilman, J. "Metapolicy Transition and Policy Implementation: New Federalism and Privatization." *Public Administration Review,* 1987, *47* (6), 468–478.

Kelley, J. *Costing Government Services: A Guide for Decision Making.* Washington, D.C.: Government Finance Officers Association, 1984.

Kettle, D. "The Fourth Face of Federalism." *Public Administration Review,* 1981, *41* (3), 366–371.

Kettler, R. "Federal Employee Challenges to Contracting Out: Is There a Viable Forum?" *Military Law Review,* 1986, *12,* 3–9.

Kirlin, J. "The Impact of Contract Service Arrangements upon the Los Angeles County Sheriff's Department and Law Enforcement in Los Angeles County." *Public Policy,* 1973, *2* (3), 533–584.

Lambright, H. *Governing Service and Technology.* New York: Oxford University Press, 1976.

League of California Cities. *More California Cutback Management.* Sacramento: League of California Cities, 1981.

Levinson, R. *Government by Private Contract: Experimentation in South San Francisco.* Davis: Institute of Governmental Affairs, University of California, 1976.

Los Angeles County. *Contract Development Manual.* Los Angeles: Los Angeles County, 1984.

Los Angeles County. *Agreements Providing for Services to Cities by the County of Los Angeles.* Los Angeles: Los Angeles County, 1985.

McEntee, G. "Privatization's Financial Arguments Flawed." *City and State Magazine,* 1986, p. 10.

Marlin, J. *Contracting for Municipal Services.* New York: Wiley, 1984.

Meyer, M., and Morgan, D. *Contracting for Municipal Services: A Handbook for Local Officials.* Norman: Bureau of Government Services, University of Oklahoma, 1979.

Miller, G. *Cities for Contract: The Politics of Municipal Incorporation.* Boston: MIT Press, 1981.

National Association of Counties Research Foundation. *A Practical Guide to Intergovernmental Agreements/Contracts for Local Officials.* Washington, D.C.: National Association of Counties Research Foundation, 1977.

National Commission for Employment Policy. *Privatization and Public Employees: The Impact of City and County Contracting Out on Government Workers.* Washington, D.C.: National Commission for Employment Policy, 1988.

National Institute of Justice. *The Privatization of Corrections.* Washington, D.C.: U.S. Justice Department, 1985.

"New Facility Treats Scottsdale to Up-Front Savings." *Privatization,* Apr. 7, 1987, pp. 2–3.

Orlans, H. (ed.). *Nonprofit Organizations, A Government Management Tool.* New York: Praeger, 1980.

Pestle, J. *Finance and Service Alternatives for Municipalities.* Grand Rapids, Mich.: Varnum, Riddering, Schmidt, and Howlett, Attorneys at Law, 1987.

"Philadelphia Costs." *City and State Magazine,* 1986, pp. 1–10.

Pierce, N., and Susskind, R. "Fewer Federal Dollars Spurring Cities to Improve Management and Trim Costs." *National Journal,* 1986, *18* (3), 504–508.

Platt, T., Barnes, K., and Bishop, B. *Government Not for Profit: The Case Against Contracting Out.* San Francisco: Institute for the Study of Labor and Economic Crises, 1983.

Poole, R. *Cutting Back City Hall.* New York: Universe Books, 1980.

Powers, R. "The Five-Way Test." *Public Management,* 1980, *46* (4), 3–5.

Prince George's County. *101 Ways to Squeeze More Out of Your*

Local Tax Dollar. Upper Marlboro, Md.: Prince George's County Productivity and Cost Reduction Plan, n.d.

"Private Effort Thanked." *City and State Magazine,* Jan. 1987, p. 1.

"Privatization Abroad: It's Different from America in the Decade of Privatization." *Privatization,* Mar. 21, 1987, pp. 1–8.

"Privatization Central to Future Public Works." *Fiscal Watchdog,* Sept. 1987, pp. 3–5.

"Privatization Fire Burns Fort Walton Beach." *Privatization,* Dec. 21, 1986, pp. 7–8.

"Privatization Helps a City Pass Legislation." *Privatization,* May 21, 1987, pp. 4–5.

"Privatization in Metropolitan Toronto: Snow Removal." *Privatization,* Dec. 12, 1986, pp. 1–9.

"Privatization Jolts London Bus Transit: Public Provider Pushed by Competition." *Privatization,* Mar. 7, 1987, pp. 1–8.

"Problematic Labor Relations in Privatization." *Privatization,* Sept. 7, 1987, pp. 1–10.

"Pros and Cons of Prison Contracting." *Privatization,* June 21, 1987, pp. 7–8.

Public Technology, Inc. *The PTI Member Catalog of Publications.* Washington, D.C.: Public Technology, Inc., 1986.

Quinn, K., and Olstein, M. "Privatization: Public/Private Partnerships Provide Essential Services." In B. Weiss (ed.), *Financing a Commonwealth.* Washington, D.C.: Government Finance Officers Association, 1985.

Rehfuss, J. Unpublished research, 1986.

Rehfuss, J. *Contracting Out and Accountability—The Importance of Contract Monitoring.* Paper presented to the American Society for Public Administration annual conference, Portland, Oreg., Apr. 20, 1988.

"Report on the National Association of State Personnel Executives." *State Government News,* 1986, p. 2.

Roy Jorgenson Associates. *An Appraisal of Highway Maintenance by Contract.* Gaithersburg, Md.: Roy Jorgenson Associates, 1981.

Rubin, I. "Combining Political and Managerial Advice on Cutting Back Budgets." *Managing Local Government,* 1983, *1* (3), 1–2.

Savas, E. S. "An Empirical Study of Competition in Municipal Service Delivery." *Public Administration Review,* 1977, *37* (6), 714–717.

Savas, E. S. *Privatizing the Public Service: How to Shrink Government.* Chatham, N.J.: Chatham House, 1982.

Savas, E. S. *Privatization: The Key to Better Government.* Chatham, N.J.: Chatham House, 1987.

Seader, D. "Privatization and America's Cities." *Public Management,* 1986, *52* (12), 6–7.

Sharkansky, I. *Whither the State: Politics and Public Enterprise in Three Countries.* Chatham, N.J.: Chatham House, 1979.

Sharkansky, I. "Policymaking and Service Delivery on the Margins of Government: The Case of Contractors." *Public Administration Review,* 1980, *40* (2), 116–124.

Shulman, M. "Alternative Ways for Delivering Public Services." *Urban Data Service Reports,* 1982, *14* (10), 2–6.

Slawsky, N., and DeMarco, J. "Is the Price Right? State and Local Government Architect and Engineer Selection." *Public Administration Review,* 1980, *40* (3), 269–275.

"Some States Lock in Private Prisons, Opponents Worry: Is It Legal?" *Privatization,* Apr. 7, 1987, pp. 1–6.

Sonenblum, S., Ries, J., and Kirlin, J. *How Cities Provide Services.* Boston: Ballinger, 1977.

"State Sued over Use of Private Contractors." *Sacramento Bee,* August 1986, Sec. A, p. 8.

Stevens, B. (ed.). *Delivering Municipal Services Efficiently: A Comparison of Municipal and Private Service Delivery. Summary.* Report prepared for the U.S. Department of Housing and Urban Development. New York: Ecodata, Inc., 1984.

Stevenson, W. "The Public Side of Private Security." Paper presented to the American Society for Public Administration annual conference, Portland, Oreg., Apr. 20, 1988.

Stewart, J. "The Falck Organization." *Transatlantic Perspectives,* 1982, *6,* 10–13.

Straussman, J., and Fairie, J. "Contracting for Local Services at the Local Level." *The Urban Interest,* 1981, *2,* 43–50.

Sullivan, N., and Marietta, J. "New Strategies for a New Game:

Privatizing Water and Wastewater Treatment Plants.'' *The Privatization Review,* 1987, *3* (3), 56–63.

"Supporters, Opponents Locked into Private Prison Debate.'' *Privatization,* June 7, 1987, p. 17.

Touche Ross. *Privatization in America.* Washington, D.C.: Touche Ross, 1984.

Touche Ross. *The Infrastructure Crisis.* Washington, D.C.: Touche Ross, 1985.

Touche Ross. *Financing Infrastructure in America.* Washington, D.C.: Touche Ross, 1987.

Tribbett, R. "The Contracting Out of Municipal Public Works Functions.'' Unpublished master's thesis, School of Business and Public Administration, California State University–Sacramento, 1983.

"Trying a New Way; Fairfield, Calif., Uses Private Employees to Make Firefighting Economics More Efficient.'' *Privatization,* July 7, 1986, pp. 2–5.

"Two Successful Texas Water Projects: Both Flow from Unique Privatization System.'' *Privatization,* Feb. 7, 1987, pp. 1–2.

Valente, C. "Local Government's Capital Finances: Options and Decisions.'' In ICMA's *1986 Municipal Year Book.* Washington, D.C.: International City Management Association, 1987.

Valente, C., and Manchester, L. *Rethinking Local Services: Examining Alternative Delivery Systems.* Washington, D.C.: International City Management Association, 1984.

Wedel, K., Katz, A., and Wieck, A. *Social Services by Government Contract: A Policy Analysis.* New York: Praeger, 1979.

Wesemann, E. *Contracting for City Services.* Pittsburgh, Pa.: Innovations Press, 1981.

"Westchester's Privatized Resource Recovery Plant: Energized by a Full-Service Contract.'' *Privatization,* May 21, 1987, pp. 3–6.

Whitcomb, C. *Contracting for Residential Services.* McLean, Va.: Community Systems and Services, Inc., 1983.

Woodson, R. "Day Care.'' In R. Q. Armington and W. Ellis (eds.), *This Way Up.* Lake Bluff, Ill.: Regnery Gateway, 1984.

Young, P. "Privatization in Great Britain." *Government Union Review,* 1986, *5,* 14–15.

Young, S. "The Nature of Privatization in Britain, 1979–85." *Western European Politics,* 1986, *9* (4), 235–252.

Zimmerman, J. "Meeting Service Needs Through Intergovernmental Agreements." In ICMA's *1973 Municipal Year Book.* Washington, D.C.: International City Management Association, 1974.

INDEX

271